Paragon Publishing Ltd
Paragon Ho...
St Pete...
Bourne...
Dorset B...
United K...

Tel: +44 (0...
Fax: +44 (0...
Email: boo...
http://para...

The Pocket Book Of Windows Answers
© 1998/99 RDT Ltd
© 1998/99 Paragon Publishing Ltd

British Library Cataloguing-in-Publication Data
A catalogue for this book is available from the British Library

ISBN 1 873650 73 6

Printed in the UK by: Mackays of Chatham, Badger Road, Lordswood, Chatham, Kent, ME5 8TD
Published by: Paragon Publishing Ltd, Bournemouth
Edited by: John Taylor
Designed by: Nicky Bartlett
Thanks to: Mark Kendrick, Steve Gotobed, Ross Andrews, Graham Taylor, Louise Wells, John Coates, Chris Hankins, Sue James, Mike James, Rex Last, Lee Hancock

Check out **http://made-easy.net** for other great books and magazines!

WINDOWS ANSWERS
The No.1 Source for all your PC Questions
95/98

CONTENTS

COMMON QUESTIONS

APPLICATIONS

WINDOWS 98

WINDOWS 95

GLOSSARY

WINDOWS ANSWERS
NOW TURN THE PAGE...

WINDOWS TEASERS

Can you solve some of those knotty problems which have puzzled many of our readers? Here's a challenge to keep the grey cells busy - but never fear, you don't have to be a Windows guru to solve them. It just takes a bit of low cunning and perhaps the odd peek at the Windows Help file.

Most problems are pretty easy to crack if you put your mind to them and, with experience, you'll find that you can work out the majority of them. But just occasionally, a real hard nut of a problem emerges, resulting in some serious head scratching.
The whole object of the exercise, apart from having a bit of fun being an electronic Sherlock Holmes, is to help you to help yourself find your own way round the system and hopefully solve many more of your problems by yourself.

So, what we've done is to put together a variety of top teasers which could easily cause a few furrowed brows. With each question there's a handy hint to help you along the way. The answers in full are printed after the Teasers - just in case you need them!

TEASER NUMBER ONE

"I've customised my Start Menu by putting the programs I use most often on it and renaming them so each begins with a number. However, I can't put any more on because they go off the top of the screen and Windows won't let me load the ones that have disappeared. What can I do?"

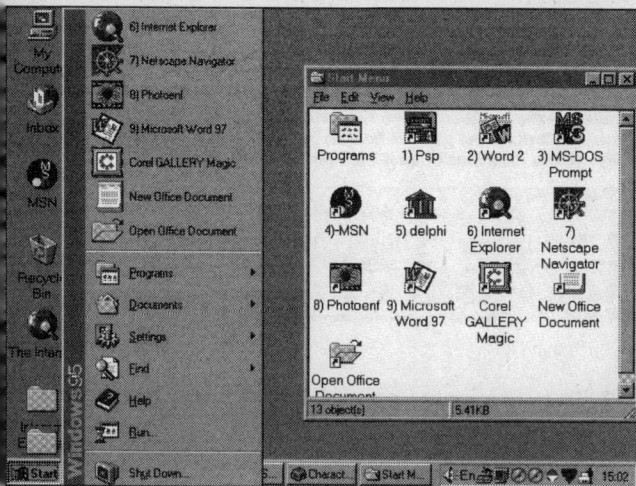

Here you can see what can happen. A whole pile of applications has been added to the Start menu and it looks as if Word 97 has reached the final straw, pushing the first five items off the top of the screen. I've also shown the Start menu folder.

NOTE:

Items are added to the Start list by dragging the icon of the application from a folder or the Desktop on to the Start button, then letting go. If you then find the Start menu folder, which is in the Windows folder, and open it, you can change the names of the icons so they begin with numbers. This means that all you have to do to launch an application is press Ctrl+Esc to bring up the Start menu, then press the number you want. You can, of course, use letters rather than numbers if you wish.

Nevertheless, if the numbered icon names disappear off the top of the screen, this little trick doesn't work. And that's the problem you have to solve.

To change the name of any icon, click on it, which should highlight it, pause for a moment, then click again. This will put the name in a box, with a cursor allowing you to edit the contents. To finish editing, click anywhere outside the box.

Clue:
Small can be beautiful...and that applies to icons, too.
A right click could also be helpful.

TEASER NUMBER TWO

"I am delighted with the help that Word 97 gives me with grammar and spelling. However, there's one drawback: I can't right click on a word with a wavy underline and get the normal pop up menu which appears to relate to the grammar or spelling fault. Can I get round this?"

Here's a composite image of what happens when you right click (a) on a word which isn't underlined; (b) on a word underlined by the spell checker; and (c) on a word underlined by the grammar checker.

Another composite image, this time showing what happens when you right click (a) on the desktop; (b) on a file icon; and (c) on the Taskbar.

NOTE:

It seems that Word has grabbed the pop up menu and more or less told you that you can't have the normal functions. You have to deal with the grammar or spelling issues or else.

This isn't such a hard nut to crack, and one of the reasons for putting it forward is to demonstrate to you that there are lots of these menus which pop up when you click on the right mouse button. Try right clicking on the desktop, for instance, and do the same on a empty space on the taskbar. In both cases, explore the Properties option - you'll find a lot of useful stuff there.

Clue:
Trying resolving one thing at a time - or cut the wavy
lines altogether, perhaps.

TEASER NUMBER THREE

"A friend of mine sent me material for our church newsletter the other day and it came up on the screen looking more like a pile of bricks than a file. I had to retype the whole lot. Is there (a) an explanation and (b) a way round the problem? Both of us are using Word."

This is what happened to our newsletter editor when he tried to open what seemed to be a perfectly normal DOC file.

NOTE:

There is an important difference between a text file and a document and that is that the text file contains... just plain text, as the name suggests. No formatting, no different fonts, images, colours or other bells and whistles. Any text editor or word processor can read a text file. However, that does not apply to word processors. They contain all kinds of formatting and style information and are typically much bigger files as a consequence.

Word 6 in particular is notorious for the size of its document files. And if you try and read one manufacturer's word processor document into another's, it will end in tears. However, the teaser states that both users had Word installed on their machines. So what is going on? And is there a crafty way in which the editor of the newsletter could have overcome the problem?

Clue:
For (a), it's all to do with numbers; for (b), it depends how you make savings. As for the crafty way, it's a matter of what accessories you have.

TEASER NUMBER FOUR

"This problem stems from a child's logic. I had designed a nice looking image using Paint Shop Pro for my five-year-old. It had a bright sun and a picture of a tree. She looked at it and said: "The tree doesn't have a shadow." How do you give it one?"

This is what the picture looks like before it grows a shadow and there's also the Skew dialog box, which may be of use in cracking this problem.

12

NOTE:

There are actually two problems lurking here. The first is: How do you make a shadow, or, in other words, a grey-scale image from a colour image? And the second goes like this: How do you take that image, stand it on its head and twist it so that it looks like a genuine shadow?

Incidentally, this is not just a Paint Shop Pro question. Any graphics package can resolve the problem in a similar way - even the basic Paint program which comes with your system can do the trick, but, depending on the kind of image, it doesn't handle the grey scale conversion too well.

Once you get the general idea of how to solve this problem, you will be amazed at the number of different things you can actually do to a whole image, or just part of it.

> *Clue:*
> *Help might get you the grey-scale - and the technical*
> *term for standing on its head is flipping; for twisting an*
> *image, skewing.*

TEASER NUMBER FIVE

"I have some foreign language text to type but there are no accents on the standard keyboard, except for the carat, and that's a separate letter. Can it be done?"

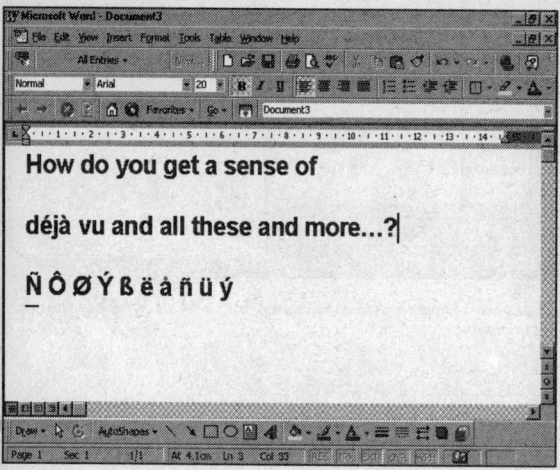

How do you get a sense of

déjà vu and all these and more...?

Ñ Ô Ø Ý ß ë å ñ ü ý

These are just some of the exotic characters you can get from your computer, but the question is - how is it done?

NOTE:

There are two kinds of situation in which you might well need special accented characters. The first is a one-off situation, where the title of a book or a foreign word or phrase to be incorporated into your text needs an accent. The other is where you wish to type large amounts of foreign language material.

Clue:
It could be a matter of Character - or of the Keyboard.

TEASER NUMBER SIX

"My Computer opens window after window like Crystal Palace. Can it be stopped and how can I change its silly name?"

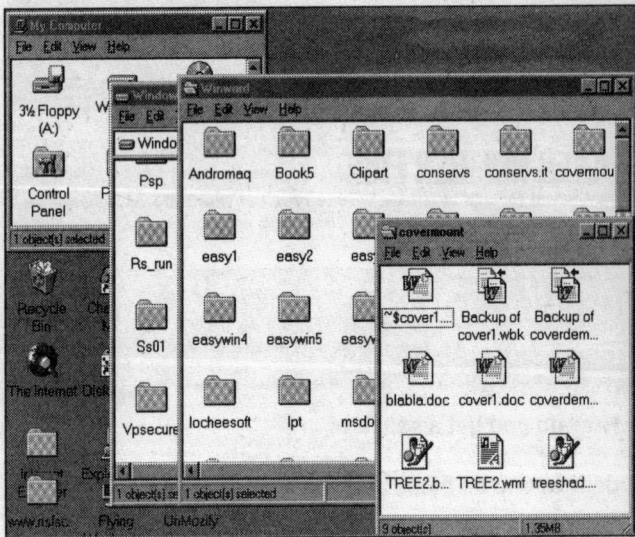

Here's a typical case of double glazing gone mad, with a whole array of windows opened in My Computer.

NOTE:

There are two main ways of looking at the folders and files on your machine: My Computer and Explorer. My Computer is probably more use-ful when you know more or less what you are looking for. If, for example, you have a folder called Business correspondence 98 and, beneath that, one folder for each month, then you can readily use My Computer to find the file you are after.

Explorer is much more flexible and allows you to wander at will around the machine. If you are really stuck for a file or folder, try the Find option on the Start menu. This is a very powerful tool indeed.

If you know the name, or at least part of the name of the file you want, let me be heretical and suggest you open an MS-DOS Window and type CD \ which gets you to the root directory. Then:

DIR name*.*/S/P

where name is the text you know about and the two asterisks and the full stop mean 'look for name plus anything else'. The slash and the S mean look in all subfolders.

The /P means print the result on screen a screenful ('page') at a time, in case there are a lot of files to display. For more information on DIR, type DIR/? to get the help information.

> *Clue:*
> *It's always useful with any application to explore the options. And the name problem is just a couple of clicks away from being solved.*

TEASER NUMBER SEVEN

"I like using Notepad for small notes, but what annoys me is that the text keeps disappearing off the right-hand side of the screen and I have to keep horizontally scrolling to read it. Is there a solution, apart from pressing Enter every now and then in the middle of a paragraph?"

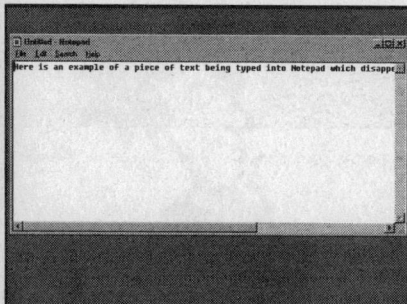

The case of the Disappearing Text - why does it go off the right-hand side of the screen, and what's to be done about it?

NOTE

The problem: There are actually three editors which come with Windows, one of which is a cut-down word processor, while the other two are strictly for plain text. Starting at the bottom, so to speak, is the MS-DOS EDIT program, which is available from the MS-DOS window.

As old-fashioned editors go, it's pretty good. The version in Windows 95 allows you to have up to ten files open at one time. It too suffers from the disappearing text problem, for one very good reason.

EDIT was designed to allow people to edit AUTOEXEC, CONFIG and batch files which consist of a sequence of - usually quite short - command lines. That you can also edit text files is an added bonus, but there can be a lot of horizontal scanning involved.

Incidentally, if you take a dislike to the colours used with edit, the Options menu item offers you a wide choice of colours to play with.

Next in line is Notepad, which is the subject of this teaser. It's pretty restrictive, not even allowing for search and replace which is available with EDIT. However, it is useful for short text files.

Top of the pile and well worth a look is WordPad, which is a (very) cut-down version of Word 6. It doesn't allow for fully justified text and is pretty basic, but it will handle a number of styles and a full range of fonts. Try it out.

Both Notepad and WordPad are accessed from the Accessories continuation menu. Go to Help, Add/Remove programs if you can't find them.

> Clue:
> The answer is just a menu item away...

TEASER NUMBER EIGHT

"Looking at my keyboard, I noticed that the Num Lock also has an icon on it which looks like a computer mouse. Does that mean anything in particular?"

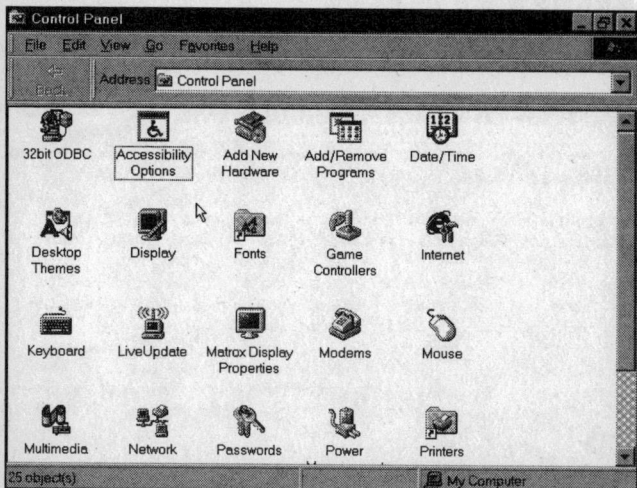

Maybe the solution to this little teaser lurks somewhere on the Control Panel?

NOTE:

One of the big advances inaugurated by Windows was the fact that it allowed commands to be carried out not by typing them in laboriously at the command prompt, but by pointing and clicking with the mouse.

Windows 95 greatly increased the number of ways in which the mouse could be used, and in particular the right mouse button came into its own.

In Windows 98, you can customise the left mouse button so that a single click, rather than a double, carries out a command, to be compatible with clicking on a link on an Internet web page.

> *Clue:*
> *You need either Help or the Control Panel for this one.*

ANSWERS

ANSWER TO TEASER NUMBER ONE

Here's a composite screen shot showing two different solutions to the Start menu problem.

EXPLANATION

On the left, you obtain the small-sized list by right clicking on the Start menu and then holding the mouse pointer over the Contents option. Just click on an item to launch it. That's one way round the problem.

But that doesn't speed things up in the way we want. The alternative option is to right click on a blank space on the Toolbar, then go for Properties, and check the box which allows you to put small icons on the Start menu. Then you can get up to twelve items on a 640 x 480 display.

HOW YOU COULD HAVE SOLVED THE PROBLEM:

Taking the cue from the Clue, go to Windows Help, and under icons you'll see an item telling you how to change the size of Start menu icons. And the 'right' hint suggested you should right click on the Start menu. Try right clicking on the Desktop, on your Taskbar and while running applications - you'll be surprised at the added computing power it gives you!

On the other hand, you could always get a higher resolution monitor - if you can afford one, that is!

ANSWER TO TEASER NUMBER TWO

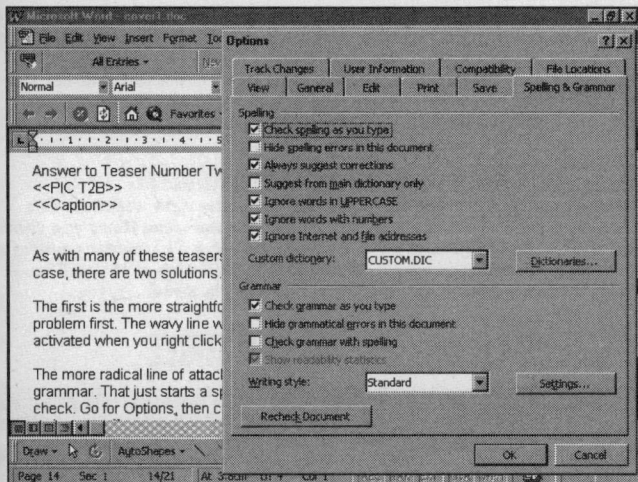

The Options from the Tools menu item, with a check against the option to look for grammar faults as the document is typed. Remove that and you will not have the green underlines - switch off the check spelling as you type option, and the red lines go too.

EXPLANATION

As with many of these teasers, there is more than one solution to the problem. In this case, there are two.

The first is the more straightforward approach. Resolve the grammar or spelling problem first. The wavy line will disappear and the normal pop up menu will be activated when you right click on the mouse.

The more radical line of attack is to go to Tools, but don't click on Spelling and Grammar. That just starts a spelling and - if you have checked the box - grammar check. Go for Options, then click on the Spelling and Grammar tag. Amongst the options on offer, you can choose to switch off the spell and grammar check altogether.

In general, it is worth thinking about taking this course anyway; the reason being that the best way to prepare a document is to concentrate firs on the words that you want to use and then on the spelling and grammar afterwards. Having Nanny State constantly tapping you on the shoulder as you write can severely interfere with your concentration.

Equally, it makes sense to wait until the checking is over before you concentrate on the broader aspects of the appearance of the text, including items like headers and footers. Get the basics out of the way before doing the fancy stuff.

A word of warning: The grammar checker is a pretty blunt instrument, and won't pick out all of your grammatical slips. So don't be over-reliant on it. The same goes for the spell checker, which won't necessarily differentiate between there and their - an example of a pair of perfectly valid words which are nevertheless used in different contexts.

HOW YOU COULD HAVE SOLVED THE PROBLEM:

Help isn't particularly helpful in pointing you in the right direction. This really is a case where you should browse along the menu items and check out what's what. A general tip when you can't solve a particular problem is to look for an option marked Options, or Preferences or Properties. There's usually a lot of useful stuff buried away in there.

ANSWER TO TEASER NUMBER THREE

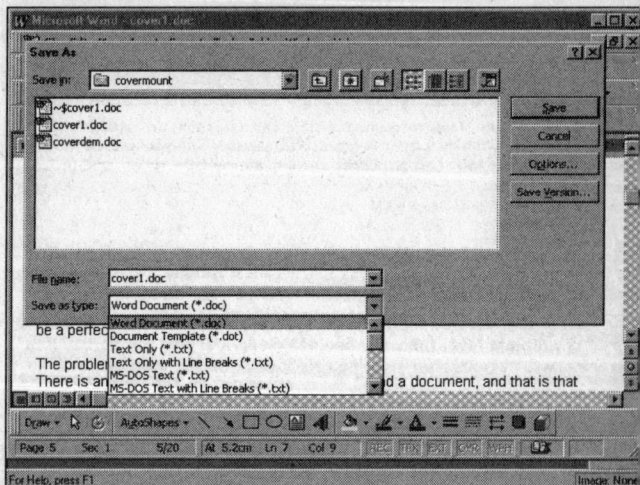

How to Save a file As a different format from the default Windows format.

An example of an RTF file. All the
style markers are in angle brackets;
somewhere in there lurks the actual
text.

Here's the part of Word 97 Help which
explains the file conversion problem
in great detail.

EXPLANATION

As you may have guessed, this is all to do with what's known in the trade
as upwards compatibility. In other words, if you have version 5 of
Wonderprog, you should be able to read stuff written in versions 1-4 of
Wonderprog, but you would probably get in a mess with versions 6 and
above.

So, what has happened is that the user who wrote the copy for the editor has a higher version of Word than the editor. Result: trouble. There
are several ways of cracking this particular nut. The most expensive and
foolproof of these is for the editor to ask the vicar nicely if he can
afford to upgrade him to the latest version of Word, currently Word 97.

The reason why this is the most foolproof solution is that the writer of
the article may have used a feature which is only available in Word 97
and not in previous versions.

Plan B is for the writer, if he has Word 97, to use Save As to save the
file in Word 6 format - and that will work if the editor has Word 6.
Another way is to get on the Internet and, from www.microsoft.com, copy
the Word 97 file converter program.

Interestingly, if the editor has a lower version number of Word and the
writer has Word 6 or the file is saved in Word 6 format, the Accessories
solution I was hinting at should work. WordPad can read Word 6 files,
which will at least get the text in manageable form as long as it is then
saved as text.

The most generally valid solution is for the writer to save the document
as an RTF file; in other words, in Rich Text Format. This is a text file containing markers which indicate style and format and is a standard which
enables documents to be transported amongst different word processors.

In the last resort, of course, the editor could have resigned and let the writer become the new editor!

HOW YOU COULD HAVE SOLVED THE PROBLEM:

This isn't too easy, unless you get wise to the idea that Save As allows you to change formats. If you hunt around under Help, though, you will see File formats and a sub-heading, Troubleshooting, converting file formats.

ANSWER TO TEASER NUMBER FOUR

The sun casting quite a credible shadow. The inverted (flipped) grey-scale image of the tree is also shown, together with the skew deformation preview panel.

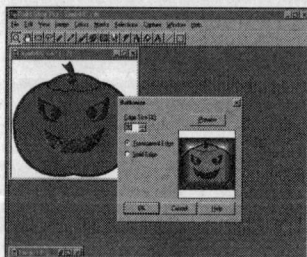

Here's another little twist that Paint Shop Pro offers: This special effect is called Buttonizing.

This is an original image and what happens when you opt to Circle it. There are quite a few other tricks you can play - look on the Image menu for them.

EXPLANATION

The task of making a shadow effect is not so difficult as it first seems. You simply need a copy of the original object, in this case, a tree, which you need to convert to grey-scale. That's because shadows don't usually come in colour, at least not in the conventions of drawing.

Then you need to turn it on its head and then skew it. Finally, you need to paste it under the actual tree so that it looks like a proper shadow.

Assuming that the sun is on the right of the tree, this is what you do. Copy the tree into a separate file, and go for Colours, grey-scale. Now go for Image and flip, which turns the image upside down. Back to image again, opt for deformations and skew the image so that the shadow looks right. That's easy with Paint Shop Pro, as it does the work for you in a preview window.

When you want to perform special effects or deformations, you may well have to increase colour depth to do so. That's done from the Colour menu.

HOW YOU COULD HAVE SOLVED THE PROBLEM:

Look in Paint Help topics under grey-scale and the other topics.

ANSWER TO TEASER NUMBER FIVE

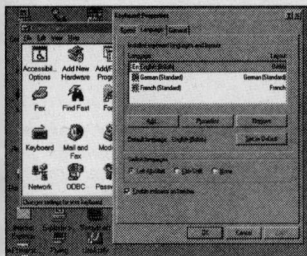

You can add or remove languages by going to the Control panel and then opting for the Language tab.

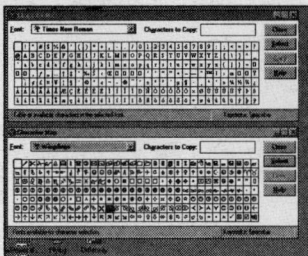

Two instances of the Character map. The first shows a conventional typeface, the second is Wingdings - and the Character map is the best way of finding out which key generates what special character.

EXPLANATION

The solution depends on the amount of work you intend doing in the language concerned. If you just want the odd accent, the easiest way to achieve that is to go to the Accessories continuation menu and opt for the Character map. If it isn't there, look in help for Add/Remove programs and add it.

Once you find your way round the Character map, you will find it easy to insert small amounts of foreign accented letters. Note that you can enlarge individual characters by clicking on them; then you can insert them in the panel at the top right one at a time or in a sequence, and finally copy them to the clipboard.

Return to your application and you can copy the character(s) back from the clipboard. In the bottom right-hand corner, the equivalent keystroke or combination of keys for the character is given and you can make a note of that and type it in. It is important to remember, though, with Word, if the combination begins with Alt followed by a number beginning with zero, you must (a) have the Num Lock switched on and (b) use the numbers on the numeric keypad.

For a more radical solution, go to the Control panel, Keyboard and click on the Languages tab, then on the Add button. You can then add new languages, such as French and German, to the list of languages. You can switch from one to another from the tray in the right-hand corner of the taskbar.

However, Character map does not recognise other keyboard sets, so if you don't know the layout of a French or other foreign keyboard, you will have to use trial and error and have a print out of the characters in front of you. Some manuals contain a diagram of these alternative character sets showing how they map out on to the keyboard.

There are many other tricks to learn. In French, some of the keys have three options. For example:

unshifted 9 = c cedilla
shifted 9 = 9
Ctrl+Shift+9 = dash

In German, the equals sign has to be hit twice to generate double open quotes, but if you press left delete only one quote is erased, giving access to 'proper' open and close double and single quotes. The close quotes come from Shift+ equals sign.

HOW YOU COULD HAVE SOLVED THE PROBLEM:

Look under help at Character map and Languages.

ANSWER TO TEASER NUMBER SIX

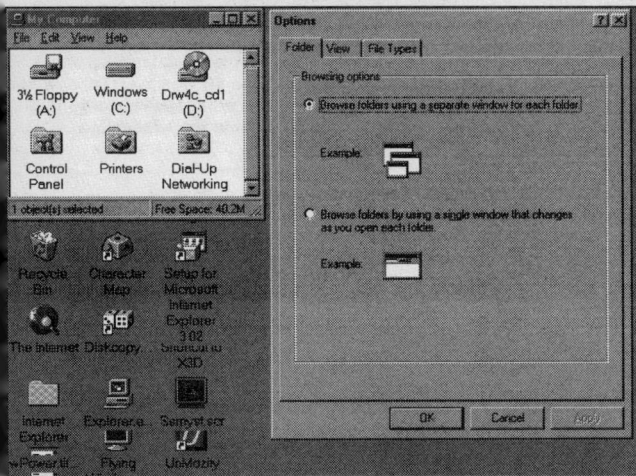

This the Folder tab, reached via View, Options. This enables you to switch off multiple windows.

EXPLANATION

With My Computer, things really begin to get messy when you are way down the tree of subfolders and want to backtrack. The easiest way of going back up the tree is by pressing the left delete key, but that leaves a trail of opened windows behind you.

So, the solution is to go to View, Options and uncheck the box which makes My Computer open a new window for every new folder.

Other tips to note: The icon of a folder with a bent arrow on it means: 'go back up one folder', an alternative to pressing the left delete key.

On the View menu, there is a section with four options, and a radio button against one of them. This means that only one option at a time can be shown. They are: Large icons, Small icons, List and Detail. Click on each one in turn to see how they affect the contents of the window.

Note also that the opening window for My Computer allows you instant access to the Control Panel and the Printers folder.

Finally, in case you haven't yet found out, if you click on the name of a folder or file, pause after it is highlighted, then click again, you can edit the name. Double click on a folder to open it and double click on the

relevant file to open that. Right click on an icon to see an impressive list
of options, including Properties, which is always worth exploring.

HOW YOU COULD HAVE SOLVED THE PROBLEM:

This is another situation where Help is not very helpful. Instead, scroll
along the menu items across the top bar of the My Computer window and
look for Options. That - or Properties, or some other similar word - indicates that there are things which you can alter in the application.

ANSWER TO TEASER NUMBER SEVEN

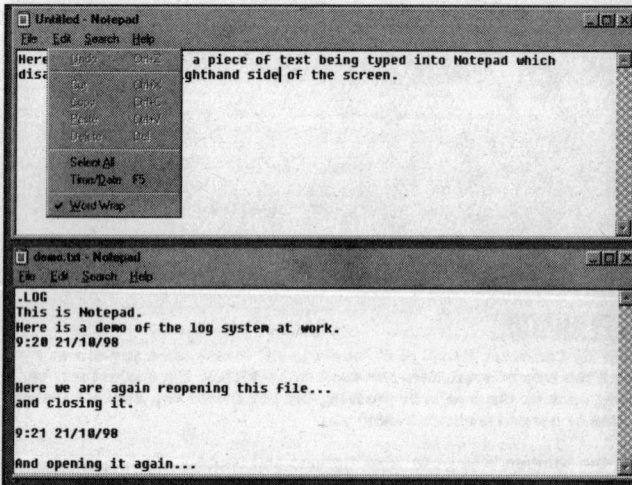

```
┌─────────────────────────────────────────────────────────────┐
│ ▣ Untitled - Notepad                                _|□|×|    │
│ File  Edit  Search  Help                                      │
│ Here │ Undo      Ctrl+Z │ a piece of text being typed into Notepad which │
│ disa │                  │ ghthand side│of the screen.          │
│      │ Cut       Ctrl+X │                                      │
│      │ Copy      Ctrl+C │                                      │
│      │ Paste     Ctrl+V │                                      │
│      │ Delete    Del    │                                      │
│      │                  │                                      │
│      │ Select All       │                                      │
│      │ Time/Date  F5    │                                      │
│      │ ✓ Word Wrap      │                                      │
│      └──────────────────┘                                     │
└─────────────────────────────────────────────────────────────┘
```

```
┌─────────────────────────────────────────────────────────────┐
│ ▣ demo.txt - Notepad                                _|□|×|    │
│ File  Edit  Search  Help                                      │
│ .LOG                                                          │
│ This is Notepad.                                              │
│ Here is a demo of the log system at work.                     │
│ 9:20 21/10/98                                                 │
│                                                               │
│                                                               │
│ Here we are again reopening this file...                      │
│ and closing it.                                               │
│                                                               │
│ 9:21 21/10/98                                                 │
│                                                               │
│ And opening it again...                                       │
└─────────────────────────────────────────────────────────────┘
```

*The answer to the problem in a nutshell - note that you can have more than one
instance of Notepad open and swap text between them. See below for an
explanation of the text in the lower window.*

EXPLANATION

The View menu allows you to word wrap the text, but it's only under
Windows 98 that the program 'remembers' when you switch the option on.
In addition, you can insert the date and time.

There is another little trick lurking up Notepad's sleeve, which can be
useful if you regularly use it for note making. If you add the four characters '.LOG' at the very beginning of your document, Notepad keeps a
record of every time the document is opened. The letters LOG have to be
in upper case.

If you have more than one instance of Notepad open, move the mouse pointer to the bottom of the window until the vertical two-headed arrow appears, then hold the left mouse button down to resize it so both windows fit on your screen.

But don't ask why the middle 'p' in Notepad is in lower case and the middle 'p' in WordPad is in upper case. That's far too deep a riddle to solve.

HOW YOU COULD HAVE SOLVED THE PROBLEM:

On this occasion, a trawl through the menu items reveals all. For the well-hidden information on .LOG, though, you would have to delve into the Help information that comes with Notepad.

ANSWER TO TEASER NUMBER EIGHT

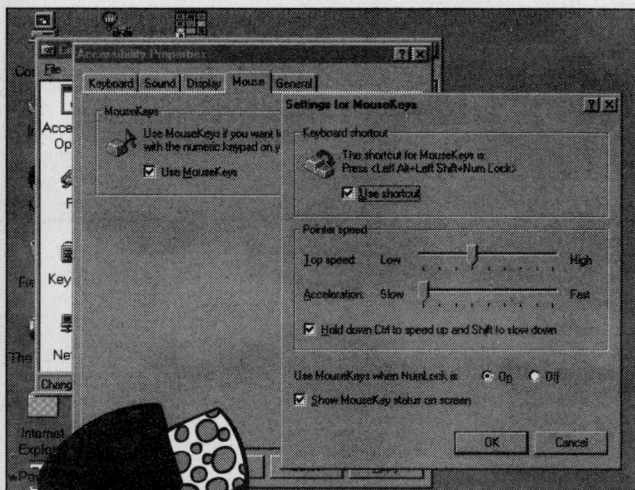

Go to the Control Panel, Accessibility features (not Mouse), then click on the Mouse tab and opt for MouseKeys.

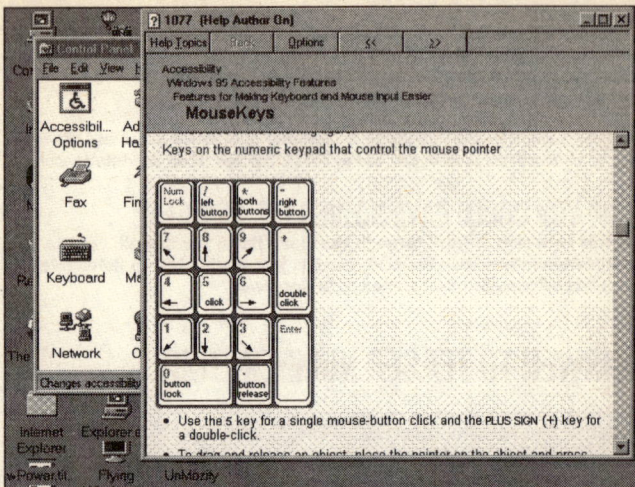

As for what keys do what, this is the information straight from the Windows Resource Kit help file.

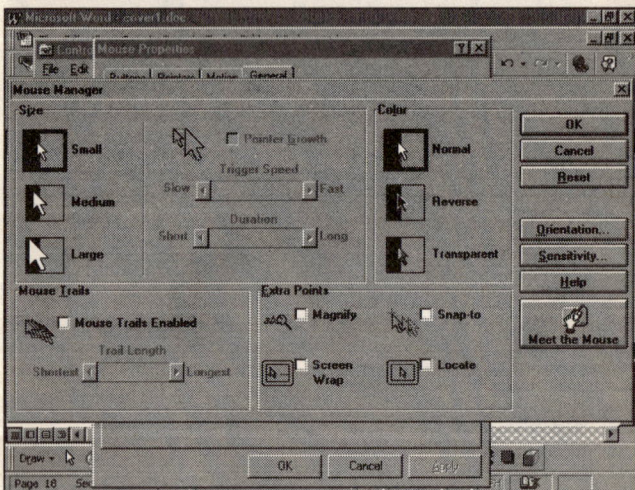

The Mouse icon on the Control Panel does have its uses, though. Do explore it, especially the Options button on the General tab. One of the delights on offer is a mini-guide to the mouse. Click on the Meet the Mouse button.

EXPLANATION

The feature which enables you to use the numeric pad as a mouse is called MouseKeys and is one of the excellent range of Accessiblity features for the handicapped which Microsoft have introduced and much enhanced.

Windows 98 actually goes one stage further for those with seeing problems. There is a rather nice device which magnifies part of the screen with a number of different settings.

Back to MouseKeys: the keys round the edge of the pad move the mouse in the directions of the arrows. 7, 9, 1 and 3 move the mouse diagonally.

Key 5 is the equivalent of a mouse click. Ins is mouse down and Del is mouse up. If you hold down the Ctrl key while pressing one of the direction keys, the mouse will move a long distance. Shift, on the other hand, moves the mouse a pixel at a time.

Note that MouseKeys is disabled unless Num Lock is switched on.

To gain access to the Windows Resource kit, you will find it on your Windows CD-ROM. It's packed with all manner of advanced help information.

HOW YOU COULD HAVE SOLVED THE PROBLEM:

The Accessibility icon is the key to MouseKeys. However, the 'obvious' choice of the Mouse icon isn't any help to you in this case.

HARDWARE

MOUSE PROBLEMS I

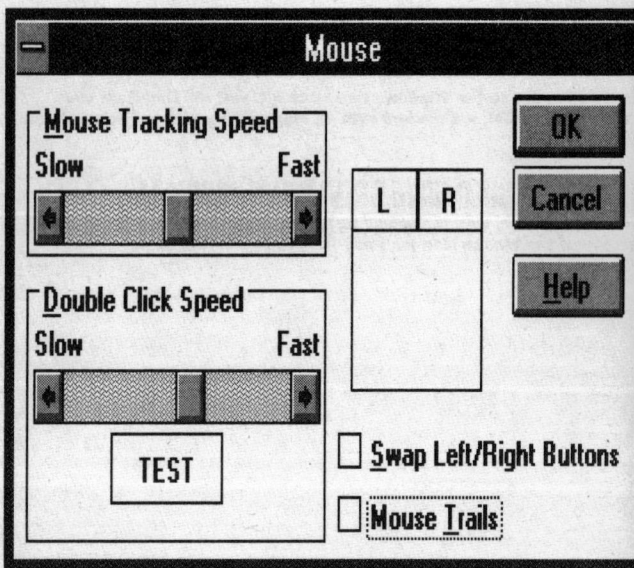

In Windows 95, Mouse Trails become Pointer trails and you can actually vary their length

Q Sometimes my mouse pointer flickers or even disappears. It seems to happen most when there's some animation happening on the screen. What's going on?
Karen Oram, Manchester

A The answer to your question appears to be Mouse trails, one of the options available to the user wishing to customise their mouse. It's likely that the option is switched on - to solve this, switch Mouse trails off.

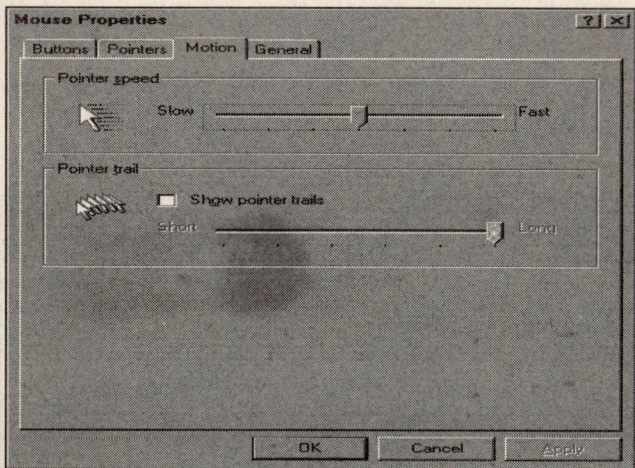

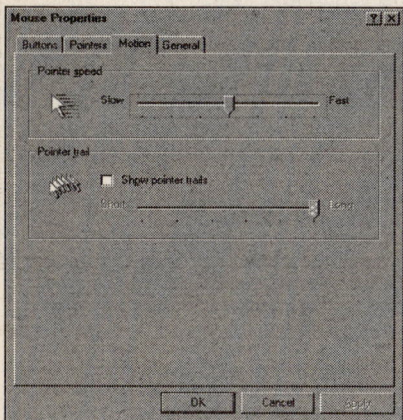

Access the Mouse properties menu, and you're able to fully customise your mouse

For those of you wondering what this means, the Mouse trails option is very useful if you cannot see too well or have an oldish laptop with a less than brilliant screen. It allows the mouse to leave a short "trail" of pointers behind it, enabling you to see it more clearly. If you can't find the mouse pointer, wiggle the mouse back and forth - you'll soon see where it's got to.

How do you select this option? In Windows 95 go to Start menu, Settings, Control Panel and double click on the mouse. Click on the Motion tab, and you will find two options. One is the mouse speed, the other the Pointer trails on/off button. Click the button to try it out to see if it will help you.

Note that Windows also allows you to vary other ways in which the mouse operates, and these may also help people who have difficulties operating their mouse.

PROTECT YOUR PC

Q In the office, the computer I use is sometimes also used by other co-workers. One of them is rather prone to change my screen saver to some ghastly Simpsons picture which he has dragged up from somewhere (the Internet perhaps?). Is it possible to stop anyone tinkering further with the computer's display?
J. Flyn, Bristol

A Indeed it is. This may take some time, but the trip is worth the trouble. You need your Windows CD-ROM and a spare quarter of an hour. Load the CD-ROM and let it autorun. [1] Select Browse, and click your way through ADMIN via APPTOOLS to POLEDIT. Go for POLEDIT.EXE (the icon showing the face next to the computer screen), and you will find yourself in the territory of the System Policy Editor.

The next bit is a touch fiddly, so follow closely. [2] From the File menu of the Policy Editor, choose Open Registry. [3] You will find yourself faced with two icons. One is called Local User, and the other is Local Computer.

Double click with your mouse on the face icon [4] (Local User), and you will see a list of items under Local User, beginning with the Control Panel.

Double click on the "Control Panel" [5], and you open up yet another list of items under Control Panel, beginning with Display.
Double click on Display and you will see a check box next to the words Restrict Display Control Panel. [6] Tick the box, and up comes a whole raft of options in the panel at the bottom of the Window. If you select "Disable Display Control" panel then any unwanted screen savers are a thing of the past.

[7] While you are at it, why not keep this Simpsons fan from being tempted to tinker with your Registry. Follow the same route through the CD-ROM's folders, and when you've got as far as selecting Open Registry

from the Files menu of the Policy Editor, go for Local User again, but this time select System and thereafter Restrictions. You'll see that one of the options you can tick is Disable Registry Editing Tools. This will stop further fiddling.

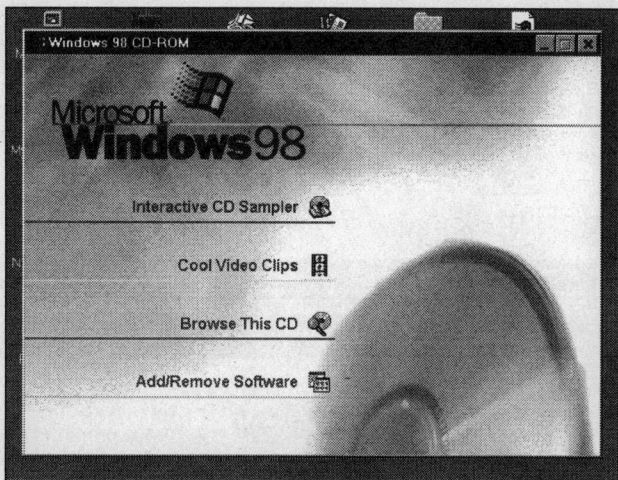

: Windows 98 CD-ROM

Microsoft Windows 98

Interactive CD Sampler

Cool Video Clips

Browse This CD

Add/Remove Software

1 *The Browse option on the Windows 95 CD-ROM front panel*

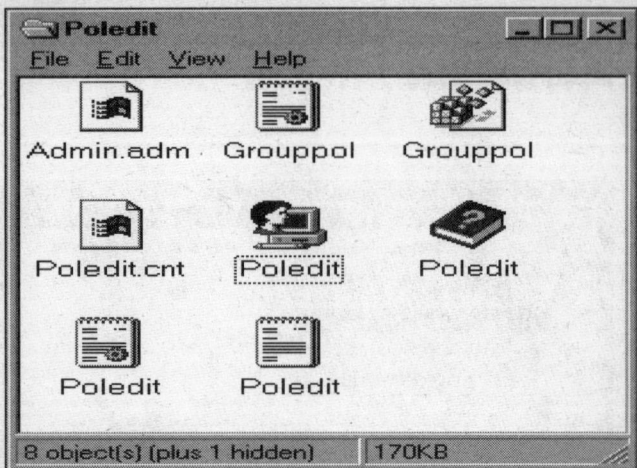

2 The Poledit (Policy Edit) folder on the CD-ROM

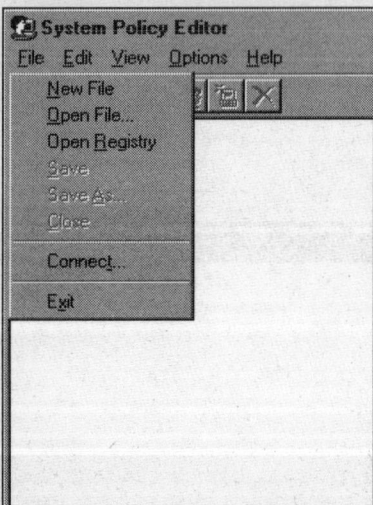

3 Opt for Open Registry

System Policy Editor - Local Registry

File   Edit   View   Options   Help

Local User   Local
                  Computer

4   *Choose the Local User icon*

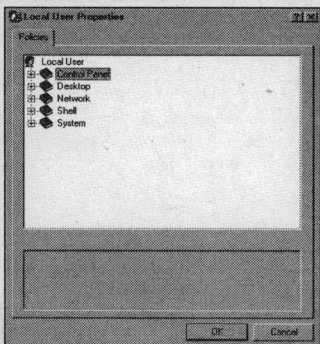

Local User Properties

Policies

- Local User
  - Control Panel
  - Desktop
  - Network
  - Shell
  - System

OK   Cancel

5   *Next, go for the Control Panel*

Local User Properties

Policies

- Local User
  - Control Panel
    - Display
      - ☑ **Restrict Display Control Panel**
    - Network
    - Passwords
    - Printers
    - System
  - Desktop
  - Network
  - Shell
  - System

Settings for Restrict Display Control Panel

- ☐ Disable Display Control Panel
- ☐ Hide Background page
- ☐ Hide Screen Saver page
- ☐ Hide Appearance page
- ☐ Hide Settings page

[OK]   [Cancel]

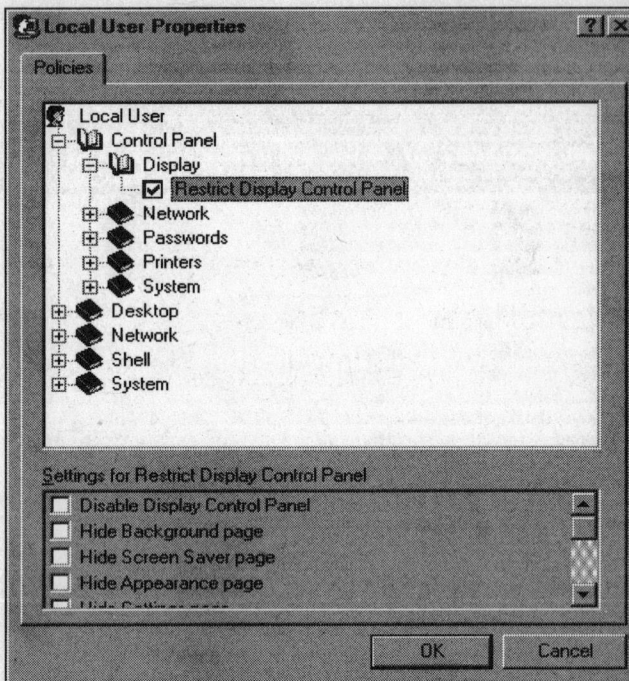

6 *And here, at last, is where you can restrict modifications to your Display Control Panel*

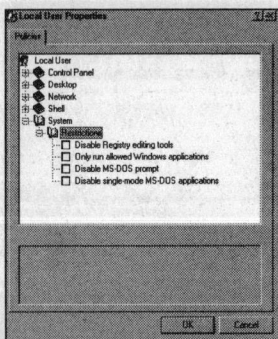

Local User Properties

Policies

- Local User
  - Control Panel
  - Desktop
  - Network
  - Shell
  - System
    - Restrictions
      - ☐ Disable Registry editing tools
      - ☐ Only run allowed Windows applications
      - ☐ Disable MS-DOS prompt
      - ☐ Disable single-mode MS-DOS applications

[OK]   [Cancel]

7 *Here you can restrict other aspects of the system*

MOUSE PROBLEMS II

Q I find it difficult to double click the mouse as I have a stiffness in my fingers. I also find it difficult to control the mouse for small movements. Is there a way round these problems?
Aled Jones, Blackpool

A If your stiffness problem is restricted to one hand, try swapping the mouse over to the other side of the keyboard and use your other hand. If the cable reach is a problem, you can buy a special extension cable.

For movement control, you might consider a trackball as an alternative to a mouse. You roll the ball with your thumb and there are two buttons serving as the left and right buttons, respectively. Their function can be reversed for left hand use by a switch located usually underneath the trackball.

If that solution doesn't suit you, the software can help a great deal. You can move among the icons in a Group or folder using the cursor keys. Then all you have to do to run the application is press Enter. To select items in a dialogue box, remember that Tab moves you round them in forward order, Shift+Tab goes backwards through them.

To control the mouse via the keyboard, go to Start, Settings, Control Panel. Highlight Accessibility options, press Enter and up comes Accessibility Properties. Have a browse through all the choices which the system offers the handicapped user - or indeed, the able-bodied user who finds them helpful. The one you want is the Mouse tab. Select Use MouseKeys, then opt for Settings. Now it gets a little bit complicated. If you use Num Lock for typing in numbers, it may well be best to opt for MouseKeys to be on when the Num Lock is off, otherwise you might be happier with things the other way round.

You can also choose to tick the Shortcut box, in which case you can turn MouseKeys on and off altogether by pressing Alt+Shift+Num Lock. When using Mouse keys, the arrows move the mouse in the four directions of the compass, so to speak.

To move the mouse diagonally, hold down an arrow key and press the appropriate key next to it. To move upwards and to the right, for example, press up arrow and the PgUp/9 key, and to move down and to the left, press down arrow and End/1.

Settings for MouseKeys   ? X

Keyboard shortcut

The shortcut for MouseKeys is:
Press <Left Alt+Left Shift+Num Lock>

☑ Use shortcut

Pointer speed

Top speed: Low |———————⊔———————| High

Acceleration: Slow |—⊔———————————| Fast

☑ Hold down Ctrl to speed up and Shift to slow down

Use MouseKeys when NumLock is: ⦿ On   ○ Off

☑ Show MouseKey status on screen

[OK   ]   [Cancel   ]

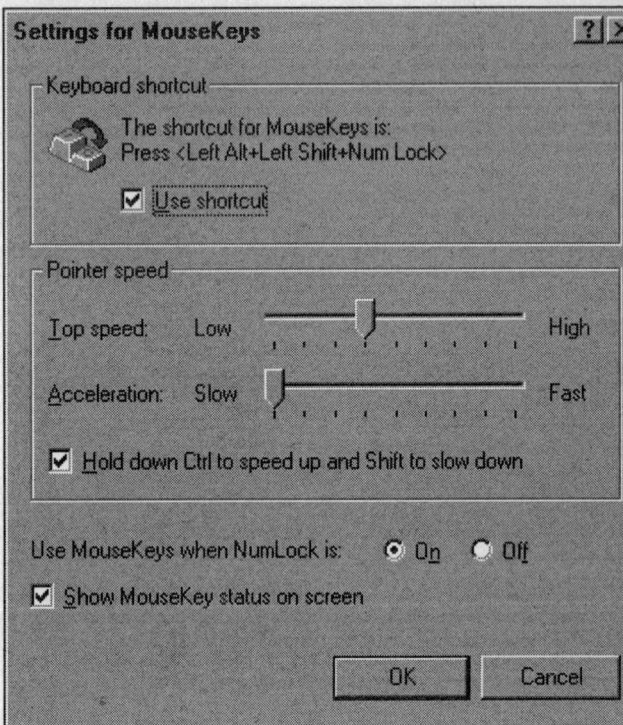

The MouseKeys check box. Click on Settings

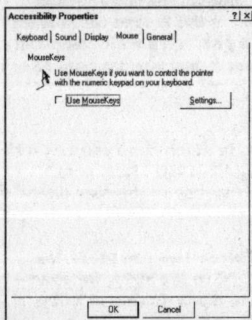

Accessibility Properties   ? X

Keyboard | Sound | Display | Mouse | General

MouseKeys

Use MouseKeys if you want to control the pointer
with the numeric keypad on your keyboard.

☐ Use MouseKeys   Settings...

[OK   ]   [Cancel]

*The Settings determine how you set up the
options on your MouseKeys*

FINGER TROUBLE

Q It's all very well for you to say "double click" on an icon. I have arthritis and find this most difficult. What can I do to get round this?
Jeremy Thompson, Surrey

A Easy. Just click on the icon, which will highlight it. Then press Enter and Bob, as they say, is your Uncle.

PRINTER BLUES

Q My poor old printer needs to be fed a page at a time, so I keep getting this wretched time out message when I don't need it. Is there a way round it?
U W Schmidt, Frankfurt

A Get a new printer. Seriously, though, if you can't afford to do that, open the Printers folder in the Control Panel. Then, right click on the printer you are after and change the delays in the Timeout settings to something much longer. Apparently, though, this doesn't always work, but I don't know why.

INTERNET

WHAT IS THE INTERNET?

Let's start by telling you what the Internet isn't. It's not the "information superhighway" you've probably heard about. That's an imaginary future network of interactive TV game shows and home shopping and every imaginable fragment of information at your fingertips. The Internet is the start of this, a foundation stone if you will, but there's a very, very long way to go.

Nor is the Net a wicked haven of pornography, witchcraft and instructions on how to make your own bombs. Yes, it is probable that some of these dubious topics can be found on the Internet if you look hard enough, but in exactly the same way you can find information on art, bushwalking, dinosaurs, education, food, genealogy, gardening, home brewing, literature, films, music, sport, travel and, of course, computers. The beauty of the Internet is that it belongs to everyone - quite literally so because no government or corporation "owns" the Internet - so you'll find the content of the Net as richly diverse as humanity itself.

OK, BUT JUST WHAT IS THE INTERNET?

The Internet is a vast, sprawling mass of computers, millions of them in fact, ranging from desktop PCs to large university and corporate machines which look like something bought from an ASIO garage sale. They're all interconnected, like the strands of a spider's web, so that any one computer can, with the right equipment, connect to another.

WHAT IS EMAIL?

Electronic mail, or email, is one of the simplest things you can do with the Net, and it's great. Imagine having instant, or near instant, written communications to a friend, a relative or someone in a company. Just type your message, hit the Send button and it's away, travelling across the Internet to its destination.

WHAT ARE NEWSGROUPS AND CHAT CHANNELS?

Newsgroups are places where you can swap electronic comments, notes, tips, questions, answers, jokes and more, with people who share your interest in just about anything. These discussion groups cover almost every possible interest, from hobbies to professional subjects.

You can also 'talk' (well, 'type' to be more accurate) live to anyone else on the Net using the Internet Relay Chat. There are chat 'channels' for any topic you care to mention and it's a real buzz to sit in front of your PC typing away to some fellow soul who could as easily be in the next room as in Alaska.

BUT WON'T MY CHILDREN STUMBLE INTO PORNO SITES?

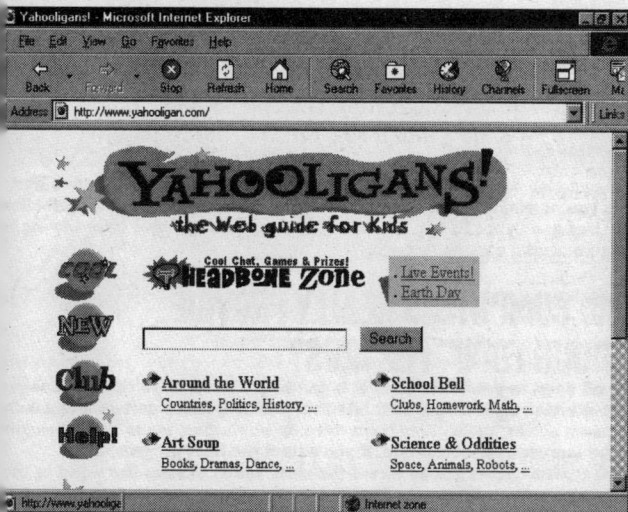

Young children are unlikely to simply stumble into porno sites. Even if they do accidentally find themselves at the front door of one, they are likely to need a credit card or password to get through. However, it can still happen and even the front page of some of these sites can be of concern to families. The best way to protect your young children is to be with them. Surf with them and search with them, just as you do outside the home. Treat the Web as the outside world, and the kids will be safe under your watchful eye.

If they are a bit older, put the computer in a central place where you can see what is happening without breathing down their neck all the time, and bookmark lots of favourite (and safe) sites.

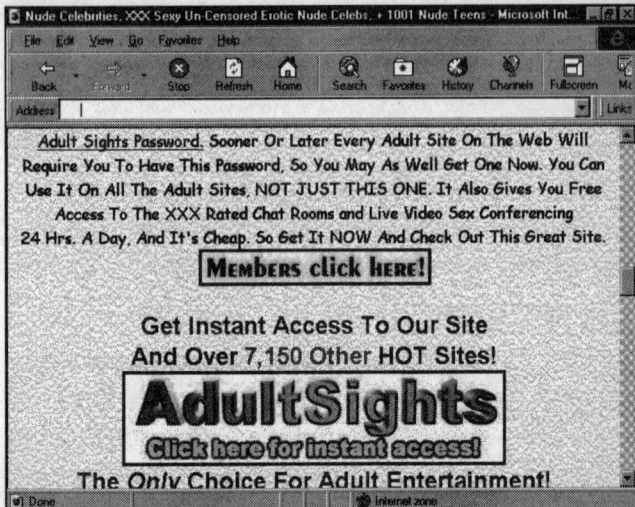

You can also use kiddie-safe search engines like Yahooligan, or one that
lets you nominate rated sites only for your search. As an extra protection
you can use Cyber Patrol, Net Nanny or one of many other filters to stop
some material coming through.

CAN COMPUTERS REALLY PROVIDE "BRAIN FOOD" FOR KIDS?

We all need to think. The computer can help kids learn to think and not
just exercise their thumb as it hits that joystick! Some software can build
problem solving skills, help them develop strategies, focus their thoughts
and encourage concentration, if you select the best programs.
Look for adventure games where the child needs to save the world or the
main character (such as the Putt Putt series for young children and the D
Brain series for older kids).
Programs that allow children to build and create (such as SimTown and
SimCity or creativity programs) also encourage them to make decisions,
plan their actions and evaluate their results. Best of all, most of these
programs will be viewed as games by the kids.

IS THE INTERNET THE SAME THING AS THE WEB?

The World Wide Web is the newest and most amazing part of the Internet.
It's a network within the Internet consisting of millions of computers that

42

an display wonderfully colourful "pages" on your PC screen.
licking a button on a page can connect you to another related screen
information. On the Web, you can be connected to a computer in your
uburb and, with the click of a button, you
et a connection through to another PC
a London museum, a French uni-
ersity or a Canadian company.
e best bit is that Web pages
an include gloriously colourful
ctures as well as text. They
an also contain sound and
deo clips which you can
ay on your PC screen
hile you're connected or
ownload" (transfer across
e phone line onto your
omputer) to replay anytime
u choose. The great-look-
g interface coupled with the
int-and-click ease of use has
ade the World Wide Web the
ost exciting part of personal
ting.

TART ME UP

Q When I installed Windows 95 it asked me if I wanted to make a startup disk I did not have any floppy disks at the time so I answered no.
ow I am worried that I did the wrong thing. Should I make a startup
sk?
Andrews, Preston

A The startup disk contains a handful of basic utilities you can use to
fix your broken Windows 95 installation, and even un-install Windows
. The traditional DOS utilities for disk management are in there, as is
version of EDIT, REGEDIT, and the un-installer.

make a startup disk, answer "YES" to the question about the startup
sk. If you skipped this part and want to make up a startup disk, run
ntrol Panel, Add/Remove Programs, and press the "Startup Disk" tab.

RONG FILE TYPE

Q I am learning how to design a Web site, and I have a problem with
images. Text is fine, changing font sizes and colours is simple, but I
st cannot get images to work. I enclose a disk with the images I want
use, but can't. Can you help me with this problem?
arren Arthur, Liverpool

A The HTML language you use to write web pages supports two kinds
of file: JPG and GIF. Don't try to work with anything else.

DECODING MIME

Q What's a MIME? I got an email in this format, and I can't make sense of it.

Y Hawthorne, E Lancs

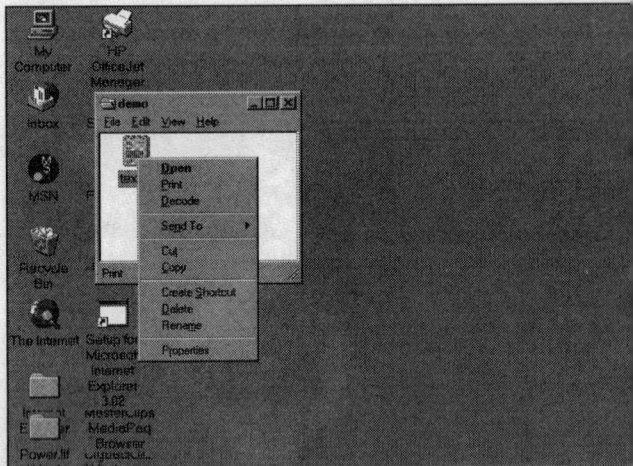

With the right software in place, you can right click on a text file and you will see the option to Decode

A It's an encoding system for messages and, if you haven't got a decoder, go to ftp://ftp.funduc.com/setupdx.exe which downloads a decoder for installation. When you save your encoded file as text and highlight the file icon, right click on the mouse and then click on Decode and follow the instructions. The program is freeware.

CRASH COURSE

Q Help! I was online using the Microsoft Network and something crashed. Now whenever I try and log on, the computer thinks it's still plugged in and throws an error message at me saying it can't find anything.

Wilson, S London

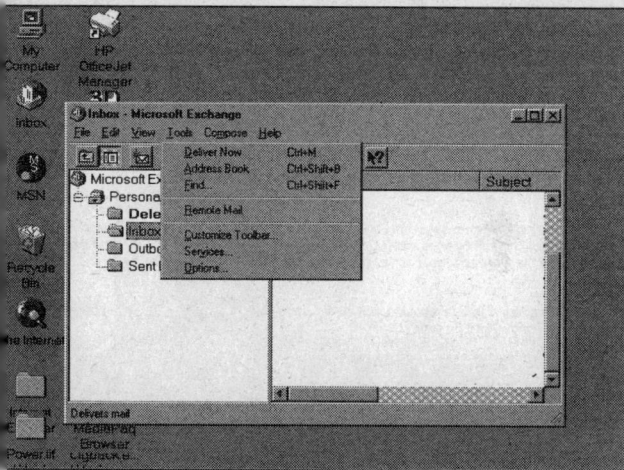

The way to kick start MSN again is to go to Inbox, opt for Tools and Deliver now

A Assuming you haven't already contacted the help line (0870 6011000), the problem can be resolved by resetting your email. Double click on Inbox, Tools, and Deliver now. That will force the system into resetting itself and all should now be well.

45

SCREEN-RES SORTED

Q I need to change screen resolution 'on the fly' so I can see the effe
Q on Internet pages I am designing. Can it be done?
Vicky Parks, Chester

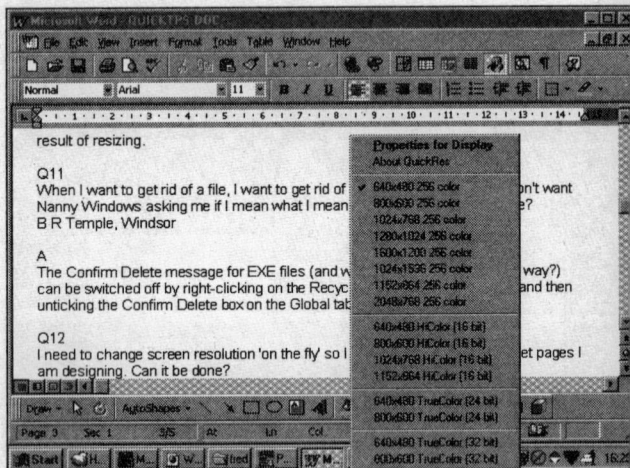

result of resizing.

Q11
When I want to get rid of a file, I want to get rid of ~~~~~~~~ n't want
Nanny Windows asking me if I mean what I mean ~~~~~~~ e?
B R Temple, Windsor

A
The Confirm Delete message for EXE files (and w ~~~~~~ way?)
can be switched off by right-clicking on the Recyc ~~~~~~ and then
unticking the Confirm Delete box on the Global tab

Q12
I need to change screen resolution 'on the fly' so I ~~~~~~ et pages I
am designing. Can it be done?

Properties for Display menu showing:

- About QuickRes
- ✓ 640x480 256 color
- 800x600 256 color
- 1024x768 256 color
- 1280x1024 256 color
- 1600x1200 256 color
- 1024x1536 256 color
- 1152x864 256 color
- 2048x768 256 color
- 640x480 HiColor (16 bit)
- 800x600 HiColor (16 bit)
- 1024x768 HiColor (16 bit)
- 1152x864 HiColor (16 bit)
- 640x480 TrueColor (24 bit)
- 800x600 TrueColor (24 bit)
- 640x480 TrueColor (32 bit)
- 800x600 TrueColor (32 bit)

To use the QuickRes tool, which appears on your Taskbar in the tray where the time is displayed, click on it and up comes a bewildering array of options

A No problem. You need a utility called QuickRes, which is part of
A PowerToys - this can be obtained from the Microsoft website at
www.microsoft.com. The collection contains a great deal of useful programs to enhance your working.

STRANGE DIALS

Q Can you help me? My windows 98 machine at strange times will autodial my Internet provider. Even when I am not home, I will ring home to find my phone engaged for hours at a time, due to auto dialling.
Bev Carney, West Drateton

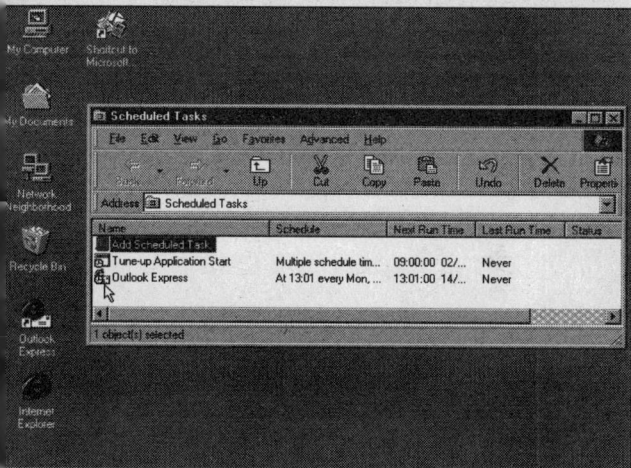

A Check your task scheduler and see if you have auto-updates scheduled (some were automatically scheduled on our Win98 - we didn't choose them). Also look at any utilities that also might have auto-update.

Also, are you using the channel update feature? If I remember correctly, that dials in and downloads selected channels for you. We don't use the channels -perhaps they have a few channels pre-selected for you?

GHOST IN THE HOUSE

Q I recently deleted a folder with an Internet program in it (there was no uninstall), along with some other files associated with it. One was a dialler program that Win 95 ran automatically at startup. The problem is that Win 95 still looks for it and I keep getting that annoying "Looking for dialler.exe" box with the flashing light. How can I make Win 95 quit looking for that file? Jim McPherson, Aberdeen

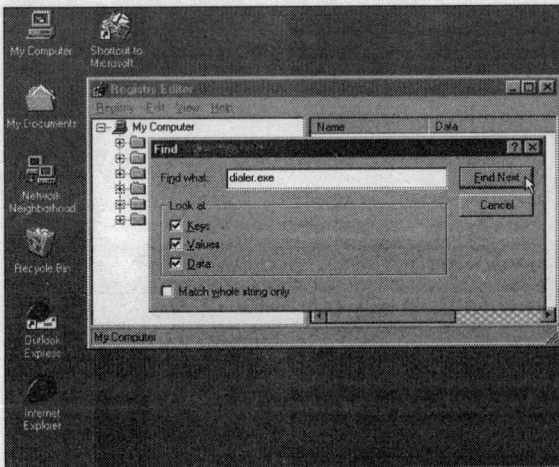

A Re-install it through add/remove programs. Then try removing it throughAdd/Remove programs, or run Regedit, and search for registry entries that contain "dialler.exe".Once located, delete it.

NET GAMING?

Q My friends and I are getting together for our monthly "net" session to play Quake, Unreal and so forth. Some upgraded to 98 and a few of us still have 95. I was wondering if anyone knows if we can still network the computers- we usually use IPX protocol. but have to use TCP/IP if we want to play Unreal. I really don't want to buy 98, my CD ROM is older and I can't get it to read any CDR disks.
Scot Mann, Darlington

Should be no problem. Windows 95/98 network works perfectly using IPX and TCP/IP.

WHAT ARE COOKIES?

Q What is a cookie which appears in Temporary Internet file? Is it safe to delete them.
John Colvin, Stourbridge

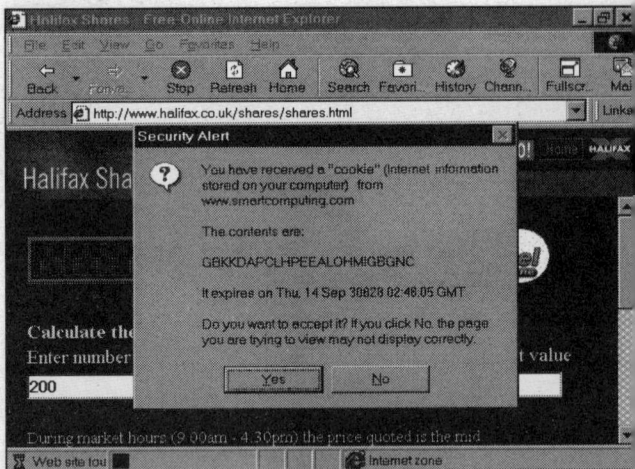

A A cookie is similar to a saved game. It records your progress through a website and stores it on your hard disk. The next time you visit that web site, it is set up according to your cookie. They can be deleted but you will lose the information they contain, so the next time you visit that web site will be like your first time. If you have IE4 and would like to be prompted before accepting further cookies, go to Start|Settings|Control Panel|Internet|Advanced. Scroll down to the Cookies options and select "Prompt before accepting cookies".

ATTACHMENT DANGER

Q I read that it wasn't a good idea to open attachments from unknown users. Does that also mean not to download attachments from unknown users either? I don't think I have that option in Outlook Express; when I download my mail all my attachments are put in my computer, aren't they?
Alan Harris, Hatfield

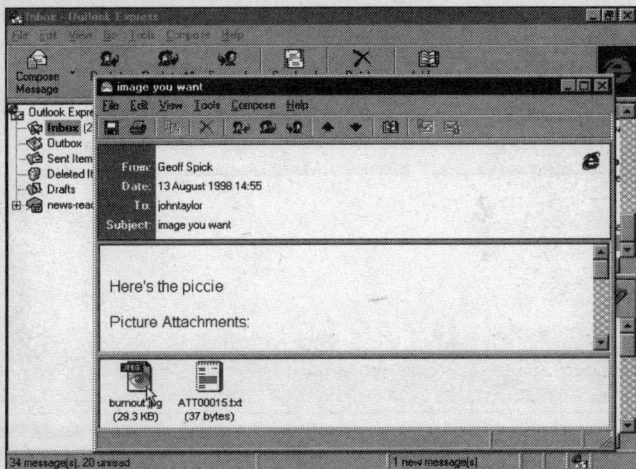

A You shouldn't open files from users you don't know. On a POP system, the attachments are downloaded automatically. However, you're safe until you execute or open the file. You're not going to get a virus from an image or text file, but be cautious with executables and Microsoft Word documents. Yes, the attachments are put in your computer, but you need have no fear. There is ZERO danger of getting a virus from an attachment that you don't open. Simply delete it after it's downloaded.

EMAIL - THE BASICS

Q I don't follow what the Inbox icon means. It asks for a post office address when I click on it. Do I need the Internet to use email?
Dave Mendham, Bridgnorth

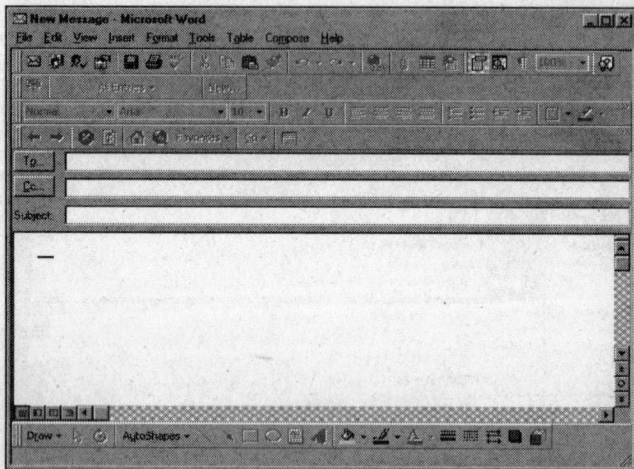

Once you have got on line, you will be able to use Mailbox to send and receive messages - here you are ready to send a new message

A The easiest way to get an email address is indeed to plug into the Internet, using one of the service providers, from AOL or MSN to Line One or even Tescos, who have jumped on the bandwagon. The packages on offer are pretty competitive, so check on what you want. Some offer multiple email addresses, which is useful if several people use your machine, as in a business environment.

Some offer free space on their machine to allow you to create your own web pages. Also, there are offers of free time or unlimited access time. Check them all out and go for the one which suits you best.

"NORMAL" SERVICE RESUMED

Q Help. I got an email from someone and tried to incorporate it into my text, but the line spacing appeared to be all over the place. I checked Format, Paragraph and all was well. In the end I had to retype it. What is going on?
Reg Carter, South Devon

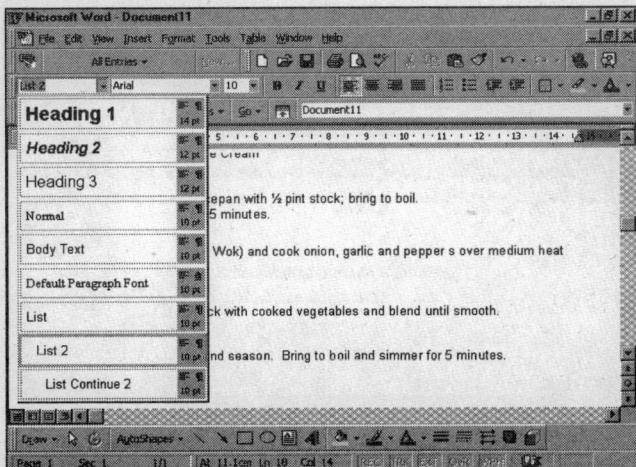

How to get confused about line spacing - List has a different interline space than Normal

A This is a really tricky little problem which took me a while to fathom out. I took an email message like the one you sent me a hard copy of and pasted it into this question and answer session and the same thing happened. It required a glance up at the top left-hand corner of the screen to resolve the problem.

The text in the main document was in Normal style, but part of the email came across as List style. All you need to do to restore "normal" service, so to speak, is to highlight the email copy and reset it as Normal from the drop-down menu.

53

REFRESH YOUR WEBSITE

Q I'm designing a website and have come across a tiresome inconvenience. Whenever I click on the Refresh button, the program insists on reloading the home page of the site and I have to click my way back to the page I am working on. Is there a way round this?
Peter Jones, Cambridge

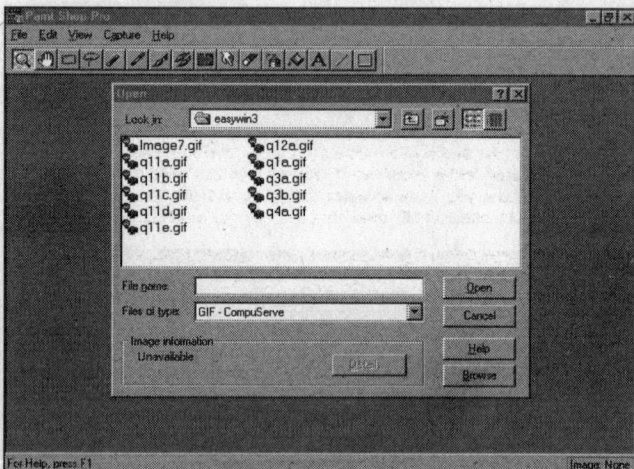

The commands for telling a user without frames how to get to browsers that support frames

A What is happening is that you are probably editing raw HTML code and using Internet Explorer. In addition, you have a website with frames. This is a technique to allow two or more distinct areas of the screen to be established. Most commonly, you'll find a fixed menu on the left-hand side from which you can link to a variety of pages on the right-hand side. The Microsoft website uses this approach.

At least with Version 3 of IE, if you click on Refresh, you end up at the main calling page, usually MAIN.HTM. The way round it is to use Netscape, which reloads the page you are actually working on. Incidentally, if you are creating a serious website it's worth remembering that you should check everything out with both Netscape and IE, and also on the main page have a NO FRAMES section which points users without frames support to a frames browser.

A STICKY WEB

Q I'm working with a colleague on a web page. To ensure that we don't get muddled as to which version is what, we have a couple of master floppy disks which we swap whenever we update parts of the page. It's terribly slow working from the A drive, though. Is there a better route?
G Garforth, Wolverhampton

A A rather odd way of working, methinks. If you are responsible for different parts of the site, why not upload new versions separately to the Internet Service Provider, and download them as required to your own machine for off-line browsing. I hope you are not simultaneously working on the same page. That sounds like a recipe for disaster to me. Anyway, you asked a question, and here is an answer.
To access a folder and its folders and browse them offline more quickly, move the master folder from the floppy disk to the hard drive like this. I'm assuming that you have a folder called something like MYSITE with subfolders TEXT and IMAGE, following the normal conventions.

(1) Minimise all Windows (if you have a Windows keyboard, Win+M, where Win = Windows key).

(2) Open My Computer, which should be on your Desktop, by double clicking it, first checking you have the disk in the drive, and then double click on the floppy disk icon in the floppy disk folder which appears.

(3) Move the mouse pointer over the folder, hold the left button down, drag the folder over to the Desktop and let go. It may take a while, but you now have a copy of the folder and its contents in the Desktop folder.

(4) Open Internet Explorer or Netscape and type the full address into the edit box. Alternatively, you could use Alt+F, Browse and find your way to the file you want.

And that's it. Immediately add the address to your list of favourites to avoid having to type all that stuff in again.

NAVIGATING NAVIGATOR

Q Netscape Navigator starts with a blank page. Why?

Sam Richardson, Slough

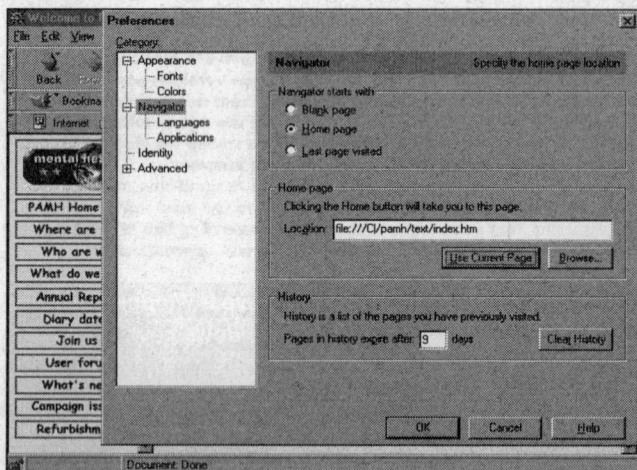

The Edit, Options dialog box of Netscape Navigator which allows you to determine which is the start up or Home page

A It's not easy to say why it happened, but the solution is to go to Edit, Preferences and you'll see a set of radio buttons allowing you to specify where Netscape starts. Note that it can be programmed to revert to the last page visited. It's well worth having a look round the options and help files that come with your favourite browser just so that you can see how many bells and whistles are available.

One extra trick of the trade, especially if you have both a high resolution and large screen, is to have more than one window open at a time.

SYSTEM SHOCK

Q When trying to load my Internet software, I got an error message saying that I should add certain device drivers to my SYSTEM.INI file. When I opened the file, I found that the drivers were already there, but the program insisted they weren't. So, I am stuck. Help!

C Stevens, Perth

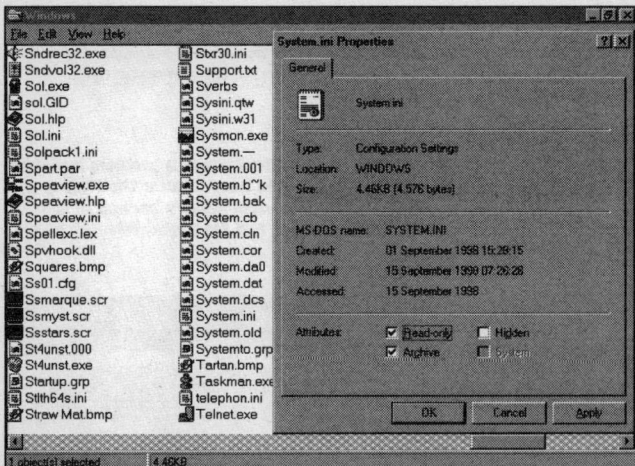

Caught red-handed! The SYSTEM.INI Properties shows that the file is read-only and can't be updated. Uncheck the box to allow other programs to access it

A You don't say which software you have been trying, but I sincerely hope you have got on to the technical help-line and had this sorted out, rather than waiting for the magazine to print a response. With the number of letters we get, that can take a long time. Open My Computer, go for the hard drive, Windows and look for the SYSTEM.INI icon. Right click on it and go for Properties.

The chances are that there is a tick in the box marked Read only. This means that you cannot alter the contents of the file. Untick the box, uninstall the software and start all over again. It should work this time.

ISDN?

Q What is ISDN and do I need it? F F Tenant, Glasgow

A The acronym stands for Integrated Services Digital Network, and it's basically a high-speed dedicated data line. You need a terminal adapter and a pretty deep wallet. It's more for businesses at the moment, but, who knows, more speed and bandwidth will be available for us all in the near future. In addition, faster access via satellite or power lines may well be alternatives for the future for the domestic user.

LOST IN THE REGISTRY

Q I sent an email to a software manufacturer about a problem and they helpfully wrote back saying that I should have to alter the Registry, which they explained in detail, but first I should make a backup of the Registry. They didn't explain how to do that and I'm stuck. What do you do?
T T Thompson, Ely

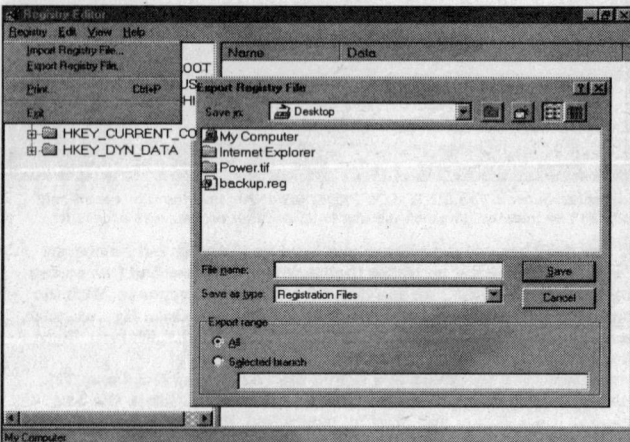

Exporting the Registry file - the image has been doctored so you can see the Registry drop-down menu and the Exporting dialog box

A This little problem is caused by a variation in terminology. First, you load the Regedit program by opting for Start, Run and type in Regedit. Instead of the expected File option on the menu bar, you get Registry. Click on that and now opt to Export Registry. Why someone didn't simply put File, Save Registry As beats me. However, the silver lining is that if it was that easy, all of us on the magazine would be without a job, and that would never do.

SECRET CODES

Q Is there a quick way of encoding text so no one can read it on the screen or if I send it by floppy disk or email?
Harriet Wood, Isle of Man

A The easiest way I know is to Select All and then choose a font which contains odd or foreign characters, like Czar, Home Planning, or Wingdings. The recipient loads the file, chooses Select All and then opts for a standard font. Of course, this isn't the best of ideas with hard copy! If you email it, send it as an attached file or you will probably get garbage.

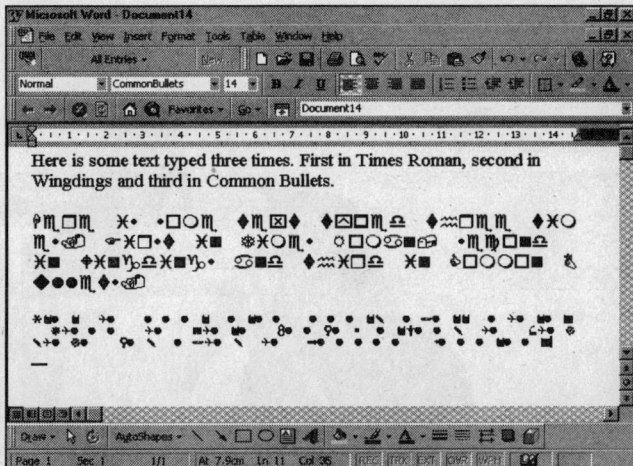

Three samples of the same text, the latter two highlighted first then converted to Wingdings and CommonBullets

BROWSING AROUND

Q I like to browse stuff off-line, but it's a nuisance that loading Internet Explorer always goes to the same file and I have to browse to the one I want. Is there a way round this?
Carmen Davids, Edinburgh

A Why not put all the files you want into a folder, open it using Explorer and double click on the first one you want - the Quick View program will then load Internet Explorer (so long as it is associated with Internet documents) and display that file. To go from one file to the next, double click on the icon on the folder you have opened.

COMMON QUESTIONS

THE FIRST CHOICE

Q Which PC should I purchase?

E Devana, Leicester

A The answer to this question is almost as difficult as answering the meaning of life. Computers change so fast - there are three product cycles a year, which means to keep up-to-date you would have to upgrade your PC three times a year. This is obviously not an option for many people. Basically, shop around and buy the best PC you can afford.

CRASH!

Q Every thing on my screen has frozen and I cannot click on anything. Nothing works, not even the Start button. What do I do?

Clarissa Page, Kettering

A When a computer stops working like this it's called a crash. Don't worry too much as most of the time it wasn't your fault and there won't be any hardware damage. However, there is only one thing you can do - switch your computer off at the mains switch, wait 20 seconds and then turn it on again. Your computer should now start up as per normal and be fully functional.

CRASH! II

Q What do I do if my system hangs up? Switch off and start again?

B Johnson, London

A When a computer stops working like this it's called a crash. Don't worry too much as most of the time it wasn't your fault and there won't be any hardware damage. Anyway, there is only one thing you can do - switch your computer off at the mains, wait 20 seconds and then turn it on again. Your computer should start up as per normal and be fully functional.

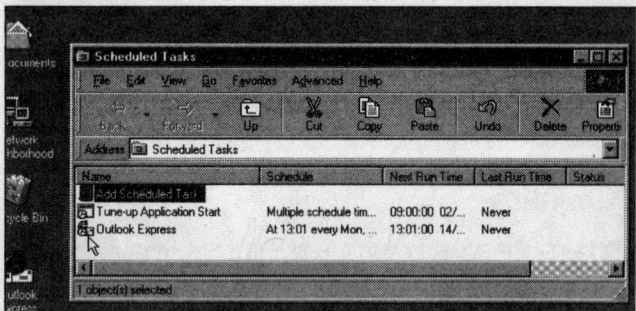

The Task list which allows you to inspect and close programs that are running

DELETE FILES THE FAST WAY

Q How do I delete files quickly?

Al Jones, Cardiff

A To delete files without sending them to the Recycle Bin, first hold down the Shift while pressing the Delete button.

A FRESH START

Q How do I go about changing my Start menu?

Jacques Petroc, Paris

A To quickly edit the Start Menu, use your mouse to right-click on the Start button, and then choose the Explore option.

CLEANING WINDOWS

Q How do I know what I am seeing on screen is the latest information when I have made changes, yet it still looks the same?
Scott Warner, London

A To quickly refresh the desktop or an Explorer window, press F5. This also works in Microsoft Internet Explorer.

PC BABIES

Q I would like to give my baby a head start in life, so when should I start my child on the computer? What different types of software are there for kids? G Dixon, Kent

A Between their second and third year most children are ready to get a lot of use out of the home computer. Some children will start earlier than this, even before their first birthday, while many will not be too impressed until a little later.

This is a reflection on their personality and often it is family decision.

Sometimes it is a matter of when the parents themselves are ready to introduce their baby to the computer. Getting ideas from other parents is often a good idea.

As for the second part of your question, there are curriculum-based programs that help kids improve their numeracy or literacy skills. Then there are creativity tools available that let them paint and create like a real artist.

Problem-solving or thinking-skills games really get the grey matter ticking over, and the games can be a happy diversion.

For children of many ages there are also some great reference titles on CD-ROM and even simple authoring tools that allow them to put together their own simple programs.

ERGONOMICS EXPLORED

Q Is it worth while getting an ergonomic keyboard, or are they just a marketing gimmick? I do get twinges in my arms and neck after working for long periods at the computer.
Julian Harris, Swindon

A A couple of points to answer here. To take the last one first - never work for long periods at the computer, even if you are young, supple and in the best of health. Hunching before a computer monitor cannot be at all beneficial and, if maintained over a long period of time, will only cause problems in later years. These can range from RSI (repetitive strain injury) in your hands and lower arms, to back problems which will necessitate visits to the doctor or physiotherapist. "Neck breaks" are now recommended by medical experts - a walk round the building or a stroll in the local park for example.

Now for the ergonomic bit. The idea behind such keyboards is that they force your arms away from the side of your body, which in turn releases tension in the neck and shoulder area. However, it only works to the full if you are a touch typist.

Two other little points. The first relates to the special keys you may find on these keyboards (specifically to be used in conjunction with Windows 95), and the second to the price. Do shop around, but do also try to test out the keyboard of your choice before you commit yourself to one.
One of the cheap keyboards tried recently in a well-known store was pretty poor and not up to the job, but another one obtained from a well-known supplier was both cheap and of high quality.

COPY-CAT

Q How do I copy a file?

R W Barnes, Manchester

A A quick way to copy files is to highlight the file by clicking on it and pressing Ctrl-C. When you are at the location you want to move the text or files to, and press Ctrl-V. For moving, Ctrl-X will cut the selection. If you make a mistake, you can press Ctrl-Z to undo it; Explorer has three levels of Undo.

COPY-CAT II

Q How do I move a file from one folder to another without having to go back and delete the original file?
D S Sanders, Bristol

A When dragging files from one folder to another across the desktop, holding down the Ctrl button forces a copy, and Shift forces a move.

COPY-CAT III

Q I was copying stuff to a floppy disk to make a back-up when an error message came up. The other files on the disk are OK. What should I do?
H Poulenc, La Rochelle

A As the disk becomes full, the data is more closely packed and the likelihood of error increases. In a case like this, it's safer to throw the disk away.

COPY-CAT IV

Q Is it possible to make an exact copy of a file in a folder without having to load it into an application and fiddle around with Save As?
S Richardson, Newbury

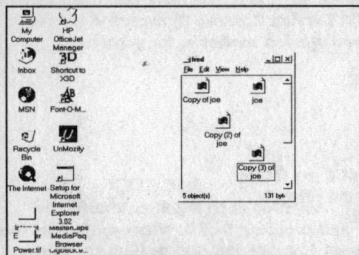

A folder with identical files in it, created by dragging with the Ctrl button down.

A Your prayer is easily answered. Hold down the Control key, click on the file you want and drag it to another part of the window. Release the mouse button, then Control. If the file is called Joe, you end up with a file called Copy of Joe. And if you make another copy, it's called Copy (2) of Joe, and so on.

SHUTTING DOWN

Q I switched my machine off the other day without shutting it down. Have I damaged anything?
B Davids, York

A Probably not, but if you have Windows will let you know. However, do not make a practice of doing so, as the shut-down process tidies things up ready for your next session.

PUT A STOP TO SETUP

Q Every time I put the Windows 95 disk in my CD drive, it runs the Setup and browser program. This is very annoying - how do I stop this from happening?
Kim Hartley, Lancs.

A When inserting an AutoPlay CD or an audio CD, you can prevent it from automatically playing by holding down the Shift button for a few seconds after you close the CD drawer.

UPDATES

Q Is there a new/updated version of Windows 95 available?

H J Matthews, Brighton

A Updated (Service Packs) are available for download free from Microsoft's Web site under Free Software. These updates provide new drivers and functionality. All of these service packs have been consolidated for a version (Windows 95 OEM Service Release 2) available on new PCs only. Currently, there is no new version available for purchase.

ABC...

Q An odd question, perhaps, but if my floppy drive is Drive A, why is the hard drive C and not A? George Crossly, London

A Not such a daft question, but don't rush to play around with this. If you do then there's a chance your system will crash when in Windows 95, so if you don't want to be stuck in MS-DOS mode, do not try this at home, or anywhere else for that matter.
In the old days, when the PC first came on the scene, it had a single floppy drive, courtesy of IBM. This was a low capacity, single-sided 5.25 inch

disk. Hard disks were unheard of (and when they
first came on to the scene, hideously expensive
and relatively low in capacity).

In order to copy from one floppy to another, you
needed a second drive, Drive B.

However, if you didn't possess one you could fool
the system into believing you had. Drive B was the phan-
tom alternative drive which allowed you to copy disk to disk.

QUICK START

Q Is there a quicker way of running my programs than click the start
button and look in the program list?
Steve Murdoch, Dundee

A If you frequently access files from a particular drive, you'll find it
useful to place an icon for that drive on your desktop. You can do
this easily by creating a shortcut.

Start by opening My Computer or Windows Explorer. Next, right click the
target drive's icon and drag it to the desktop. When you drop the icon on
the desktop, you'll see a context menu.

At this point, select the Create Shortcut(s) Here command and a new
shortcut to the drive will appear. You'll now be able to easily access your
drive by double clicking the new drive icon.

PASSWORD PROBLEMS

Q I'm the only person in our house who uses
a PC. Entering a password to start
Windows 95 each time I turn on the system
seems silly. Do I need to do this?
E Wiessman, Herts

A Fortunately, you can remove the default
password prompt by making your password blank. When you do, Windows 95 will
automatically start up without prompting
you for a password. It stores your password in a file that has the extension
PWL. The first part of the filename will be
the same as your user name. For example, if your
user name is Bob, then your password will be stored in a file
called BOB.PWL. You'll find this file in the Windows folder. To remove the
password prompt, begin by deleting your PWL file. Next, restart your system, and you'll see the Enter Windows Password dialog box. At this
point, simply click OK - don't type anything in the Password text box.
You'll never be prompted for a password again.

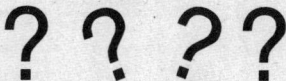

MS-DOS

Q What is MS-DOS and do I need it?
R Smith, Ipswich

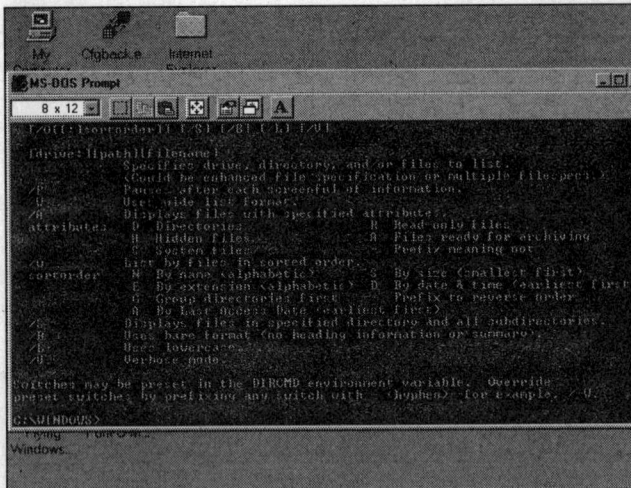

The MS-DOS Window showing the help for the DIR command

A It's the original command line-driven operating system for IBM PC and compatibles. It's available for running MS-DOS based programs and games, and you can still use the whole range of MS-DOS commands if you wish.

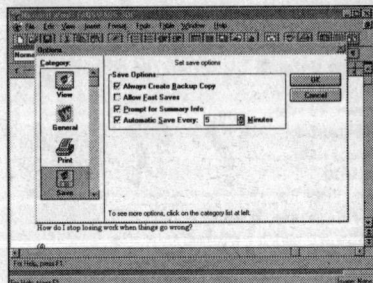

The dialog box in Word 2 which allows you to autosave documents at specified time intervals

GET SAVING

Q How do I stop losing work when things go wrong? G S Sampson, Oxford

A Two easy ways. First, press Alt+F and S every now and then to save the file you are currently working with. In addition, look at your software to see if it offers an Autosave function - if it does, use it.

STOPPING AUTORUN

Q How can I stop a music CD or a CD-ROM autoplaying when I load it into the machine?
O Fredricks, Newcastle

A There are two options available. The more flexible route, which keeps the option open for the disc to autorun, is to hold down the Shift key when loading the CD-ROM until the drive light stops flickering. To switch it off altogether, go to the Control Panel from the Settings part of the Start menu. Then double click on the System icon, select the Device Manager, then click on the plus sign against CD-ROM. When you see the name of your CD-ROM, double click on that and choose the Settings tab. Finally, remove the tick from the box marked Auto Insert Notification.

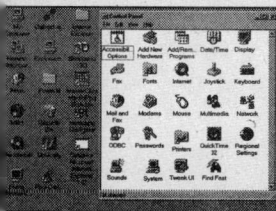

1 You access the Device Manager via the Systems icon on the Control Panel

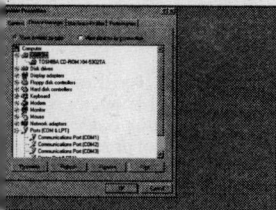

2 Click on the box alongside the CD-ROM icon to reveal the name of your player

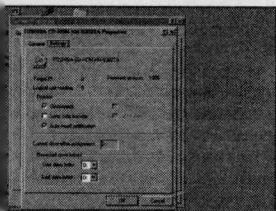

3 Use Help to get to Installing a Windows component after Windows has been loaded

ACCESSORISE YOUR SYSTEM

Q My friend's computer has a couple of accessories - Calculator and Character Map - which I don't have. Why not, and what can I do about it? James Hurtle, Manchester

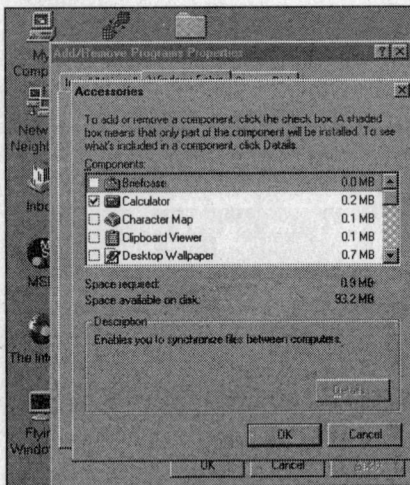

The list of Accessories is revealed by clicking on the Details button

A The quickest way is to start up Help, ask for Adding, Programs - then opt to Display Installing a Windows component after Windows has been installed. Up comes a dialog box which talks you through the adding process. The Calculator and the Character Map are under Accessories. An alternative route is via the Add/Remove programs icon on the Control Panel.

SHORTCUT TO SUCCESS

Q What's a shortcut, what use are they to me, and how do I get to use them? Helen Rhodes, Cornwall

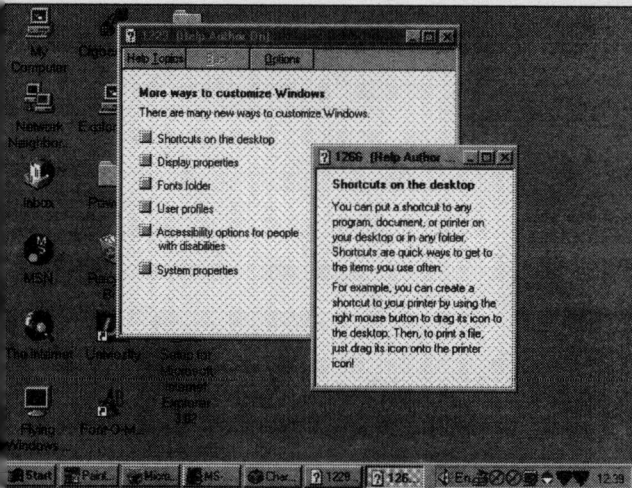

Help shows you how to make use of Shortcuts

A A shortcut is a kind of pointer which allows you to open an item quickly. If you don't want it any more, drag it to the Recycle Bin. It won't delete the item it points to, just the shortcut itself.

DOGGY DECORATIONS

Q I've a nice digital image of our pet dog. Is there any way I can use that as wallpaper for my desktop?
K Smith, London

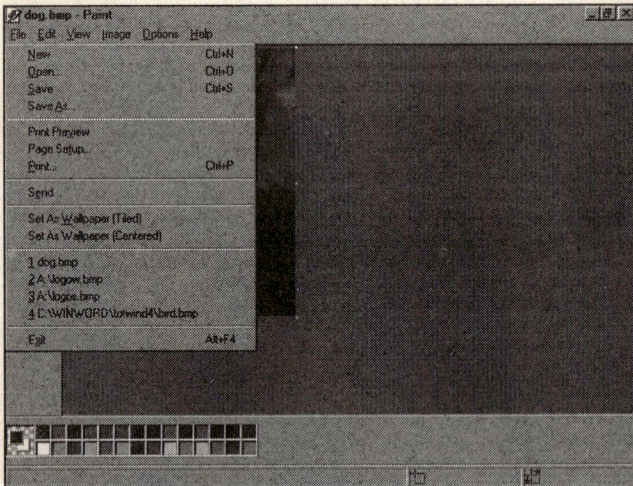

The Save as Wallpaper options in the File menu of Paint. If they're not highlighted, save the file first

The final product - dog wallpaper

A Load the file, preferably as a BMP (bitmap) or WMF (Windows Meta Format), into Paint, and then save as wallpaper. Note that Paint insists that you save the file from within Paint, even if it is already saved before it lets you save it as wallpaper, centred or tiled.

LIMITED ACCESS

Q How do I let someone else use my machine without letting them get access to my files or changing my settings?
J Jones, Birmingham

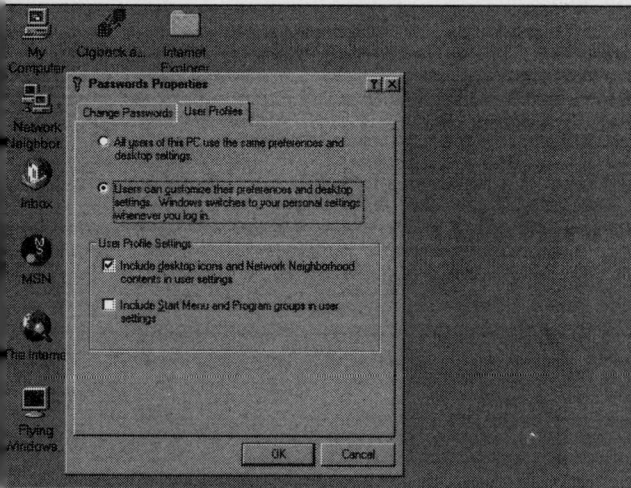

Preparing to set up different user profiles, which allows you to control access to your system

A Go to the Control panel, click on Passwords, opt for User Profiles, and that will allow you to set up "user profiles", as they are called.

WHERE'S PAINTBRUSH?

Q I've just upgraded from a Windows 3.1 machine. Whatever happened to Paintbrush?
Frank Dimly, Bristol

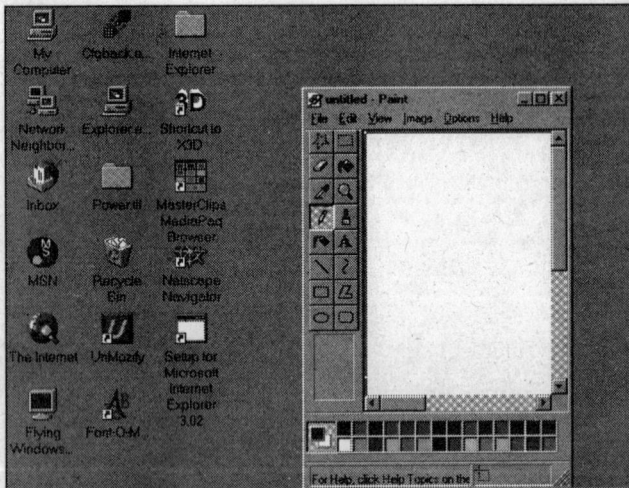

PaintBrush has been re-christened as Paint under Windows 95

A It's called Paint now, and should be on the Accessories continuation menu.

CODENAME: CHICAGO

Q Why is Windows 95 called Windows 95?

L P Wilson, Penrith

A That's the official name and more or less relates to the year it came out. Under development, it was codenamed Chicago. The next version is Windows 98 - which will become available later this year.

CUSTOMISING CLOSE-DOWN

Q Is it possible to customise the closing screens of Windows? J G Windsor, Arbroath

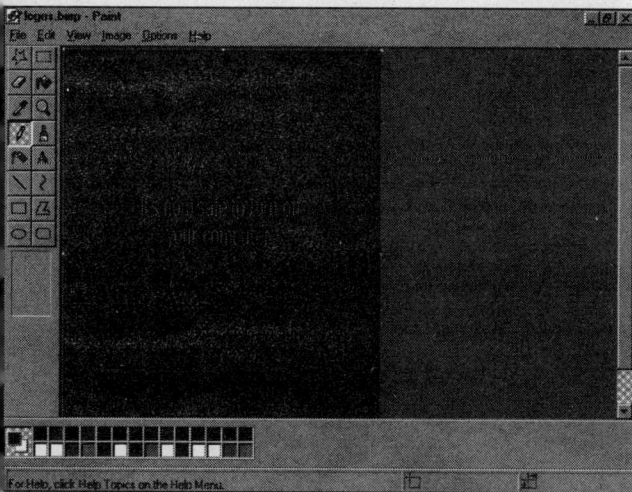

The Logos.sys file renamed as Logo.bmp and loaded into Paint

A Indeed it is. In the Windows folder, there are two files - LOGOW.SYS and LOGOS.SYS - which are the "Please wait..." and "It's now safe..." images. However, they have the SYS or system extension, which means that Paint refuses to acknowledge their existence. To be safe, copy them somewhere else, then change the extension to BMP. Load them into Paint, and you can now alter them to suit your fancy.

STARTING UP

Q I read somewhere about a Startup disk to use if Windows won't reload. How do I get one?
K L Vidal, London

A On the Start menu, go to Settings, then Control Panel. Select Add/Remove Programs and click on the Startup disk tab. Follow the instructions given.

BIN 'EM

Q I don't want to send some files to the Recycle Bin, just get rid of them. How's that done?
Carla White, Liverpool

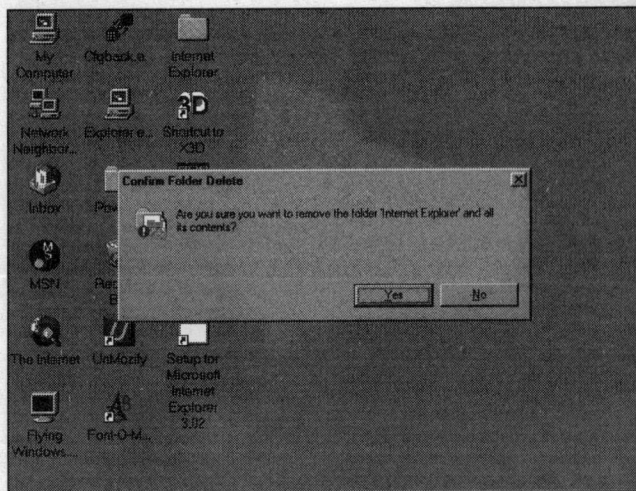

Right click on a file or folder, then Shift+D and you then get this final warning before deleting your programs

A Right click on the file, then press Shift+D and click on Yes. Make sure you really want to delete the file completely first, though.

BIN 'EM II

Q When I have a Save file or other similar window open, is it possible to delete files directly from the window?
N Dawson, Corby

A Click on the filename, then press Delete to send it to the Recycle Bin, Shift+Delete to delete it at once. You'll be asked to confirm in ___ cases. Alternatively, right click on the filename and choose the ___te option.

EMPTYING THE GARBAGE

Q Is there any way of deleting files completely while dragging them to the Recycle Bin without holding down Shift?
Durley, Devon

A Do note that if you send a file to the Recycle Bin, it just clutters up your drive until the Bin is full - by default, that takes up ten per cent of your drive which nowadays can be quite a hefty chunk. Right click on the Recycle Bin, and from the Global tab tick the Do not remove files to the Recycle Bin option.

GET MORE FROM START

Q I saw somewhere it's possible to add items to the Start menu for quicker access. How do you do that?
Bigsby, Taunton

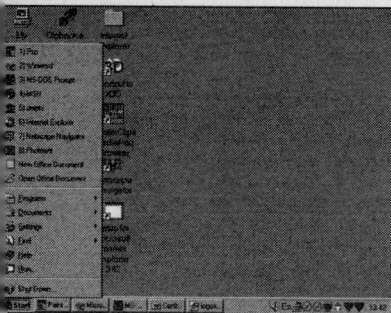

A customised Start menu. If it becomes too big to fit on the screen, opt for small icons

A Use Explorer to find the application you want, hold down the right mouse button, drag it over the Start menu, then release it. If you ave a few items, make life even easier by opening the Start menu fold-r (right click on the Start button, then opt for Open) and rename them y putting numbers in front. To run the application with the Start menu pen, just click the number you want.

TIDY DOCUMENTS

Q What's the point of the Documents option and how can I get rid of what's in it?
P Brinson, Stockport

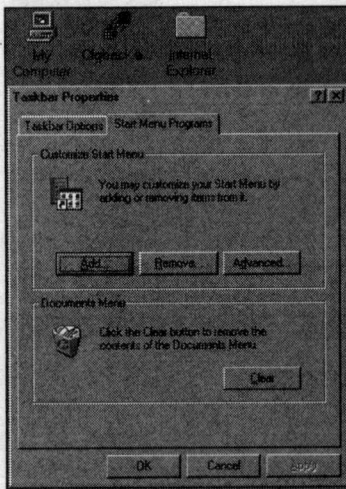

Use the Taskbar Properties dialog box to delete the contents of the Documents menu

A It contains the files you have accessed most recently - from those programs designed for Windows 95 which can use the Documents menu, that is. So Word 2 can't, but Word 97 can. Click on a file and it will conveniently open it within the appropriate application. To empty the Documents menu, right click on the Taskbar. Opt for Properties and click on the Start menu tab. You'll see an option for you to erase the contents of the Documents menu.

LOSING TIME

Q Can I remove the clock from the Taskbar?

G Lampson, Northants

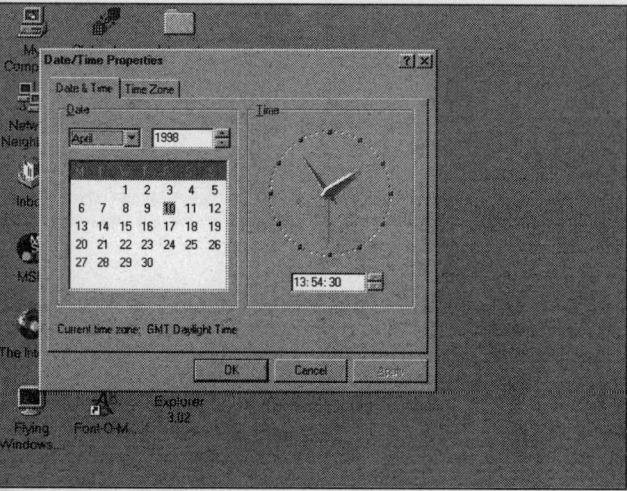

Adjusting the Date and Time - also allows you to alter time zones

A Right click on the Taskbar, go for Properties and the Taskbar Options tab. You'll now be able to remove the tick from the Show Clock box by clicking on it or pressing C.

CLEAN UP YOUR TASKBAR

Q How can I possibly right click on the Taskbar when it's fully cluttered up with items?

Ed Richards,

A If your Taskbar is across the bottom of the screen, move the mouse pointer to the extreme left or right of the bar and then right click. Up should come the menu.

TASKBAR II

Q My screen gets cluttered with the Taskbar. Can I hide it - and get it back when I want it?
Dave Beattie, Slough

A Right click on the Taskbar, click on the Taskbar options tab and then click on Auto Hide. This conceals the Taskbar until you move the mouse pointer over where it would have been if it had been there. That causes the Taskbar to reappear, until you move the pointer away again.

TASKBAR III

Q If you right click on a blank part of the Taskbar, you can Minimise Windows and do other things. What if your Taskbar is full and there is no space, what do you do then?
Simon Matthews, Brighton

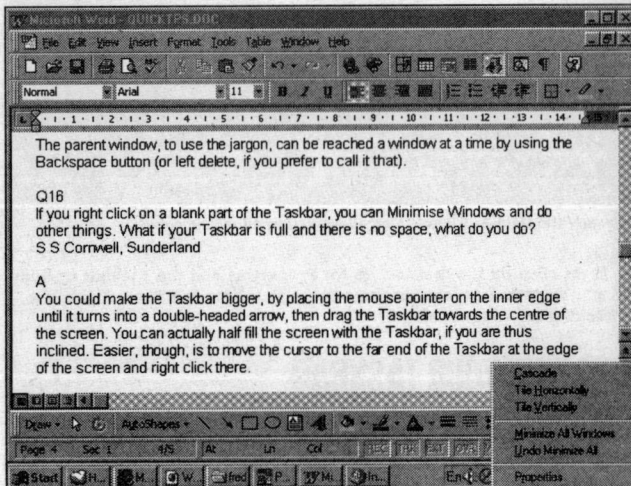

The parent window, to use the jargon, can be reached a window at a time by using the Backspace button (or left delete, if you prefer to call it that).

Q16
If you right click on a blank part of the Taskbar, you can Minimise Windows and do other things. What if your Taskbar is full and there is no space, what do you do?
S S Cornwell, Sunderland

A
You could make the Taskbar bigger, by placing the mouse pointer on the inner edge until it turns into a double-headed arrow, then drag the Taskbar towards the centre of the screen. You can actually half fill the screen with the Taskbar, if you are thus inclined. Easier, though, is to move the cursor to the far end of the Taskbar at the edge of the screen and right click there.

If you right click on the far end of the Taskbar, you'll find that however cluttered up it is, you get the appropriate pop-up menu

A You could make the Taskbar bigger by placing the mouse pointer on the inner edge until it turns into a double-headed arrow, then drag the Taskbar towards the centre of the screen. You can actually half fill the screen with the Taskbar, if you are that way inclined. Easier, though, is to move the cursor to the far end of the Taskbar at the edge of the screen and right click there.

PROGRAM MANAGER

Q I liked the Program Manager in Windows 3.1. Can I use it under Windows 95?
Dean Kelly, Dublin

A You can if you want, but it's not recommended as it doesn't support long filenames, or drag files around or rename them. It's in the Windows folder as PROGMAN.EXE.

HIDDEN EXTENSIONS

Q]Why can't I see the file extensions in My Computer?
S Jackson, London

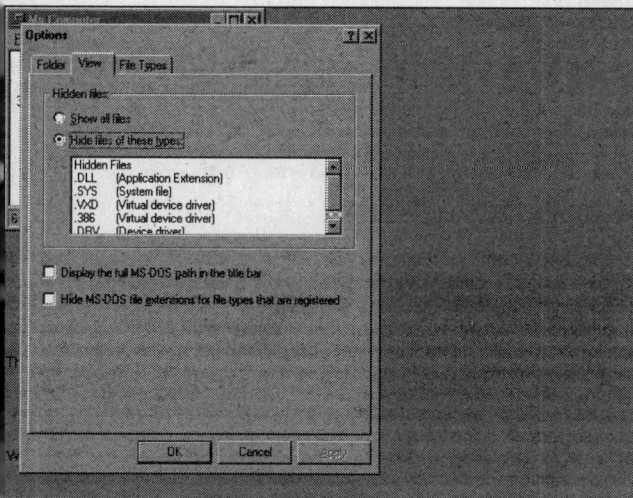

Use this dialog box to add or remove file extensions from filenames

A Because you haven't asked for them. Open My Computer, select View and Options. Then click on the View tab and ensure that the option to Hide MS-DOS extension names isn't ticked.

COMMON MISTAKES WITH DIALOG

Q I changed an option under the screen saver but it won't work. Why not?
Kelvin Gerrard, Worthing

A A common mistake is to alter something in a dialog box and then press Cancel or just move the focus away to something else without pressing OK or Apply.

THE WINDOWS KEY TO SUCCESS

Q I have a Windows keyboard which has the special Windows keys on it. Apart from bringing up the Start menu and acting as a right mouse button click, do they have any other uses?
T R Michaels, Leicester

A Indeed they do. Assuming that "Win" stands for the Windows key, try these: Win+Tab takes you round the Taskbar buttons. When the one of your choice is highlighted, press Enter to restore the application. Win+M and Shift+Win+M minimise and unminimise all tasks. Win+F1 launches Windows Help. Win+R opens the Run dialog box. Win+F starts the Find files or folders dialog, and finally Ctrl+Win+F finds computer.

BAD NEWS

Q What does a General failure message mean on a floppy disk?
Pete Hempson, Preston

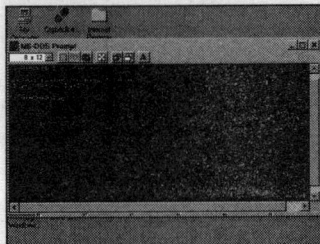

If an unfamiliar or faulty disk is accessed via the MS-DOS Window it will throw up a General Failure message

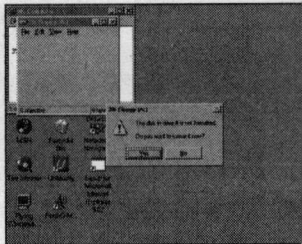

If you try and access a rogue disk with My Computer, it will think it is unformatted and invite you to format it thus losing all its contents

A Usually bad news. Try removing the disk from the drive and inserting again. If that doesn't work, try accessing it from another application. If you succeed in accessing the disk, copy any important stuff from it right away.

It sounds like you were looking at the disk from the MS-DOS Window. If you use My Computer, it treats a faulty disk in the same way as one with a format it doesn't recognise: it invites you to format it.

DISK CARE

Q I bent the metal slide bar on a floppy disk. Are its contents lost?

M Neilson, Newcastle

A No. First, remove the slider altogether, ensuring that the spring is also removed. Don't touch the surface of the actual disk inside the housing. Then insert the disk into the drive, copy the files you want, and then discard the disk.

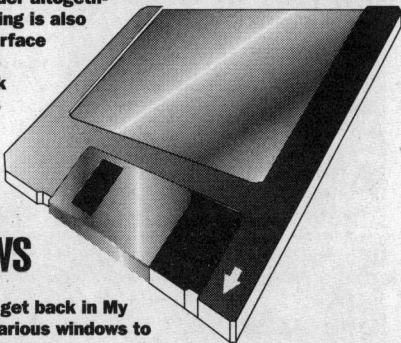

BACKTRACK THROUGH WINDOWS

Q Silly question. How do I get back in My Computer through the various windows to the one I started with?
L D Griffin, Bournemouth

A The parent window, to use the jargon, can be reached a window at a time by using the Backspace button (or left delete button, if you prefer to call it that).

EASY ACCESS

Q One thing I find annoying when opening an Open file window is that it always resets itself to showing the beginning of the list alphabetically, even if it is a big folder and the previous file I opened was at the end of the alphabet. Is there a cure?
T Kennedy, Cambridge

A Very irritating this one is, too. It would be nice if Windows 'remembered' whereabouts you last accessed a file. There are a couple of suggestions. First: give in and make your folders smaller. Secondly: click on the window, then hit the first letter of the file you are after, and it will obligingly jump to that part of the list.

BLAST OFF!

Q I read somewhere you can actually launch a Windows application from the MS-DOS Window. Is it true?B

G Jarvis, Sheffield

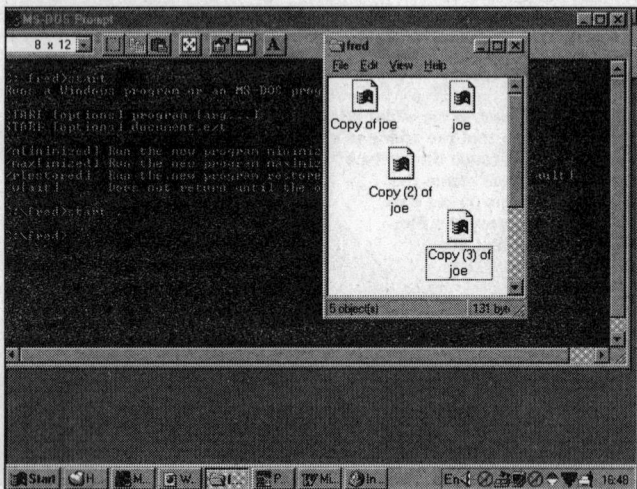

Type START in the MS-DOS Window without a parameter, and it explains what it does. START plus a folder name brings up that folder

A Yes. With a DOC file just type START plus the file name. This trick can also be used to open a folder to inspect the files in it. From the MS-DOS prompt, type START followed by the name of the folder or file you want. Type START plus a space plus a full stop, and you'll open the current folder.

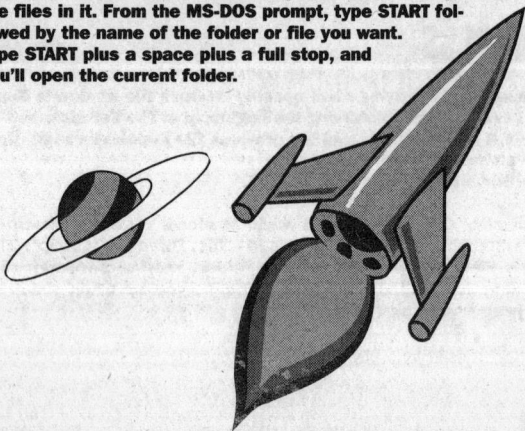

HIDDEN EXTENSIONS II

Q I want to see file extensions displayed, especially in a folder full of graphics with different types, like GIF, JPEG and so on. Can it be done?
A F Briggs, Manchester

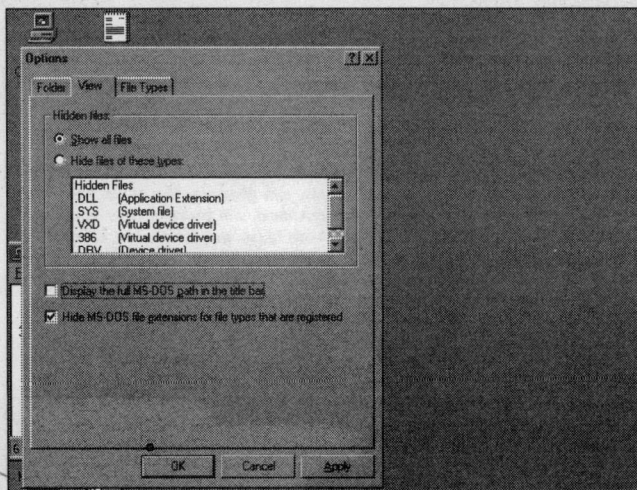

My Computer, View, Options, then the View tab lets you opt to reveal extension names

A Go to My Computer, click on View, Options, then the View tab, and remove the tick against Hide extensions.

MOUSE TROUBLE

Q I'm a bit shaky with the mouse, and when you get one of those boxes with lots of tabs on them, there are no underlined letters to allow you to press Alt+ something to get where you want. Is there a keyboard solution?
Jane Farrell, Birmingham

A What seems to work is that if you press Ctrl+Tab, a dotted rectangle appears round the tab name, then if you press Ctrl+ left or right arrow, you cycle through the tabs in the appropriate direction. Continuous pressing of Ctrl+Tab gets you round them from left to right.

APPLICATIONS

POSTER POWER

Q I offered to design a poster for the Scouts' coffee morning, but I made a complete mess of it. I thought this DTP stuff was simple. Can you help me?
Neil Jones, Nottingham

A You, like many who use computers, have made the fundamental mistake of thinking that the technology will give you the skills needed to implement it. A word processor, for instance, will correct your spelling and other errors (within limits), but there is no way it will make you a good writer, either of letters to the editor, or of a great novel.
The same applies to DTP. Now to answer your question. Point one: Keep it simple and make it striking. Point two: Posters are there to get a message across, and nothing should get in the way of this important point. To achieve the best results, think of the three key elements of any poster:

What (in other words, name the event)
When (date and time)
Where (location of the event)

When incorporating these elements into the poster, put the What into the largest typeface and nearest the top of the page. We tend to look at the upper half of a page first, and that's important when your potential customers may just get a fleeting glimpse of the poster as they are driving or walking past.

In the words of the time-honoured cliché, a picture is worth a thousand words, and so if you are advertising a coffee morning, a cup of coffee would clearly convey the message. A character breasting the winning tape will announce a school's sports day, and a pack of cards inform you of a bridge or whist evening. And a pair of sad and happy masks will tell you that there's a play on at the village hall over the weekend. But don't go overboard - too many images will produce a confusing product.
And do try to be consistent: if you are designing a poster, tickets and a programme for the event, make

sure that you follow through the design in each element, using the same typefaces, and if you have used a logo or image, put it on each part of the documentation.

A poster with all the right information on it, plus a nice logo. Note that the organisation running the event needs a mention (near the top of the page is ideal).

INTRO

Paint Shop Pro is a much-praised shareware graphics package, ideal for single-page graphics and for manipulating images for local or Internet use. Here are just a few of the questions we've received on how to get the best out of Paint Shop Pro. Except where otherwise mentioned, answers refer to Version 4.14.

Version 5 is now being tested. For regular updates, you will find the relevant information on the Internet at www.jasc.com The JASC bit stands for Japan-American Student Conference - but this is not very important.

TURN THE PAGE FOR PSP PROBLEMS!

SMOOTHING THE JAGGED EDGES

Q I'm having a spot of bother with Paint Shop Pro. I have what I hope is an up-to-date version, and I read somewhere about anti-aliasing and the way in which this technique smoothes over the rough edges in text, so that the sides of a capital A for example don't look jagged.
So I duly ensured anti-aliasing was switched on and nothing happened. The text was just as jagged as it was before. What have I done wrong?
Charlie Hobbs, North London

Anti-aliasing e

and switche

An enlarged image showing anti-aliasing switched on for the first line, and off on the line below

A Apart from getting involved with computers in the first place, the answer is buried in the small print of Paint Shop Pro. First of all, for those of you who don't know, anti-aliasing is a crafty way of smoothing over lines which otherwise would look clunky and unprofessional.
The trouble is that anti-aliasing isn't activated unless you have an image with 16.5 million colours, the standard for JPG images. Go to Colours, and increase the colour depth to the maximum.
This doesn't mean you have to save the file as a JPG - once the anti-aliasing is done, it remains in effect, all other things being equal.

GRIDLOCKED

Q I don't understand the option to show a grid when the image is expanded. It's on as far as I can see, but when I click on the magnifying glass, the image just gets bigger, but it doesn't show gridlines. I must have slipped up somewhere, but I still can't see where I went astray. Can you assist?
Werner Schmidt, Newcastle

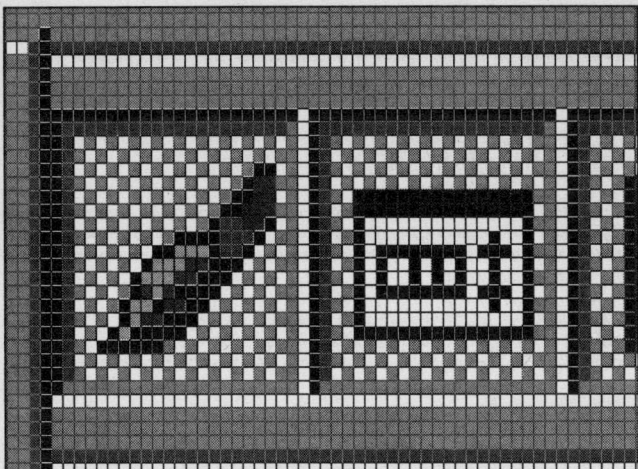

Looking like a design for a marble bathroom floor, this is part of the Tool palette of Paint Shop Pro magnified 10 times.

A You haven't been adventurous enough! The image needs to be expanded to 10:1 before the gridlines appear for the first time - and then you can really get into detail and change one pixel at a time.

NO ROOM FOR THE PICTURE

Q How do I maximise the viewing area for images - or is it even possible to make it bigger? The latest version of PSP takes up a lot of space, especially with the Colour palette on the right. I have a 640 x 480 display and it's such a nuisance having to scroll back and forth through an image.
JJ Foreman, Winchester

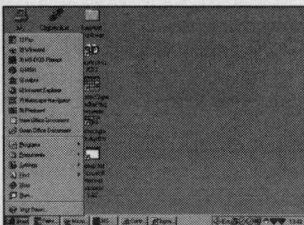

The View menu with all the options switched on - remove them and switch on the Full screen to get as much image as possible

A Click on the View menu item and clear the tick from the following (by clicking on them one by one): Toolbar, Tool palette, Colour bar, Style bar and finally Status bar. Then tick Full screen edit option.
Now you have a complete screen for your image to expand into. To access the menu items along the top of the screen, move the cursor to the top, then click - you will see that as you move along, the menus

will subsequently appear.

It's useful to have the magnifying glass tool selected in this mode. It allows you to rapidly increase or decrease the size of your image. Don't forget that you can work on an image in reduced size - it doesn't have to be at a scale of 1:1 for editing purposes.

FOUR LETTER WORDS

Q I have a program called Unmodify which allows me to archive material which I have explored on the Internet. I am anxious to copy various images and photographs, but with Paint Shop Pro I have come up against an infuriating problem.

I thought file extensions were three letters long or less, but quite often I have come up against files which, according to Paint Shop Pro, have the extension JPE. The program cannot recognise these files. What is going on?
Harold Weaver, Ely

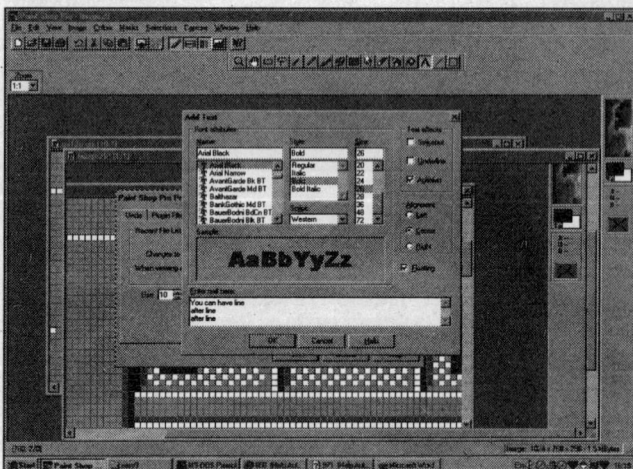

Do check out all the Preference tabs to see the range of available options in Paint Shop Pro

A There are various packages which allow you to inspect off-line the sites which you have visited, and you are quite right - there is a problem with the fact that the PC's operating system originally allowed for eight plus three filenames, that is, eight characters for the name proper, and three for the extension.
A side effect of Windows 95 allowing for long filenames is that there is rich opportunity for incompatibilities and confusions. One of these comes

with 3.1 programs running under 95.

What has happened is that you have found on the Internet a machine which supports four-character extension names (JPEG, HTML, and so on), but Paint Shop Pro picks up only the first three letters, in this case JPE. It looks up JPE in its list of graphics types, fails to find it, and then gives up, saying the file is unknown to it.

What can you do? Simple: rename the file type as JPG, and all should be well. It's possible to go back into the MS-DOS prompt, find the appropriate directory and type: REN *.JPE *.JPG, which is a lot quicker than using Windows Explorer.

MY UNDOING

Q When I opt for Undo I find the last half dozen things I have done have been undone. What's going on? Also, I wish the program allowed me to have more than one line of text.
P Williams, Isle of Man

A You have got an elderly version of Paint Shop Pro, which is quite a nuisance in this respect. Get version 4.14 - the latest one for Windows.

Turning to text: You'll find the latest version offers a much better text-handling facility with the option to left, right and centre justify, and much more than just one line of text.

INVISIBLE INK

Q I'm a beginner with Paint Shop Pro, and I am driven to despair. I can't get text to appear on screen and the whole thing has seized up on me. I enclose a disk with a screen dump to see if you can find out what is wrong.
Ken Griffiths, Grampian

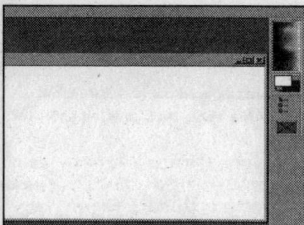

Part of the screen dump sent in by our reader - showing that the foreground colour is white and the background of the image is white, too. No wonder there is no text to be seen!

A This is one of the oldest goofs in the game, and a trap we have all fallen into with monotonous regularity. The dump you sent in shows that the background colour of the image you are using is white, and that on the Colour palette the foreground colour is also white.
This means you are placing white text on a white background; we leave it up to our readers to work out what the result is!

DOWNSIZING

Q When I reduce a photograph - I use Paint Shop Pro, it can get rather muddy-looking. Is there a way round this?
F G March, Wisbech

A If you are using JPG (JPEG) format, try converting it to GIF (CompuServe) format. That will reduce the colours to 256 and quite often does the trick. On the whole, try to fiddle around with resizing complex images as little as you can, since quality degradation is often the result of resizing.

SHADOWPLAY

Q I'm on a tight budget but I would like to have those fancy shadow effects you can get from expensive graphics packages. I just use Paint and there seems to be no way of getting them. Can you help?
S D Wright, Burslem

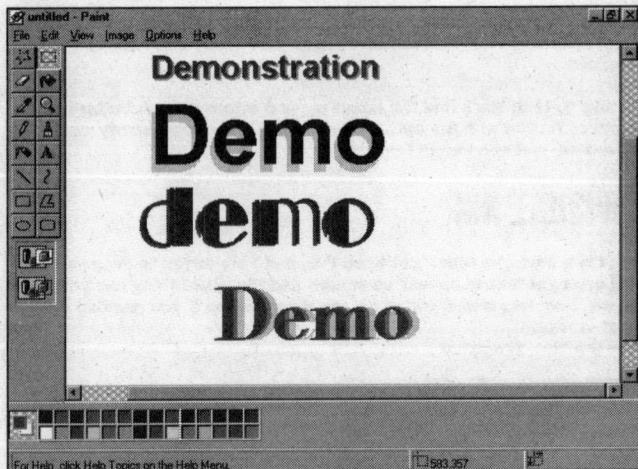

A number of effects using two or three colours of the same text, pasting one over another

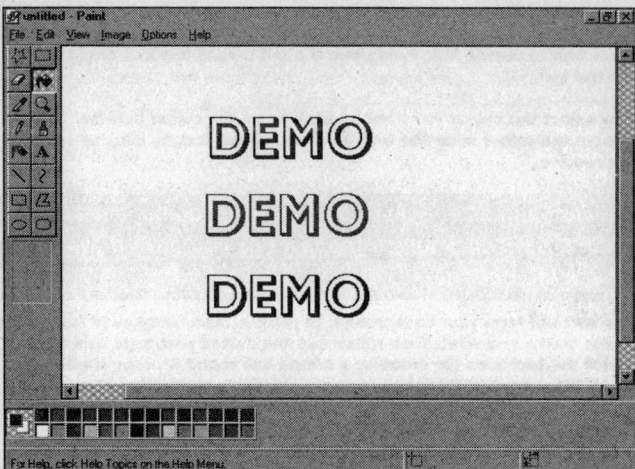
Three 'layers' ready for cutting and pasting. Work from the bottom layer upwards

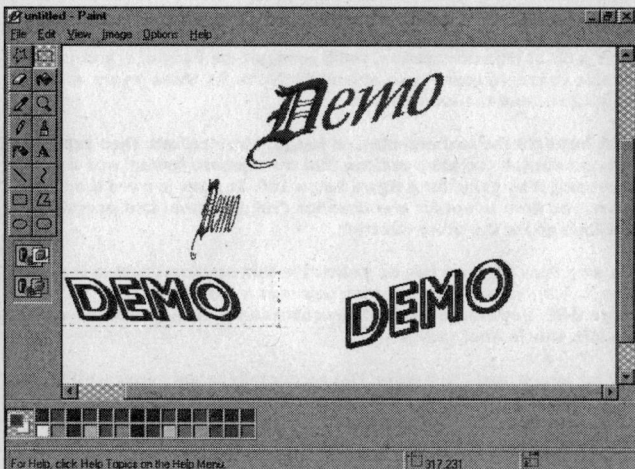
More effects, this time using stretch and skew to further dramatise the appearance

A This is a case where an ounce of ingenuity is better than a ton of money, and a great deal more fun. You will need to experiment for the best effects, but this is basically what you can do.

First, take a blank screen and put a couple of words of text on it in a light colour. You do this by clicking on the A button (the Text Tool), then use the cross hair to draw a box. Hold down the left mouse key and drag to create the box.

Now select the colour you want by clicking on the colour palette. You can change the colour once the text has been typed, too, by clicking on what you require.

> *For font and size, ensure that the Text Toolbar is visible. If it isn't, right click inside the text box you have drawn and check the option.*

This text will form your background. To get the main foreground text, click on the colour you want. Then either use the dotted rectangle tool to select the text area (by creating a dotted line round it), copy it and paste it to a blank part of the image and use the Fill tool (the tipped up paint can) to change its colour. Cut it and paste it over the background text slightly offset to give the shadow effect.

That's easiest if there are only a few letters. The alternative is to create another text box of the same size and retype the text in the foreground colour. Then select it with the dotted rectangle tool, cut it and then paste it over the background colour.

After a bit of experimentation, you'll soon get the hang of it and you will be able to create some quite stunning effects. Try three layers or more, building up from the lowest layer.

Also, highlight the text and click on Image, Stretch/Skew. Then experiment with the stretch and skew options. You can squeeze text as well as stretching it by going for a figure below 100. To skew in more than one plane, you have to opt for one direction first, complete that operation, and then go for the other direction.

You may think that you can only skew the text so that it tilts to the right (like italics), because the program demands a positive integer in the range 0-89. However, a piece of deviousness will allow you to skew text to the left. This is what you do.

Opt for Image, and Flip/Rotate. Flip horizontally to get mirror writing, then skew, then flip back horizontally. That will tilt your text to the left, like backwards italics. A few more tricks, and you can get text to cast a skewed shadow.

A SEE-THROUGH PROBLEM

Q I'm struggling with Paint Shop Pro Version 4 and a simple web page. I have a yellow background colour and want to put a banner on it consisting of text and a logo, but I want them to have a transparent background, so it looks as if they are perched on top of the yellow. The background colour of the file is white and it resolutely refuses to change, even if I opt for it to be transparent. Can you assist?

P Williams, North Yorkshire

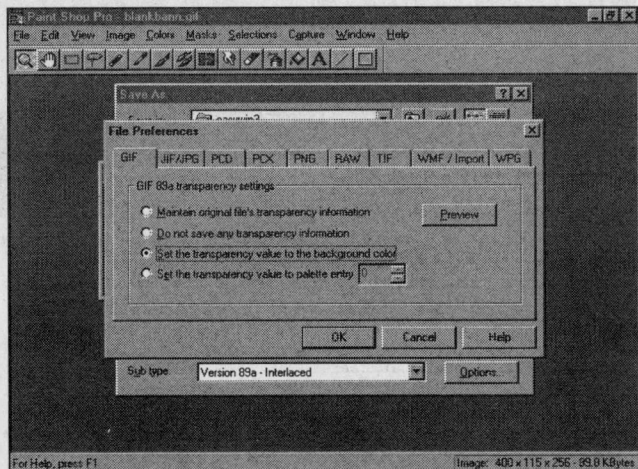

When Saving As with Paint Shop Pro, ensure that the transparency is set to the background colour and the subtype is 89A Interlaced - then it will appear just right on the web page

A A bit complicated, this. If your file is JPEG, convert it to GIF. Open the Save As dialog box, and ensure that the file subtype is Version 89a Interlaced. Then click on Options and check the radio button which sets the transparency value to the background colour. That should do the trick.

SWAP LETTER CASES

Q How do I change upper and lower case characters around in Word?

Paul Spick, Dover

A Highlight the letter or letters you want to change. Then press Shift+F3. This is a neat little three-part toggle, which goes from lower case to upper case for first letters of the words highlighted to ALL UPPER, and then back again to all lower.

It's a nice touch, but note that this trick doesn't work with WordPad, which is a cut-down version of Word 6.

HEADED LETTERS

Q A friend of mine has rather nice headed paper with a red woodpecker on a tree trunk. When I asked him which graphics package he got it from, he told me he hadn't, it was just an ordinary typeface. Am I having my leg pulled?
Jackie Rees, Lincoln

A In a word, no. This is a typeface you may well find on your machine called Animals. It has all kinds of beasts of the field and birds of the air, but you will have to print them in a pretty large typeface to have any impact in your letter.

A menagerie from the Animals font - note that 72 point is as big as WordPad goes, so you'll need a full-blooded word processor to get a more striking effect

LOCATE THE QUOTES IN WORD FOR WINDOWS

Q It's only just occurred to me that you are supposed to be able to get proper single and double quotes in Word for Windows, not just the typewriter up-and-down marks, but I don't seem to be able to find them. Where are they concealed?
R. Hamid, Hull

A If you type Alt+0145 with the NumLock on, you get open single quote, and Alt+0146 gets you the closing single quote. For double quotes, Alt+0147 and Alt+0148. With Notepad, the single quotes work,

Accessing the Symbol option under Word 2

but the double ones don't. Both work in WordPad.

If you can't remember those numbers, press Alt+I (for the Insert drop-down menu), and opt for Symbol. Make sure that you have Symbol in the font box on display in front of you.

Then, double click on the Symbol you are after. Do beware of one little snag, though: there are some fonts which do not support "proper" quotes. One of the commonest is Arial.

As an alternative to Insert Symbol, you can use the Character Map accessory if you like. That has the added advantage of allowing you to insert more than one exotic character at a time.

97

SFX

Q I saw some fancy effects in Word. Is it possible to have shadow text, outline and so on?
M. Etheridge, Manchester

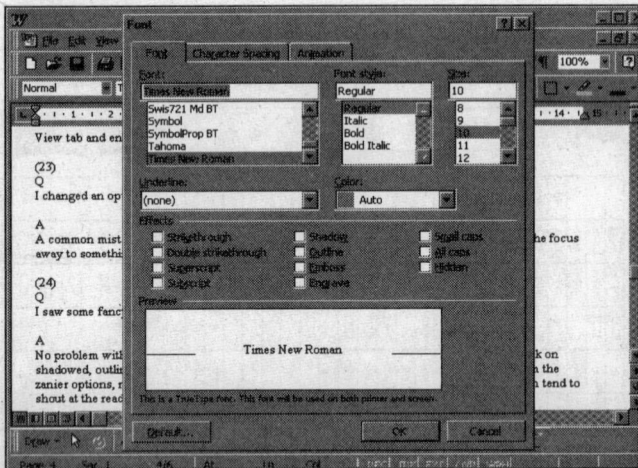

Fancy effects can be achieved via Fonts on the Format menu

A No problem with the later versions of Word. Go for Format, then Font and the Font tab. Click on shadowed, outline, emboss and so on and watch the effect in the preview window. Note the small caps option, which can be more effective than ALL CAPS which tend to shout at the reader too much.

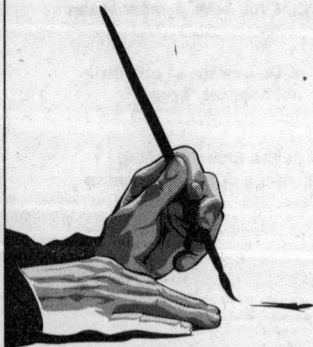

CHANGE YOUR FONTS

Q Can you change fonts in a Word document using Find and Replace?

Betty Johnson, Reading

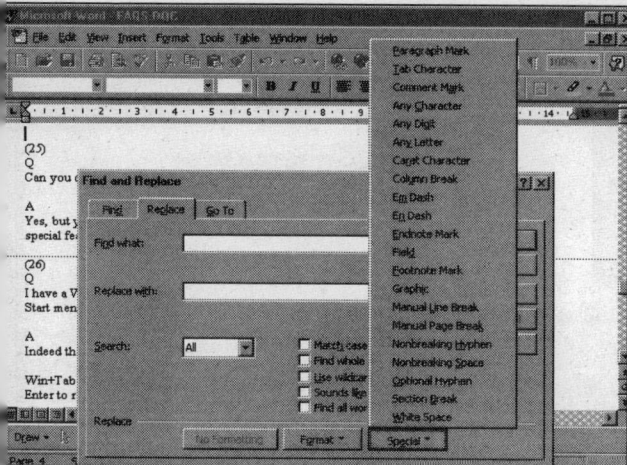

Special Find and Replace in Word 97 - from Find and Replace, click on More, then Special

A Yes, but you must use Special Find and Replace, which allows you to try out the various special features of Word. Go to Edit, Find and Replace, click on More, then Special. There's a preview window to let you see the effect of your changes.

CORRUPTION!

Q I have a floppy disk with three files on it which are somehow corrupt and I want to get as much out of them as I can. Is there a way of doing this?
Brian R Wetherall, West Yorkshire

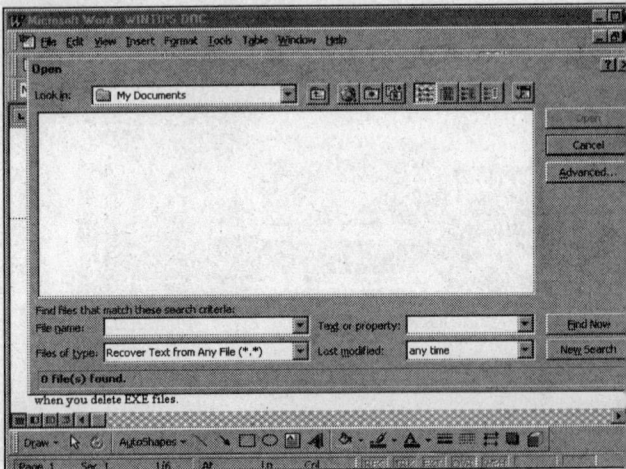

How to recover damaged files using Word 97

A There is, actually, using Word 97. If you have a file which is a text file - it doesn't have to be a Word 97 file - press Alt+F and Open, and click on the file you want to try and recover.

Under 'Files of type' you will find 'Recover text from any file'. Go for Open and see what Word 97 can restore for you. By the way, don't save any recovered material on to the suspect disk. Once you've extracted from all you can, bin the disk - and not in the Recycle Bin, either!

SFX II

Q I have Word 97 and love the special effects you can get with characters. I can't get these effects in my graphics program, though. Is there any way of using them in images?
W Jones, Cardiff

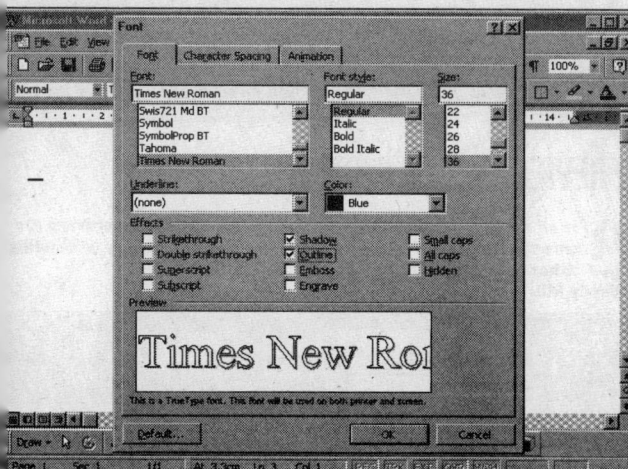

Special text effects using Word 97

A Try setting the effect out in Word then press Print Screen. Switch to Paint Shop Pro, press Alt+E and paste as new image. Now cut and paste the special effect into the image file you are working with. You may have to resize the image or experiment with the size of the Word text, but it's a workable solution.

HIDE AND SEEK

Q When using Word, can I make comments in the text which don't appear when I print a document?
Wilson, Aberdeen

A You are referring to what is known as 'hidden text'. You can enter notes and other information in a variety of ways. The easiest is to press Ctrl+H to toggle hidden text on and off. To be able to see it - it appears with a dotted underlining - go to Tools, Options, Modify view settings and tick the box. To print the hidden text, go to Print, Options and select hidden text.

MACROS EXPLAINED

Q What's a Word macro and do I need one?

J James, Birmingham

A Probably not, if you haven't felt the lack of one. A macro is a command which causes a whole number of pre-stored commands to be carried out, and it's used when you want to repeat a sequence of commands time and again. Have a look at Word Help to see if there is a role for macros in your computing. It's not too difficult once you get the hang of them.

PREVIEW PROBS WITH WORD 97

Q I'm all confused. When I had Word 2 I used Find File to preview file contents - easy. With Word 97 I'm lost, and I see no way of deleting files either. Can you help?

Wendy Hill, Ely

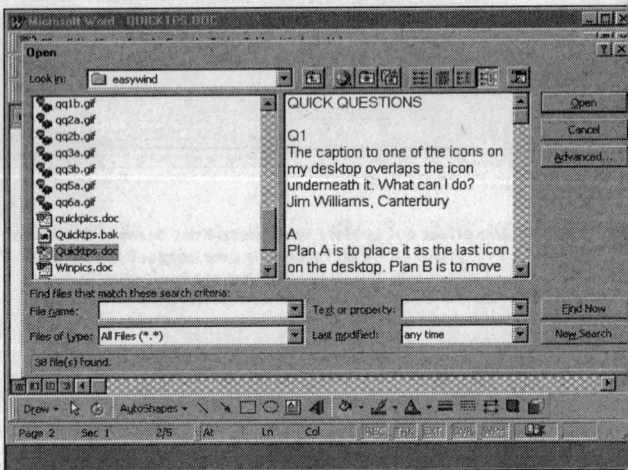

This is the way to preview documents in Word 97 - click on the Preview box at the top of the window

A Word 97 goes about things differently. Click on the Open box, select the folder you want to look in, then press the Preview box. To delete a file, right click on its name with the mouse and up comes the menu with Delete on it.

HOW MANY WORDS?

Q How do I do a word count in Word?

H Allardyce, Chester,

In order to get to the Statistics, go for Alt+F then I (Properties), then click on the Statistics tab

A You don't say which version. In early versions of Word for Windows, go for Alt+F, I (for Summary Info), then go for Statistics. In later versions, Alt+F, I (for Properties, this time), then click on the Statistics tab.

COLUMN SPACE

Q When using narrow columns, sometimes big gaps appear in the text, especially with long words. What do I do?
G Annan, Doncaster

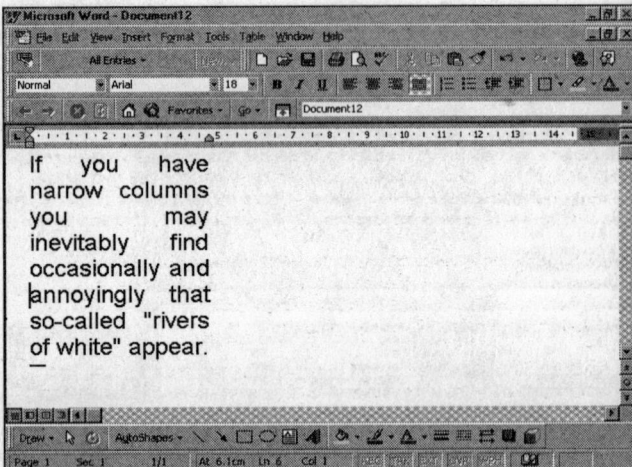

> If you have narrow columns you may inevitably find occasionally and annoyingly that so-called "rivers of white" appear.

An example of ugly white spaces appearing, typically when you have very narrow columns

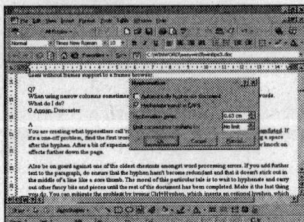

The Hyphenation dialog box with its various options, including automatic hyphenation

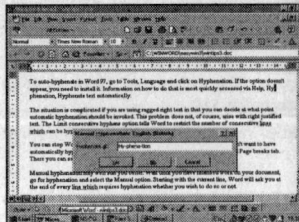

A manual hyphenation session in progress, stopping at a pretty appropriate word. Pure chance, honest

A You are creating what typesetters call 'rivers of white' down the page and they look pretty ham-fisted. If it's a one-off problem, find the first word on the next line and hyphenate it if you can, leaving a space after the hyphen. After a bit of experimentation, the text may sort itself out, but watch out for knock-on effects further down the page.

Also, be on guard against one of the oldest chestnuts amongst word processing errors. If you add further text to the paragraph, do ensure that the hyphen hasn't become redundant and that it doesn't stick out in the middle of a line like a sore thumb. The moral of this particular tale is to wait to hyphenate and carry out other fancy bits and pieces until the rest of the document has been completed. Make it the last thing you do. You can avoid the problem by typing Ctrl+Hyphen, which inserts an optional hyphen, and which disappears if it is not needed.

A better approach is to let your word processor do all or some of the work for you. At this point, do bear in mind the difference between soft and hard hyphens. A soft hyphen is one which goes into the text at the end of a print line as and when needed. A hard hyphen is one which has to be retained wherever it appears on a line, in words which need them.

To auto-hyphenate in Word 97, go to Tools, Language and click on Hyphenation. If the option doesn't appear, you need to install it. Information on how to do that is most quickly accessed via Help, Hyphenation, Hyphenate text automatically.

The situation is complicated if you are using ragged right text, in that you can decide at what point automatic hyphenation should be invoked. That issue does not, of course, arise with right justified text. The Limit consecutive hyphens option tells Word to restrict the number of consecutive lines which can be hyphenated.

You can stop Word from hyphenating part of a document by highlighting the bit you don't want to have automatically hyphenated. Then go to Format, Paragraph, and click on the Line and Page breaks tab. There you can see a check box which inhibits hyphenation.

Manual hyphenation may well suit you better. Wait until you have finalised work on your document, go for hyphenation and select the Manual option. Starting with the current line, Word will ask you at the end of every line which requires hyphenation whether you wish to do so or not.

Word is also brainy enough to remove a hyphen if you change the wording of your document in such a way that the hyphen is no longer relevant. However, you will have to go over the hyphenation process again for that paragraph.

As for a hard hyphen, type Ctrl+Shift+Hyphen.

BLAST FROM THE PAST

Q For a number of years I have been using an Amstrad 8512 with LocoScript and an external 3.5 inch drive. I now have a PC and having written three books, several lectures and numerous short stories on my Amstrad, how can I make the disks compatible with Windows 95?
A R S Aston Cannock, Staffs

A Those of us with long memories will recall the fact that the personal computing revolution began with Alan Sugar's little Amstrad machines, the Personal Computer Word processors, the famous little green-screen PCW and its more elaborate descendants. Some of us will admit under torture to having in the past written a few thousand words about the machine, its native word processor LocoScript and the CP/M operating system.

The question is, how do you get the data which you hold on PCW format disks on to a PC? This is quite a complicated issue, dependant on a number of factors. The first is that there were two sizes of disk, 3 inch and 3.5 inch. The second is that LocoScript documents, like those of any other word processor, are not plain text but full of codes and so forth which are peculiar to it.

Let's start with the best case scenario. If you have a version of LocoScript for the PC and a PCW with a 3.5 inch disk drive, then you are almost home and dry. All you need is a program which you mount on your PC which reads PCW formatted disks and your documents with all their styles, layouts and so forth are copied across.

The next best situation is that you decide that only the text of your documents is important, so export them as plain ASCII text on the PCW, then use the program to read the disk on your PC.

It gets worse. If you have a 3 inch drive, or if you have no version of LocoScript on your PC (or worse still, both apply) then you need help. Try www.locomotive.com on the Internet, which offers various products for transferring material from the PCW to the PC. And, if you are really stuck there is a disk transfer service on offer too.

(NOT SO) QUICK VIEW

Q Somewhere I read about Quick View and how to use it. I tried to follow the instructions but nothing happened. I guess it must be me. What's wrong?
Cartier, Paris

Opening the Add/Remove Programs dialog box via Help is the quickest route to the facility

When you've highlighted Accessories, opt for Details, scroll down, and there you will find Quick View

The Quick View program up and running, this time showing the contents of an RTF file

The document in page view, with the curled over page ends for you to click on to move through it

A If you remember the Meccano set, the golden rule always seemed to be that if you had Set number 1 then the exciting model you wanted to build needed the more expensive Set number 2, and so on. You are in a similar situation, except that there is no need to go out and buy an add-on.

What you need is your Windows CD-ROM and the Add/Remove Programs dialog box. The easiest way to get to that is to opt for Help, Add/Remove Programs, Installing a Windows component after Windows has been installed, and click on the box with the bent arrow to load it. Alternatively, Start Menu, Settings, Control Panel, Add/Remove Programs will get you there. The next bit is a touch fiddly, so follow closely.

The second item on the list is Accessories. Ensure that there is a tick in the check box against Accessories, then click on that line to highlight it.

Now look down for the Details button and click on that.

A whole list of options appears. Most of them are extremely useful, and you don't have them already, check at least on the boxes against: Calculator, Character Map, Clipboard Viewer, Games, Paint, Quick View and WordPad. Do take time out to see what each of these does. They will all appear on the Accessories continuation menu, except for Quick View which snuggles unseen into the system.

Now click on OK when you've got all the options you want. Incidentally, this technique can be used for removing items, if you untick the appropriate box. At this point, ignore the Have Disk button and just click on OK.

After a moment or two, everything will be loaded. Now let's give Quick View a whirl. Open Explorer and highlight the file you want to use Quick View with. Now click on File on the menu bar, and you will find Quick View as one of the options, but only if Quick View will work with that kind of file.

You are pretty safe with DOC or TXT files, and WMF and BMP are acceptable too. Click on Quick View and up comes the text. If there are embedded graphics, these are not shown. Complicated DOC files with lots of graphics won't load, or at least they won't on my machine.

There are a couple of very nice touches to this program. The A boxes allow you to increase or decrease the size of the text, but not just between two options. You can keep on clicking to enlarge or reduce the text.

If you opt for View, Page View, you can not only see the text a page at a time; if there is more than one page a folded over corner with arrows, you can click on them to go forward or back one page.

When the Quick View Window is open you can quickly load another file into it by dragging its icon on to the Window, either from a folder contents Window or the Desktop. You can also change the font and size of text by using the View, Font option.

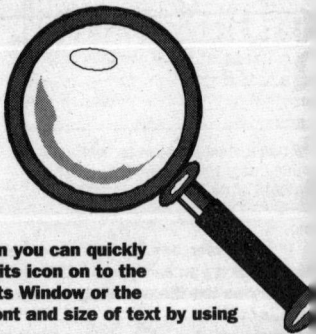

And finally, if you want to edit the file you are viewing, just click on the Word icon or opt for Files, Open File for editing. Incidentally, this will work even for a file which won't load into Quick View.

GIVING LONG DOCS THE CHOP

Q I'm using Word 97 and I want to chop long documents in half, but it takes an age with holding down the mouse. Also, I fear losing half the text. I also need to number the pages. What do I do?
Dora Mullins, N London

A A bit of planning and some fancy keyboard work will solve the problem. First, get the complete document and make two copies of it. Assuming it's 64 pages, call the first copy Pages 1-32.doc and the second one Pages 33-64.doc.

Load the first file and go to the top of page 33. Click on the top of the page. Hold down the Shift key, then press Ctrl+End. This selects the whole of the second half of the document. Press Del to erase it. Now you have the first half of your document.

The next bit is a little more complicated. Load the second file, go to the end of page 32 and click on it. Hold down Shift, then Ctrl+Home. Then use Del to delete the first half. Now go to Insert (Alt+I), Page Numbers, Format. Select your start page at 33 to ensure that your headers and footers give the page number correctly. Also, switch off the Different first page if you have that switched on. That's on Page Set up on the Header and Footer floating Toolbar (accessed from Alt+V, Header and Footer).

LOST FILES IN DELPHI...

Q A friend of mine wrote a little file-handling program for me in Delphi, and it works fine, except that sometimes when it is running I get a message saying a particular file can't be found. I know it's there. What's going wrong?
Devana, Leicester

A Your programming friend has overlooked a problem which comes with multi-tasking: in other words, running more than one program at a time.

What happens is that your data is loaded from, I suspect, the same directory as the EXE program is running in and it is referred to just by its name, not its full path. As a result, if you now load another application and work with that, the chances are that the 'current' directory when you return to your friend's application will be in quite a different part of the hard drive altogether.

Tell him that the solution is to use a command called Application. Path, to extract the path name and bolt that on the front of any file name used in his program (and any other programs he writes, for that matter).

BALANCING THE ACCOUNTS

Q I tried setting out a price list in Word with tabs, but the pounds and pence don't line up properly. What am I doing wrong?
Perry Hampden, London

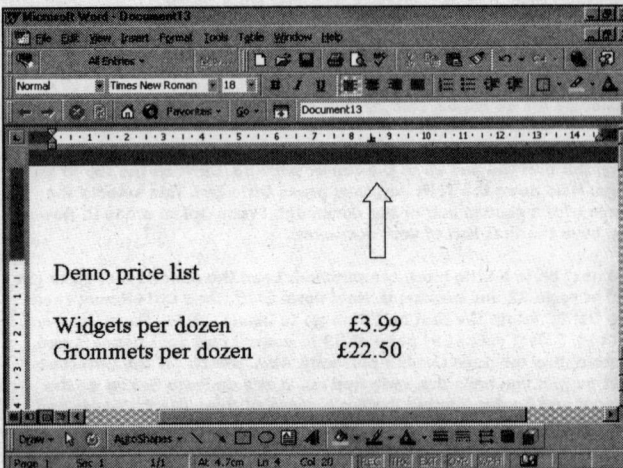

A decimal tab - the arrow in the text points to the curious looking decimal tab indicator on the tab bar

A There is more than one kind of tab. Click on Format, Tabs and, under Alignment, click on decimal. Then indicate where you want the tab to be (check with the ruler to see what value makes sense.) That will line up your money values neatly. If you were using a spreadsheet ensure that the cell(s) concerned are marked as of type currency. If you have already typed the values in, select the text you want to be affected - you may have to remove existing tabs. Also note the odd-looking decimal tab marker on the tab bar.

LEFT-RIGHT, LEFT-RIGHT, LE...

Q I want to have on one line text left justified and right justified, if you see what I mean. I'm puzzled as how to do it.
J Smith, East Lancs

A The easy way is to keep putting spaces in between until the text lines up with the left and right sides of your page. Rough and ready, but it works. Do be careful, though, if you are trying this with headers and footers. Pages 1-9 may be OK, but the extra character in page 10 may spill the text over on to the next line!

CUSTOMISING HEADERS AND FOOTERS

Q I don't want the page number to appear on the first page of my document. What do I do?
B Barber, Liverpool

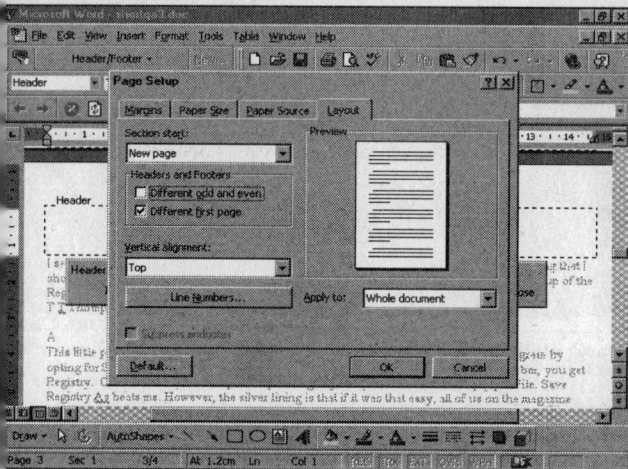

pting for a different first page header and footer under Word 97

A In any half-decent word processor you should be able to opt to have different headers and footers on the first page. In Word 97, go for iew, Header and Footer. Then opt for Page setup and the Layout tag. here you can click on the radio button which will get you a different eader or footer for the first page.

DIRTY TRICKS

Q I often play Solitaire, which originally came with Windows 3.1, I hink. Sometimes it would be nice o Undo a three-card turnover and st turn one, so that I can finish e occasional game. Not proper heating, just a helping hand. an you help?
avid Long, Bradford

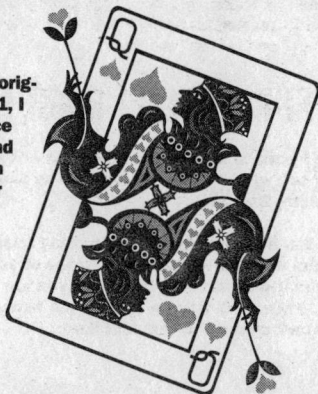

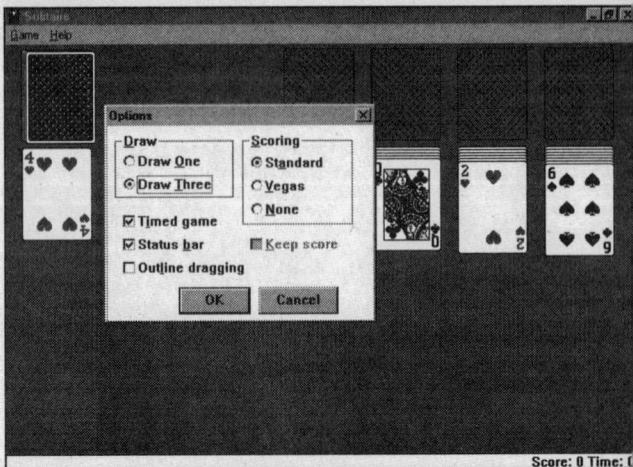

You can alter the number of cards in Solitaire turned over to one - but surely that makes the whole game far too easy

A We don't really condone this sort of thing. However, if you really must you can either go for Options and change the whole game to one-card turn over, but that will take you back to the top of the deck. A neater alternative is to go for Undo (which returns the last three cards turned over to the pack), then hold down Ctrl+Alt+Shift and - if you have any hands or fingers left at this point - click on the face-down cards to turn the next one. That will turn just one card over.

WIN98

MISSING FAX

Q Where is Microsoft fax on Win 98?

Charles K. MacKay, Email

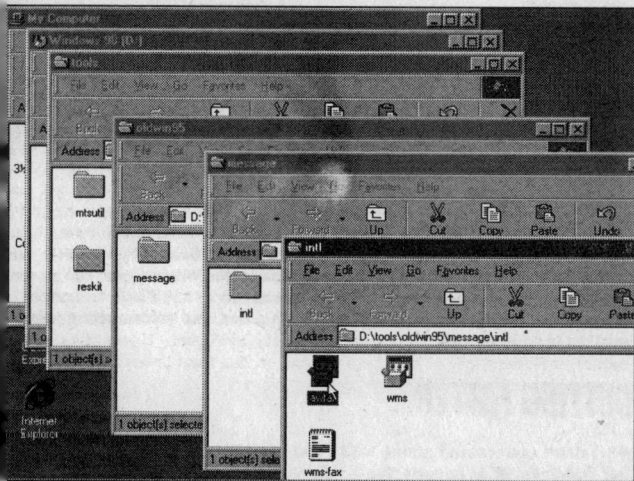

A There is no native fax in Windows 98 because most people used software that came with their modem for that function, or a third-party software like Winfax Pro. Microsoft included the old Messaging and Fax functions on the Windows 98 CD. They are in the \tools\oldwin95 folder. Or, if you download Outlook 98 from the Microsoft web site (www.microsoft.com\office), you'll find that there is a stripped-down version of WinFax included with it.

GETTING FAT

Q Are there any compatibility problems between Windows 95 and Windows 98 because of this new FAT32? Also, will all disks that have data saved under Windows 98 be readable under Windows 95? Thanks.
Kavin Karro, Email

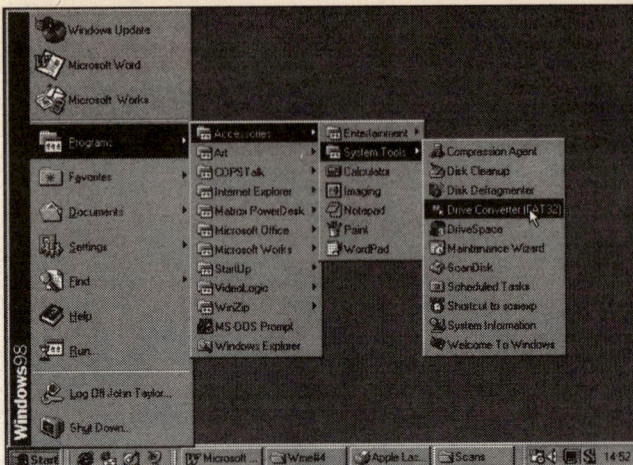

A FAT32 is not new - it came out with win95 osr2. What do you mean by compatibility problems? If someone creates a Word 2.0 document in Win 3.1, yes, you can open it in Word 6.0 on Win 98. Is this what you mean? The answer to the second part of your question is yes. The problem, if you call it a problem, is that if you convert to FAT32, you cannot use a FAT16 system again without repartitioning and reformatting your hard drive to be FAT16.

GETTING FATTER

Q I don't understand about FAT32 and what it is supposed to do for Windows 98. It sounds like a dubious slimming cure to me. Is there anything in it for me?
Sam Miller, Liverpool

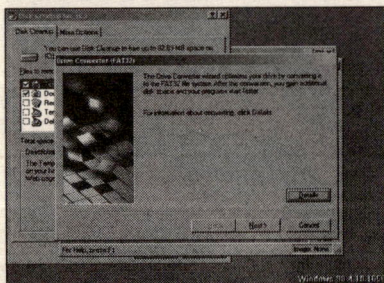

The Drive Converter program part of Disk Cleanup - and remember it cannot be reversed

114

If you look at the figures you'll see that for a 5-byte file, the memory available has dropped by 32K without FAT32

A In a funny kind of way, it is a slimming cure for your hard disk. First of all, FAT stands for File Allocation Table, and the 16-bit version was OK until hard disks with more than 1Gb started to appear a couple of years ago.

For complicated technical reasons, this meant that files were allocated space in chunks of 32K at a time, however small they were. If you want to see the full horror of this and you don't have FAT32, pop into an MS-DOS Window and type DIR. Make a note of the amount of disk space you have, then type EDIT TEMP.

This opens a new file called TEMP for editing. Type in a couple of characters, then exit from the editor, saving the file. That's done by pressing Alt+X and Y for Yes to save. Now type DIR/OD - which gives a directory listing in date order - and you will see your new file taking up a handful of bytes but the system gobbling up an additional 32K. Now multiply that across all your files and you will see the scale of the problem.

FAT32 accesses the disk using a 32-bit number, which allows the clusters to be far smaller. The size is 4K per cluster for a 1Gb drive, getting larger according to the size of your drive, and it will only revert to 32K with a 32Gb drive (hands up all those who have one!). In other words, the FAT32 system is pretty future proof. Using it can save around 20 per cent of your disk space.

On an historical note, one of the reasons why MS-DOS started off at version 1 and went on upgrading was to cope, first of all, with bigger capacity floppy disks, then the very existence of hard drives, and subsequently with the rapidly advancing technology which produced bigger and bigger drives, leaving the operating system struggling to cope with them.

You don't have to convert to FAT32 and there may be problems with some older DOS programs, especially since the process isn't reversible.

SUSPEND YOUR DISBELIEF

Q What is the significance of the Suspend option? Can I use it or the screen saver to stop prying eyes looking at my work when I am away from my desk?
Alice Carter, N London

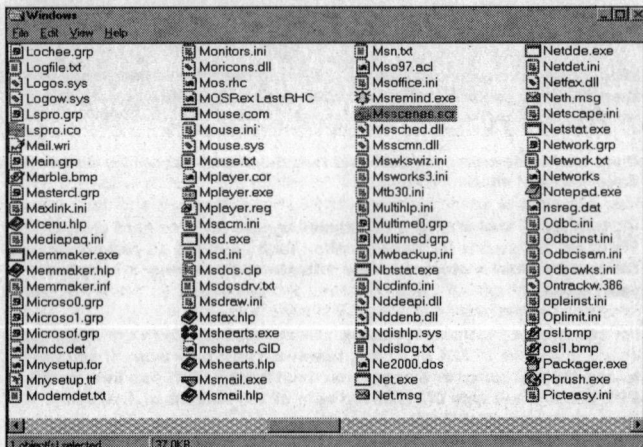

The Windows folder with a Screensaver highlighted

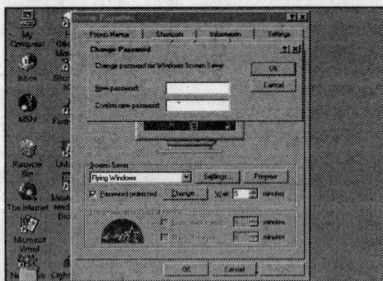

Putting a password on a screensaver - you have to type it twice for security reasons

A Later versions of Windows 95 and Windows 98 have a Suspend option, which means that the system appears to go completely to sleep, although it will wake up if you get an email or a phone call, or if a program needs to run automatically. In addition, a keypress will bring it back to life.

In Windows 98, the Suspend option is on the Shutdown menu, but you cannot really use it to protect your machine from nosy parkers. Your machine also needs to have a power-saving mode, as laptops do. What you need is a screen saver which is password protected. The problem is that screen savers only kick in after a given amount of time and you can't wait that long if nature calls or the front door bell rings.

What you should do is to open the Windows folder and look for a screen saver (it will have the SCR extension, if you have opted to show extensions). The icon is a computer screen with a keyboard beneath it. Double click on the icon to see if it's the screen saver you want.

If it is, use the right mouse key to drag it to the Desktop and copy it there. Now all you have to do is double click on it to get it going. But what about security?

Right click on the Desktop and go for Properties. Click on the Screen Saver tab and check the Password Protected box. Type a password and then retype to confirm. Do not forget your password - and don't leave it on a Post-It note next to your monitor!

The screen saver can only be cleared with the password, but there are ways round the problem like rebooting the machine. However, it at least keeps the opportunist curious colleague at bay.

MONITOR MADNESS

Q I saw somewhere that Windows 98 supports multiple monitors. How can that help me?
Judie Graham, Isle of Wight

A First of all, you need the appropriate screen driver cards. Then, you can have up to nine monitors, if you really must, and they do not have to be all of the same resolution. If you have two monitors, for example, you can spread a single window across both.

More useful, perhaps, when you are on line, is to have your favourite search engine open on one screen and the site you are currently exploring in the other. Or, with a spreadsheet; you can have the normal view open in one screen and a pie chart of the data on the other. Equally useful is having a word processor open with different documents on the separate screens, to aid pasting and copying and information comparison and searching exercises.

Also, if you like to have a load of stuff on your Taskbar, you can increase its size on one monitor - it can go as far as filling half the screen, if you really want it to.

UPGRADE OR NOT UPGRADE?

Q Do I need to upgrade? I have a recent version of Windows 95 and I have downloaded Internet Explorer version 4.01. Is Windows 98 worth it for me?
T Potter, Hillsborough

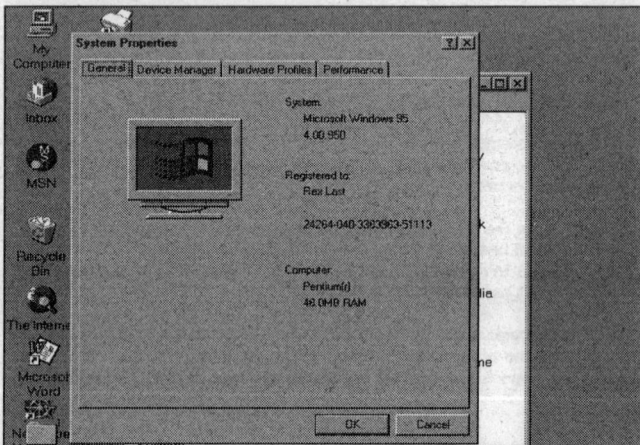

An older version of Windows 95. Only if there is a 'B' after the number or greater do you have a later version

A For you and others in a similar position, probably not, especially if you already enjoy the benefits of FAT32 which saves disk space. Why not wait until an upgrade of Windows 98 comes along - it might well contain a whole host of new things which would make it worth your while to purchase it.

If you have the original version of Windows 95 or Windows 3.1, upgrading will probably benefit you most, unless you are struggling along with a 486 and 16Mb of RAM. There are unlikely to be incompatibility problems, but on the CD-ROM includes a file called SETUP.TXT, which you ought to read thoroughly, just in case.

Another reader asked about converting to Windows NT (New Technology). NT is aimed at the business user, and my advice would be to wait until NT 5 is around - that looks like the next big upgrade for Windows, and a much more robust system, too.

CRASH-PROOF?

Q My Windows 95 keeps taking a nose-dive at the most inconvenient moments. Is Windows 98 more crash-proof than its predecessors?
Y Gardner, Yeovil

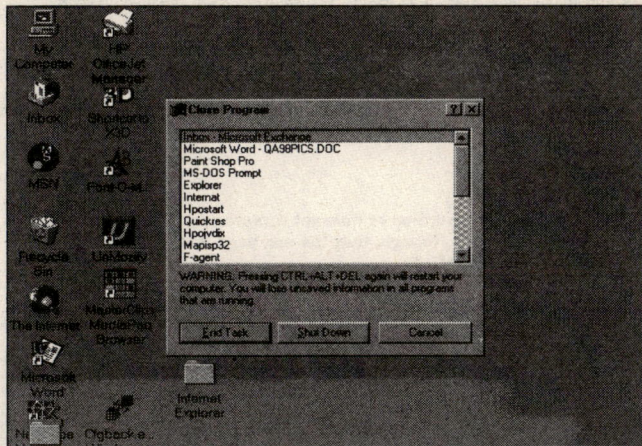

The Close Program Dialog box, accessed by Ctrl+Alt+Del, which also appears after an application crash

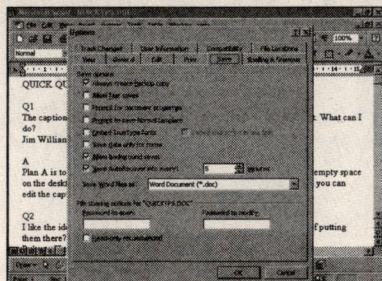

Word 97 with the dialog box showing you how to Autosave documents - and also allow you to make automatic backups

A It all depends what you mean by crash-proof. Some applications tend to crash more than others. Paint Shop Pro 4.12 falls out of the sky now and then under Windows 95, but then so do other programs, Internet Explorer among them. Microsoft does claim, though, that Windows 98 is much better behaved than its predecessors.

The problem is most often caused by one application trying to access a memory location which doesn't belong to it, and that has been addressed by NT, making it much more robust.

It is always better to expect the worst, and with MS Word, for example, you can protect yourself to some extent by invoking the Autosave option. This will save open files at a specified time interval. Press Alt+T for the Tools menu, go for options and then click on the Save tab. You can then switch on Autosave and determine the time interval between saves.

If you are running a program with no such facility, hitting Alt+F and S to save an open file every now and then is no hardship. A lot less bother, in fact, than losing all your data if the system crashes.

CACHE-BACK

Q I have the latest version of Internet Explorer and I like the caching facility. Trouble is, though, that the odd page keeps disappearing. What am I doing wrong?
E Archer, Hull

Unmozify exploring the cache - and not finding a great deal in it

A Nothing. This has been widely reported as happening, so perhaps it will be fixed in the next version. The cache is a device which saves recently accessed material. There are programs which take some or all of the material you have accessed on the Internet and save it in a form which allows you to browse off-line.

One contender is a shareware program called Unmozify, from Info

Evolution. Whichever program you choose, you will save money if you download information and view it at your convenience at a later time.

BEWARE OF THE .BAT...

Q How do I get to look at and modify Autoexec.bat from Windows 98?
John Cameron, Perth

A You should rarely have need to make changes to either Autoexec.bat or Config.sys, because if you don't know what you are doing the results can be disastrous. Still, if you insist, go for Run from the Start menu, and type:
MSCONFIG.

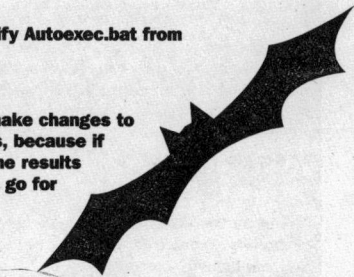

ACCESSIBLE WINDOWS

Q I am about to get a new machine and I am currently using Windows 95. My problem is that I have a mobility problem with my hands and find it hard to use the keyboard without the Sticky Shift feature. Will Windows 98 have this option?
T Perkins, Winchester

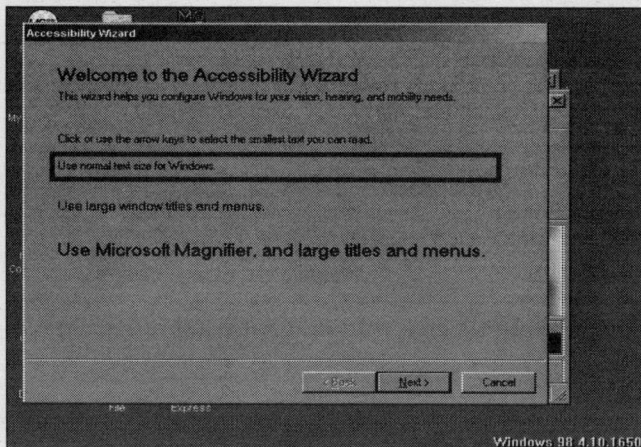

On the Accessories continuation menu, here's the opening page of the Accessibility Wizard

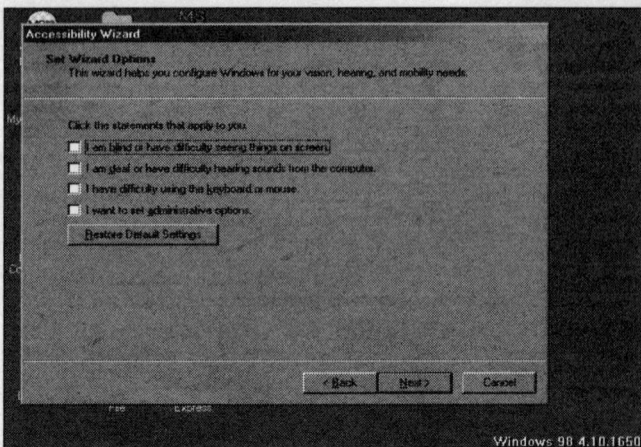

Here the Accessiblity Wizard is helping you select options based on disability

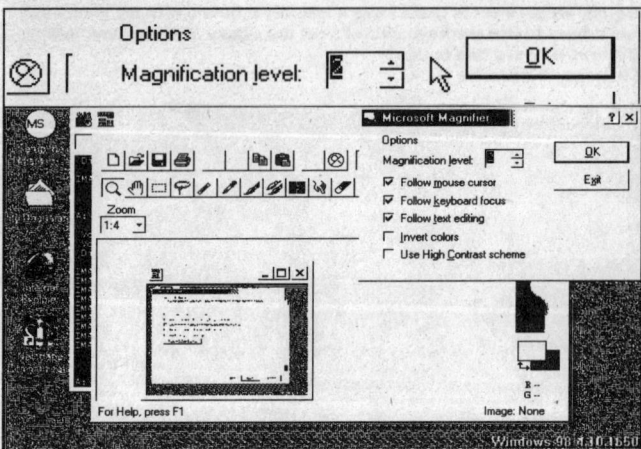

Here is the Image Magnifier at work. It's quite a neat utility with a number of options

A Yes, you will have all the options under Windows 95 plus an additional goodie, the magnifier. In addition, the Accessibility Settings Wizard should make Setup much easier.

The magnifier can help those of you with seeing problems. When you have the magnifier switched on, a fixed panel at the top of the screen follows the mouse movements and gives an enlarged version. The magnification can be adjusted and there are plenty of other options, too.

WHAT'S THE POINT?

Q What's the purpose of the Documents menu and what use is it to me?
Arthur Phillips, Winchester

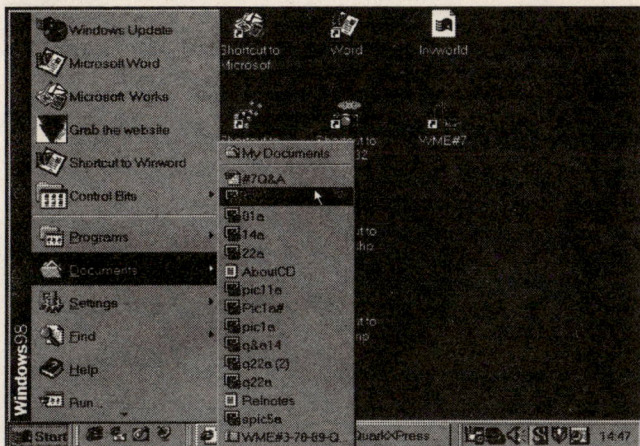

The Documents submenu on the Start menu

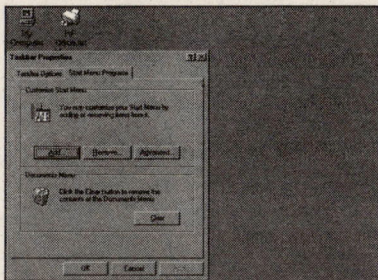

Taskbar Properties allows you to clear documents from the submenu

A Opt for Documents from the Start menu by moving the mouse pointer over it. In answer to part of another reader's question, the items on a menu with an arrow against them are those which have files or applications stored under them, and the purpose of the arrow is to indicate that there is more to come, as it were, on a submenu.

In Windows 98, a total of 15 documents can be held. These are the most recent documents you have used. And the reason they are there? Simple, just click on a document and it will be loaded into the appropriate application ready for you to use.

If for some reason or other you want to clear the Documents list, right click on the Taskbar, opt for Properties, and select the Start menu Programs tab. You will be able to remove the entire contents of the Documents Menu by clicking on the Clear button. At the same time, you can customise your Start menu.

THAT'S MAGIC!

Q What's an Update Wizard? And while I'm at it, what's a Wizard anyway? I know computers are supposed to be magic, but that's taking things a bit far.
Barry Updike, Norwich

A The Update Wizard connects you to the Microsoft web site which allows you to download updates to the operating system. A Wizard is a program which holds your hand in a user-friendly way through a series of steps to get to a particular objective, like adding on a piece of hardware or a program.

Amongst the other new Wizards for Windows 98 is the Tune-Up Wizard, which helps users defragment their disks and delete unnecessary files on a regular schedule. Then there's the System File Checker, which keeps an eye on your key files to ensure they are OK, the Accessibility Settings Wizard, along with many more to boot.

All Wizards have a similar step-by-step look and feel about them in order to make life as easy as possible for the user.

124

RESOLVING RESOLUTION

Q One of the problems with Windows 95 was not being able to change the display resolution without rebooting. Can you do this in Windows 98?
K P Larrimour, Aberdeen

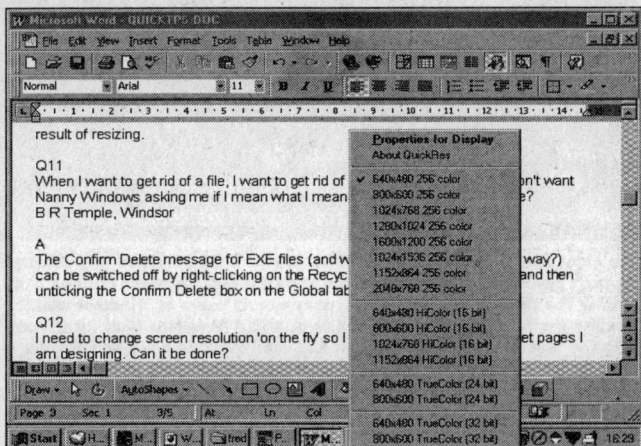

The Desktop utility in Windows 95 ready to change the resolution of your monitor

A Not strictly true. If you use PowerToys under Windows 95 you get an icon on your Taskbar to let you do just that. It's very useful for checking how material fits on various screen resolutions on a web page. In Windows 98, go to Display, Settings, Advanced.

If you have a high resolution monitor (say, 17 inch 1024 x 768) and a number of games designed for DOS or early Windows programs, you may find that the graphics look better at 640 x 480 resolution.

By the way, if you are running PowerToys with Windows 95 and want to upgrade, it should work smoothly with Windows 98.

THE WINDOWS KEY EXPLAINED IN FULL

Q I've just got a machine with a Windows keyboard. Are there any other features on the Windows buttons or keys apart from just hitting them and getting menus?
G D Jenner, S Shields

A If you press the Windows key (Win for short), you get the Start menu.

If you press the key looking like a menu with a cursor, you get the same effect as hitting the right mouse button.

That's not the end of the story by any means. You can press key combinations, too:

Win+E - opens Explorer
Win+F - Find folders or files
Ctrl+Win+F - Find computer
Win+M - Minimise all Windows
Shift+Win+M - Undo Minimise all Windows
Win+R - Open the Run dialog box
Win+Tab - Go round the Taskbar buttons
Win+Break - Run the System Properties dialog box

The most useful of these is the Minimise and Undo Minimise key combinations. It saves you the trouble of going to the Taskbar, right clicking and finding the right option. There are many expert users of Windows who, despite the fact that it's supposed to be a GUI (Graphics User Interface) with the mouse in control, find that key combinations are much quicker, especially since it saves your having to stop typing, pick up the mouse, do the clicking, and then get back to the keyboard.

Remember also that if you hit the Windows key by mistake, it can take over from some applications. MS-DOS has a particularly hard time coping, and you may have to close the Window down and start again. Alternatively, try pressing Esc - that might work.

HELP!!!

Q What's happened to Help? I don't recognise it - but it looks a lot better.
Karen Harper, Southend

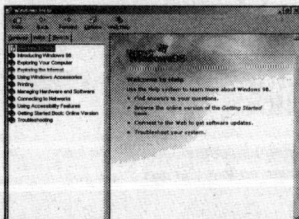

The opening screen of Windows 98 Help, which acts just like a web browser

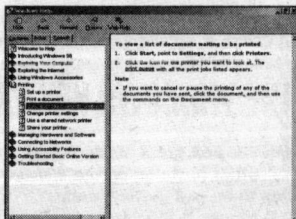

The left-hand side of the screen shows the topics and the detailed Help information appears on the right

A As part of the aim to merge your local computer with the Internet, Help has taken on a whole new appearance, based as it is now on Internet Explorer. The basic ideas behind Help and IE are pretty similar, in fact. Both use hypertext and links, and both have clickable images and other features.

Help has the look and feel of a website and the layout certainly makes finding things easier. Take time out to get yourself thoroughly familiar with it.

RESPECTABLE CHARACTERS

Q Help! What's happened to my old friend the Character Map?

Undine Falkener, Outer Hebrides

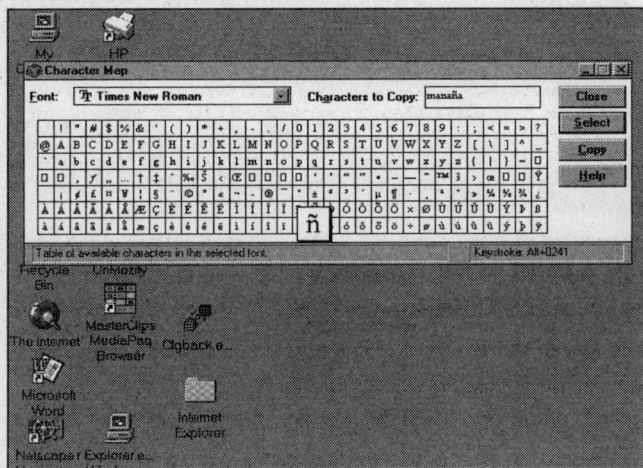

The Character Map with Times Roman on display. Note the exotic characters in the lower rows

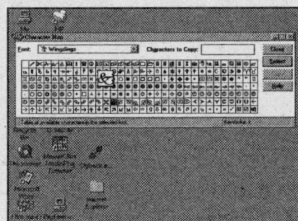

Wingdings, a collection of all manner of unusual symbols many of which have decorative use

A Nothing much, except that it has been moved, along with the Clipboard Viewer and other stuff to System Tools on the Accessories continuation menu. Why the Calculator isn't there, too, is a bit odd, but I suppose it has to go somewhere.

For those of you unfamiliar with the Character Map, do load it and see what it does. One of the obvious uses of the utility is to load Wingdings or some other non-standard font and see what key or keys you have to press to get the appropriate characters.

First, select the font you want from the drop-down menu. If you start with Times New Roman, you will see not just the standard keyboard characters, but also the more exotic accented characters. If you wanted n tilde lower case, for example, click on that item (near the middle of the bottom row). If you hold down the left button, you will see the character enlarged.

The keystroke or key combination appears in the bottom right-hand corner. Note that if you opt to key in Alt+0241 in Word you must have the Num Lock on, otherwise it won't work. The other point to note is that you must have the leading zero, if not you will not get the right ANSI (American National Standards Institute) character.

An easier approach is to double click on the character or characters you want, and they appear in the Characters to Copy box, into which you can type or double click other characters. Then you press the Copy button to send the character or characters to the Clipboard. Back in your word processor, press Ctrl+P to paste them into your document.

If you now opt for Wingdings, you will find a whole raft of exotic characters, which can be used to add, say, a telephone icon to your phone number, alternative numbers in different designs, and some of the characters make suitable borders for tickets or business cards.

Any box which contains a thinnish upright rectangle indicates that there is no equivalent character for that keystroke or key combination.

TIDY YOUR HARD DRIVE

Q Is there a way of tidying up disk space easily under Windows 98?

Larry Paterson, Halifax

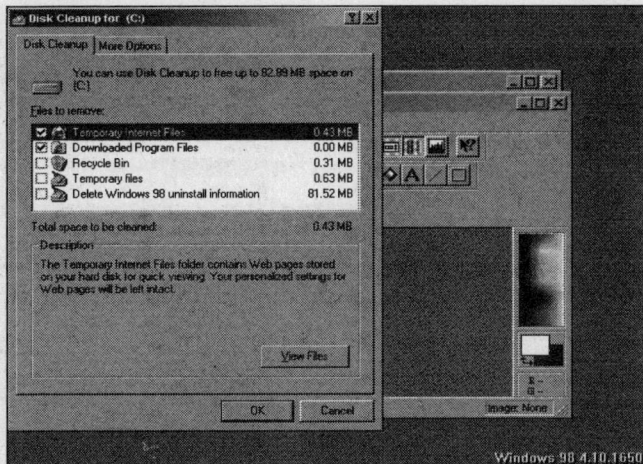

The Disk Cleanup Wizard has a number of options for you to save disk space

A There is indeed, and it's called the Disk CleanUp Wizard. This feature can be accessed in one of two ways: either from the Accessories continuation menu from Start menu or by right clicking on any drive and opting for the CleanUp tool.

The tool removes temporary files. Also, there's a More options tab which gives links to Add/Remove Programs so that you can remove programs or components you no longer require. There is also a link to the Driver Converter program which lets you convert to FAT32 for increased space saving efficiency.

Note that the Disk CleanUp tool only works on the current or selected drive.

GET MORE RESOURCEFUL

Q How do I know how much of the system is running idle and how much is being used?
Y Olderham, Chelmsford

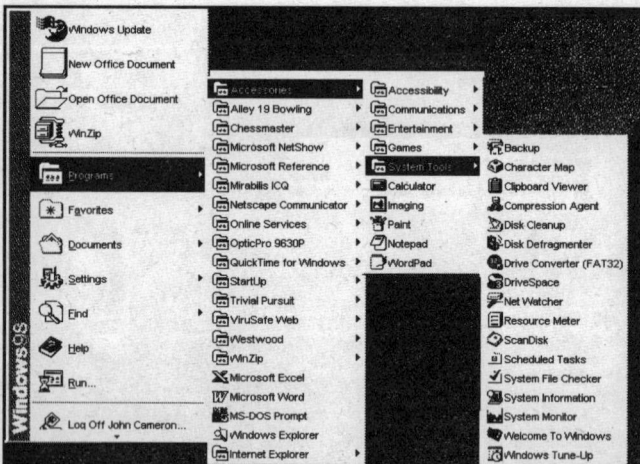

The Resource Meter can be found under System Tools

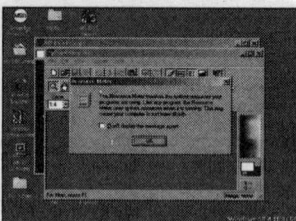

The Resource Meter comes with a friendly warning that it actually slows the system down

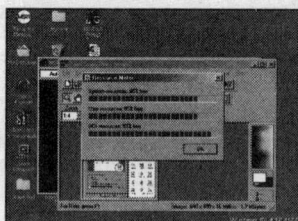

What the Resource Meter looks like when you ask for Details. Not much going on here

A The Resource Meter is what you are after. If you go to the Accessories continuation menu and opt for System tools, you will find it lurking there. When activated, it will warn you that it slows the system down. Then it sits on the tray at the right-hand corner of the Taskbar.

Right click on it and go for Details. This will show you how much of your system is being currently used. Don't forget to right click on the icon in the tray and opt to close it if you no longer want it.

FINDING THE CALCULATOR

Q Didn't there used to be a Calculator in Windows 3.1? I'd very much welcome it to help with my computing. Maybe I'm looking in the wrong place.
Gerald Haddingstone, Belfast

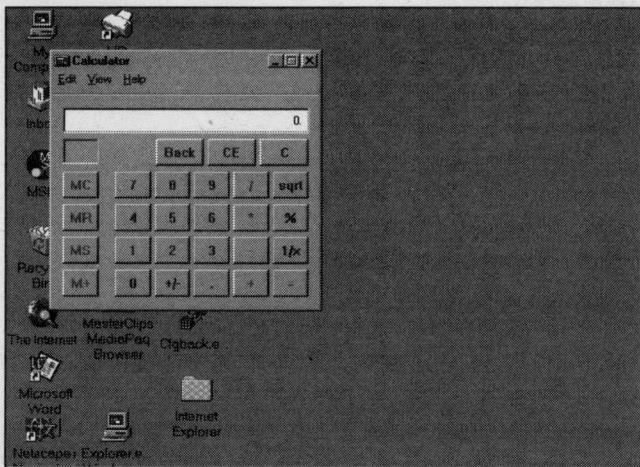

The Calculator in its default display format

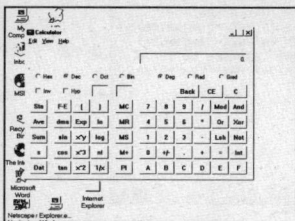

The Calculator showing off its scientific options

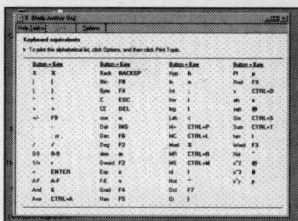

The keyboard equivalents which allow you to type into the Calculator without the mouse

A Indeed there did, and it is still there. It's on the Accessories continu-ation menu, and is well worth a moment or two trying it out.
The first point to note is that it is in fact two Calculators in one: on the one hand it's a simple, basic calculator, whilst on the other it's a pretty

complex and powerful scientific calculator. To switch between them, click on View and select.

Note that you can either operate the calculator from the mouse or from the keyboard. To find out the keyboard equivalent of a key, right click on it with the mouse (which seems to rather defeat the object, if you see what I mean).

Up pops a panel with the words 'What's this' (instead of just giving the value right away). Then click on that, and you will get the corresponding key or key combination.

Much more sensible is to go into Help, Tips and Tricks, Keyboard equivalents, and then click on Related Topics. Up at long last comes a list of keyboard sequences (which are used as functions when you paste data into the Calculator). The one you want is Keyboard equivalents, which you should made a hard copy of if you use the Calculator a great deal.

For programming buffs, the Scientific Calculator converts between the usual number bases: hex, decimal, octal and binary.

WEAVING A WEB PAGE

Q How can I design my own web pages? Do I have to learn HTML, whatever that is?
W Vaughan, Cardiff

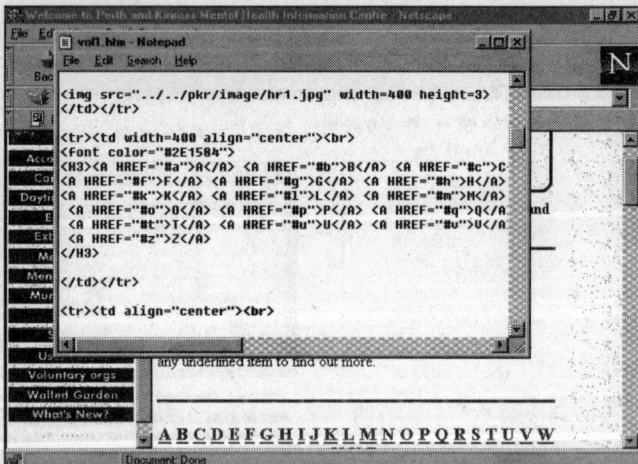

A web page with some of the underlying HTML code that drives it

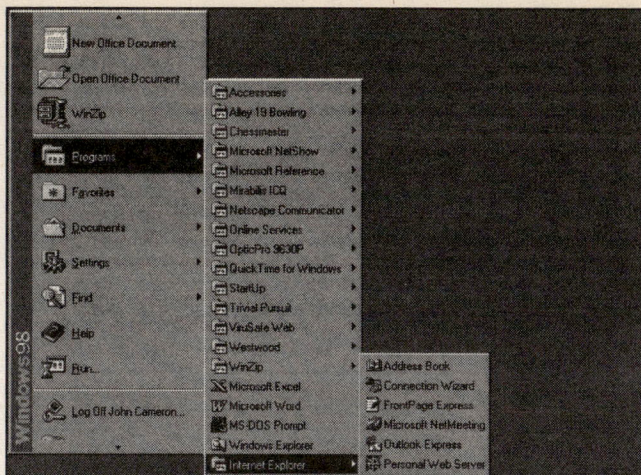

How to get through the menus to FrontPage Express

The opening blank screen of FrontPage Express, waiting for you to get going with your web page design

A First, HTML: that stands for Hypertext Markup Language, the scripting language which is used to put text, images and sound on a web page. If you are a programmer, you may well find that HTML holds no terrors, except that it can be extremely fussy and also difficult to debug, especially with complicated page layouts.

If you have Word 97, you can save a document as HTML. Alternatively, have a go at Frontline Express, a cut-down version of the program which allows you to design web pages.

WIN 98 AESTHETICS

Q One thing I found annoying with Windows 95 was the animation of windows as they opened and closed. I think it needed a Registry patch to get rid of it. Now even menus leap back and forth like young lambs. How do you stop this?
O Orchard, Aberdeen

A I suppose it is a matter of taste - and whether your machine can really cope with this gimmick (sorry, tasteful new feature). To modify this and some other aspects of the system, go to Display Properties, by right-clicking on the Desktop and opting for Properties.

There are a number of check boxes under Visual effects, and among them is menu animations, which are switched on by default. As you can see, you can also show window contents when you are dragging windows, if that is your pleasure.

Also click on the Web tab to see what goodies are on offer there.

LINK FILES: GET CONNECTED

Q I asked a friend to send me a copy of a particular program, which he duly did on a disk. When I looked at it, there was only a tiny file there with the extension LNK. What's going on?
H H Darling, Newcastle

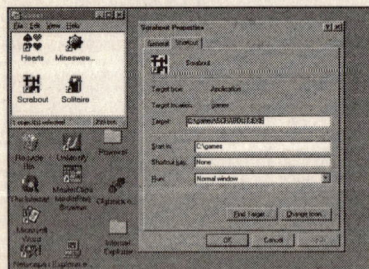

The Games folder is an example of a folder full of links to other folders, and Properties, Short cut shows you where the actual files are that run the application

A The extension LNK means that this is a 'link' file, or shortcut, as it is more correctly known. In other words, it doesn't contain the actual application, only a pointer to where the application itself is located. The purpose of this is to allow you to place links on your Desktop or Start menu without having to copy the whole application.

The question is, how to find out where the LNK file is pointing to and, ultimately, how to get to the actual application. Let me take a stab in the dark and guess that your friend was trying to pass a game on to you from the Games submenu of the Accessories continuation menu.

Let's assume that the game in question is the excellent and addictive shareware Scrabble version, Scrabout. First, open the Games folder and look closely at the icons. By default, shortcuts have a little box in the bottom left-hand corner containing an arrow, so they can easily be identified.

Now right click on the Scrabout icon. You will see a number of options, including Properties. If you click on Properties, and then on the Shortcut tab, you will see the target folder in which the game is actually located. When you get to that folder, do be sure to copy the entire contents of the folder on to floppy disk for onwards transmission.

The reason for this is that the actual program file, SCRABOUT.EXE, calls upon various other files, including Help, a dictionary and more besides, without which it won't work at all.

It may well make more sense for your friend to dig out the original ZIP or install file in which Scrabout originally came.

WOT NO PROGRAM MANAGER?

Q What's happened to the Program Manager? Maybe I'm old-fashioned but I did like it.
R Rayner, Sunderland
A touch of nostalgia - the Program Manager in Windows 95. Note the Taskbar tray is taken as the Startup Group

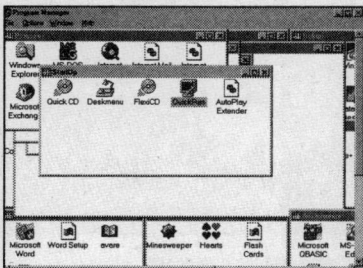

A touch of nostalgia - the Program Manager in Windows 95. Note the Taskbar tray is taken as the Startup Group

AIt's gone, that's what's happened. However, if you want a quick way of getting a look at the contents of a folder and you are conversant with MS-DOS, open an MS-DOS Window and type START followed by the path of the directory you want, or if you are already in that directory, type START followed by a space followed by a full stop (which stands for the current directory). You can also use START to launch applications.

A LOST LEGACY

Q What about legacy programs and Windows 98?

F T Brechin, Isle of Wight

AOne of the real problems designers of Windows have had to deal with is the 'legacy' of MS-DOS. Many games were written for MS-DOS and a lot of them played fast and loose with the operating system. Our understanding is that the old games programs should still run, but do check whether opting for FAT32 will have a harmful effect.

WAR OF THE PORTS

Q Has Windows 98 overcome the problem of port conflicts?

J K Arthur, Scunthorpe

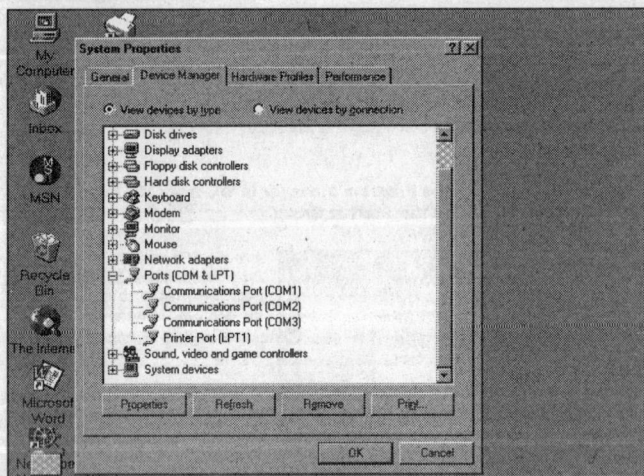

The Device Manager showing the COM ports and the printer port

A When PCs first came into existence, three COM ports were regarded as the height of luxury, but with the amount of kit you can hang on to a machine nowadays it's not suprising that there are hardware conflicts. The new idea is a USB, a Universal Serial Bus, which uses what's known as hub technology to allow you to hang up to 127 devices on to your machine, although there are speed constraints. In the future a system called FireWire will allow faster access.

NETSCAPE'S NEW LOOK

Q Can I no longer use Netscape?

William Westerman, Sunderland

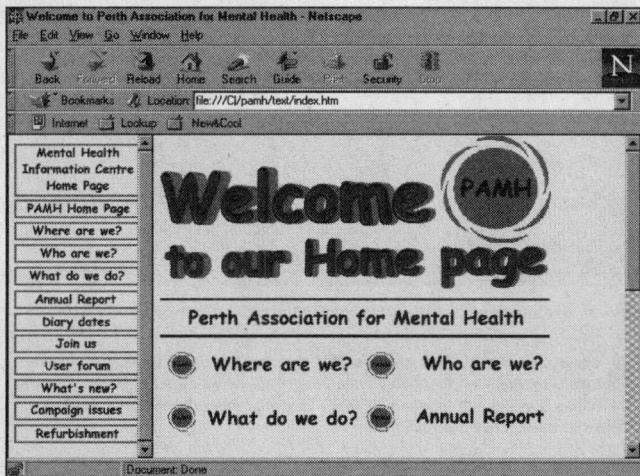

Netscape Navigator has a different look and feel from Internet Explorer and many prefer it

A You can still use it, but the idea with Windows 98 is that the Active Desktop links you via Internet Explorer to the net - and that exclusivity is what caused all the bother in the American courts. And you can't uninstall IE, either.

GOODBYE PINBALL!

Q I just got a new machine with Windows 98 installed. Where's my favourite game, 3D Pinball?
H Williams, North Shields

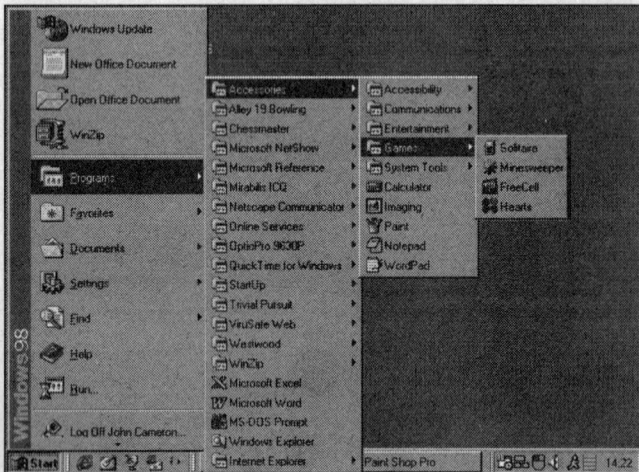

How to find your way through the menus to the Games that come with Windows 98

A Gone, I'm afraid. This came with Plus! for Windows 95 but curiously has disappeared from 98. Trial programs does contain three games, including a cut-down version of Golf. The standard games are Solitaire, Minesweeper, Free Cell and Hearts

THUNK ABOUT IT...

Q What on earth is Thunking?

G J Jones, Hartlepool

A It sounds like something Winnie the Pooh used to get up to, but actually it refers to a technique for converting information from 16 to 32 bit format and is used whilst an application is running.

138

WIN 98 AND THE 'NET: THE PERFECT COUPLE?

Q I don't have the Internet. Is it worth having Windows 98?

Barry Lyndon, Middlesborough

A One of the key aspects of Windows 98 is to make a seamless link between your machine and what's on it and the world wide web. It is possible to switch this feature off, but I guess that 98 without the web is rather like buying a car and keeping it in the garage.

SUPPORT FOR DVD

Q] What about Windows 98 and DVD?

D Player, S Shields

A The system contains built-in support for DVD and also for MMX chips.

IS THE END OF THE WORLD NIGH?

Q What about Windows 98 and the millennium bug?

A Snelley, Lincoln

A Windows 98 is advertised as millennium compliant, but that does not mean that some of your older applications will not cause a problem. By the way, Windows 95 is compliant and will work until the year 2099, so you needn't rush out and upgrade. There's no truth at all in the rumour that the next version of Windows will be Windows 00!

THE REQUIRED SYSTEM

Q How do I know if my machine will run Windows 98?

I F Oliver-Sturton, E Midlands

A There has been much discussion about this. The official minimum requirement is - rightly - regarded as a bit on the tight side, and the consensus is that for a brisk performance you need a Pentium 166 or better, 24Mb RAM (although 64 would be an advantage), 1Gb hard drive and a CD-Rom player. The system takes up over 100Mb of your drive, by the way.

SPEEDY WINDOWS

Q Is Windows 98 faster?

P Peters, Frinton

A Under the right conditions there are reports of a 9 per cent overall improvement. It can load applications much more quickly and shuts down faster, but FAT32, if loaded, is slower than FAT16 as there is more code to it.

TALKING COMPUTERS

Q Windows 98 has introduced me to the Internet, but I'm baffled by the letters http which preface most web pages. What on earth does that little lot mean?

H T Fraser, Perth

A It's all to do with protocol, not in the diplomatic sense, but in relation to the way in which computers can be persuaded to talk to each other, whatever their internal set-up is like. Text on the web is usually managed with ftp, which stands for File Transfer Protocol, but when it comes to images, text, sounds and the rest, you need a HyperText Transfer Protocol.

BACKUP BLUES

Q Do I still need to make floppy backups of my data in Windows 98?

N Burger, Paris

A Strange question. Of course you do, unless you have another backup device, like a Zip drive. It is always vital to back data up, however fancy the operating system. Make it a practice to back stuff up before you switch off the machine at the end of a work session.

PICKING UP THE TAB

Q I've noticed with a dialog box that you can go from one item to another using Tab. It's a bore having to go all the way round to get to the previous one. Is there a way round it?

William T Holmes, Holbrook

A Every Window has what's known as a 'tab order', which is set by the programmer. You're quite right, Tab gets you round the edit boxes, radio buttons, check boxes and the rest in a predetermined order.

Shift+Tab goes round in reverse tab order - that's your problem solved.

DOT-TO-DOT

Q Even though I have Win 98, I still like to experiment with MS-DOS. But in a directory listing what are the two dots and single dot items?
Dorothy Allison, Greenwich

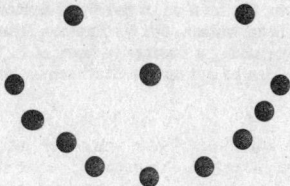

Even an empty subdirectory has the two 'dotty' entries one pointing to the current directory, the other to the next up the tree

A For the uninitiated, directory means folder in MS-DOS speak. The single dot means 'this directory' and the double dot means 'the next directory up in the tree', which lets the operating system know where it is. If you are into web page design, you will know that there are two directories side by side, TEXT and IMAGE, and to refer to the image you simply type ../IMAGE/THISIMAGE.JPEG.

CHANGE YOUR BLINK RATE

Q Can I change the cursor blink rate? My recollection from MS-DOS days is that it is fixed by the hardware and can't be altered.
V Cummings, Weston-Super-Mare

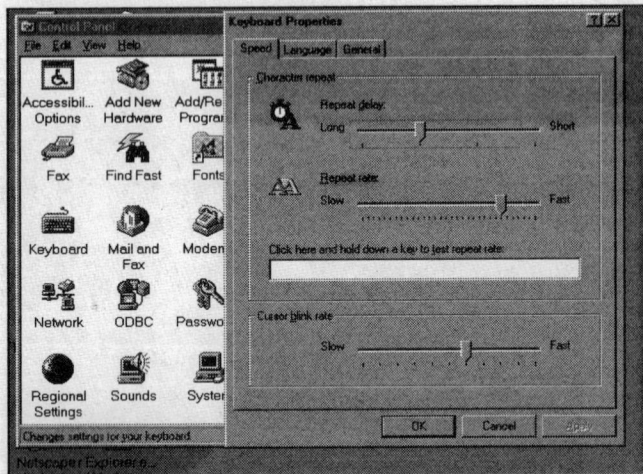

Go to the Control Panel, opt for Keyboard and you can alter the cursor blink rate

A Not so. Go to Keyboard properties in the Control Panel and move the slider to change the blink rate.

A BETTER START

Q How do I add items to my Start menu?

Quentin Dillington, E London

A Open the folder in which the application is sitting. Use the right mouse button to drag the icon on to the Start button. An additional tip is to right click on the Start button, opt for Explore From Here and change the name of the icon by putting a number in front of it. To launch the application, press Ctrl+Esc to put up the Start menu, then just press the number you want.

NAVIGATING THE 'NET

Q I'm pretty new to the Internet. How do I find out what's going on regarding Windows 98?
Keith Graves, Southampton

A You don't say who your ISP (Internet Service Provider) is. You should have a Search or Find option which will give you access to one of the search engines on the Internet: Yahoo, Lycos, and so on. In the search string edit box, just type Windows 98 and see what happens.

Microsoft has product information at www.microsoft.com/windows98. One site offering links to information is www.windows98.org and the www.annoyances.org/win98 site covers grumbles and groans about Windows 98. But there is still much more available.

EMPTY YOUR FLOPPY

Q What's the quickest way to 'empty' a floppy disk with loads of subdirectories on it? Formatting takes an absolute age.
C V Weighton, Ipswich

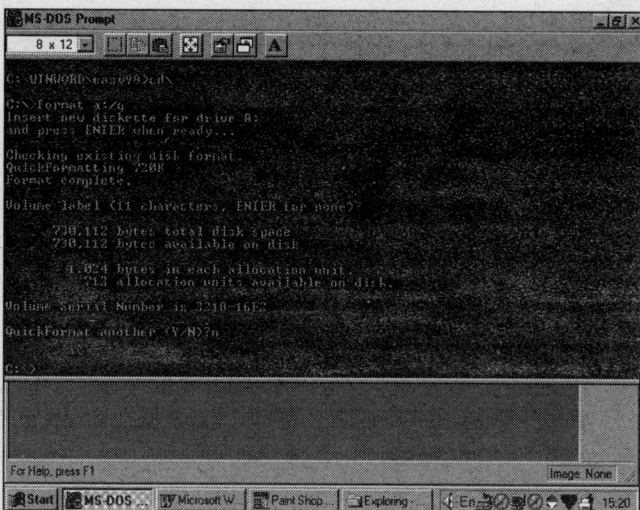

This is the sequence of events when you quick format a floppy disk in an MS-DOS Window

A So it does. The quick and old-fashioned way is to go to an MS-DOS Window and type: FORMAT A:/Q

This performs a 'quick' format on the A: drive disk and it really is over in no time at all. When asked for the Volume label, you can leave that blank or give the disk a label.

LOST IMAGES

Q I've just started trying to get to grips with designing web pages and I can't get my images to load. What's wrong?
S S Liberty, Bristol

A Not an easy one to answer from a distance, but my guess is that you have files in WMF, BMP or some other format. You need to convert them to JPG or GIF files for them to be accepted.

DESKTOP THEMES: WASTE OF TIME?

Q What are Desktop themes?

A Apart from being a bit of a waste of time and space, they are fancy patterns and sounds and designer fonts to brighten up your Desktop. If you didn't install Desktop themes, you need to go to the Control Panel and Add/Remove Programs.

WINDOWS 98 NOTEPAD

Q I see that Notepad is still around in Windows 98. Is it just the same?

I Brown, Bute

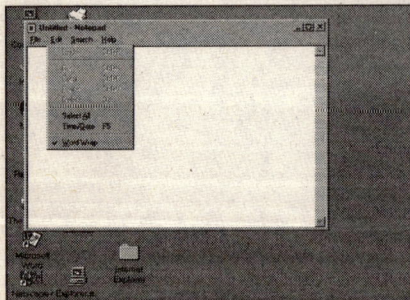

Notepad with the word wrap option set on

A Indeed it is, except in one particular facet. If you set word wrap on, Notepad will now 'remember' that you have done so when you reload it. That's either a blessing or a nuisance, depending on how you use Notepad.

THE LONG AND SHORT OF IT

Q What do I do with long filenames if I want to copy them to a floppy disk for someone running Windows 3.1?
Charlie Bell, Birmingham

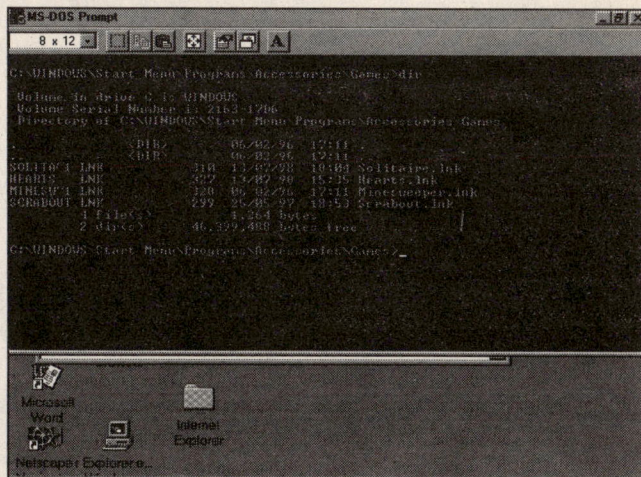

On the left, the MS-DOS filename and on the right the long filename

A The easiest way to see what happens is to open an MS-DOS Window and type DIR. On the left you will see the filename in its 8 plus 3 format, compatible with Windows 3.1 and MS-DOS. On the right is the long filename equivalent. If the name breaches the 8 plus 3 convention, it is converted to a six-character name plus a tilde plus a number.

> *This is quite ingenious and works well most of the time. One problem with Paint Shop Pro is that if you have a JPEG extension, it will not recognise it, thinking it is an unknown file type, JPE. So rename any such file as JPG. You can do that in MS-DOS with: REN *.JPE *.JPG*

CHECK OUT YOUR FONTS

Q How can I see what a font looks like?

D Eaton, Stirling

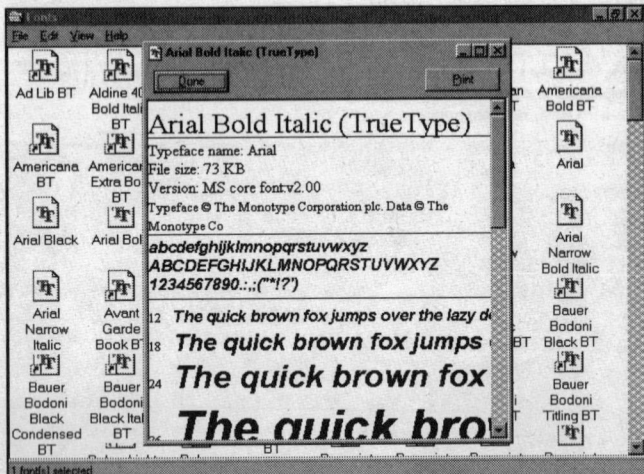

Here is a view of a font from double clicking on the icon in the fonts folder

A Some packages show you a demo, but go to Control Panel, Fonts and double click on the font you want to preview.

COME FLY WITH ME

Q I like the Flying Windows screen saver and would like to print it but I have no idea how to go about it. Can you help?

Terry Barnes, Wallasey

You can capture screen savers and copy them into your graphics package - this is Flying Windows

A When Flying Windows is running press the Print Screen key. Then open your favourite graphics package and press Alt+E then P to paste it in. From then on, it's up to you.

FAX THE DIRECT WAY

Q Is it possible to send a fax directly from Word 97?

Iain Stewart, Durham

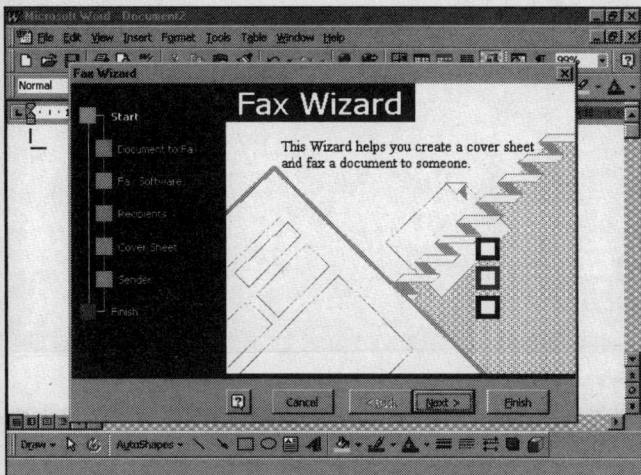

No problem sending faxes directly from Word 97 with the help of the Fax Wizard

A Not only a fax, but an email too. Alt+F then Send To - on the continuation menu you'll see a number of options. Take your pick.

IT'S GOOD TO TALK

Q Can I use the computer to dial up the phone? How can you do if?

Sally H Eveleigh, Hull

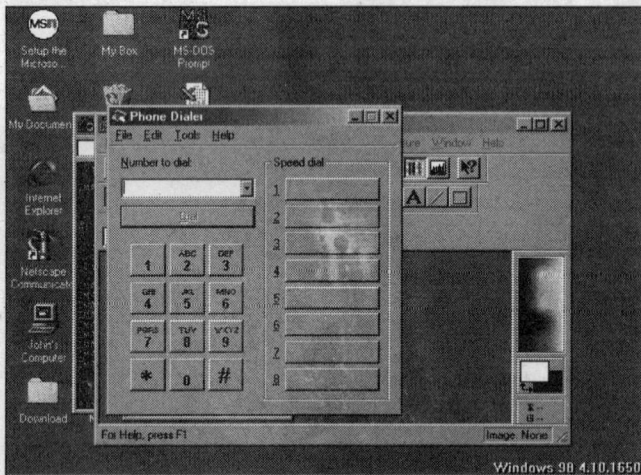

Here's the Phone Dialler program ready and waiting for you to set it up

A Summon up Programs, Accessories, Communications and you will find the same Phone Dialler program which was supplied with Windows 95.

MAKE SOME NOISE!

Q Can I vary the sound from my speakers from the computer itself?

P Parker, Harlow

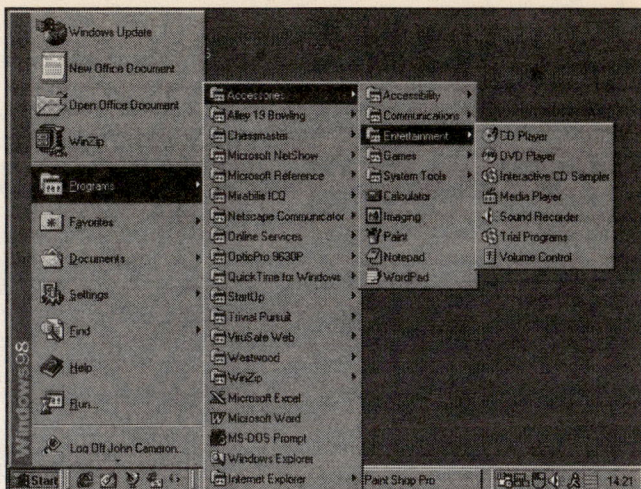

How to get to the Volume Control - as well as other media devices, and Trial Programs

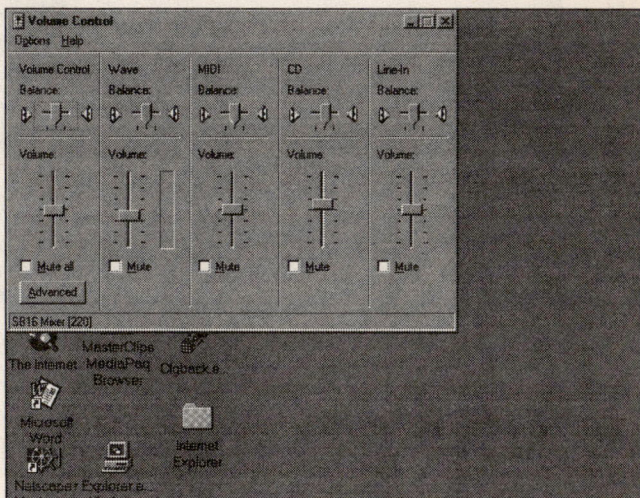

The Volume Control itself - unchanged from Windows 95 - has loads of bells and whistles for you to play with

A Indeed you can. From the Accessories continuation menu, go for the rather oddly named Entertainment option and there it is. The Volume Control is the same as for Windows 95.

KEEPING TRACK OF ERRORS

Q What if things go horribly wrong? Is there a way of tracking errors?

W Wellings, North Hants

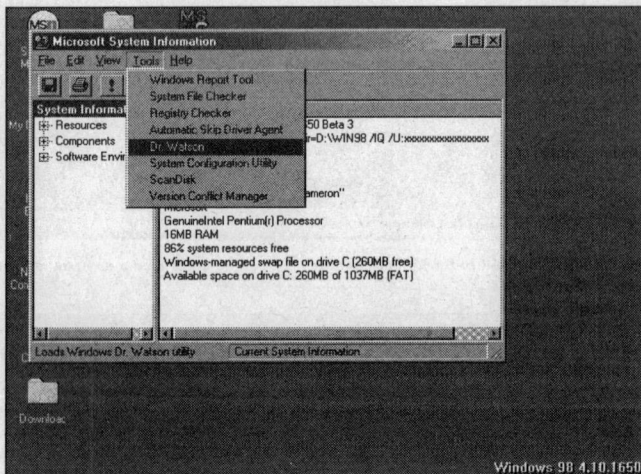

On the Accessories Continuation menu you'll find System Information with a wide range of options

A You must be referring to System Information which - if you are lucky - you may never need to invoke. It contains a number of diagnostic aids, including the curiously named Dr Watson, who, from a straightforward reading of the Sherlock Holmes books, is less than brilliant at solving problems. A Freudian slip? We hope not.

RETRO EXPLORER

Q I liked Windows 95 Explorer. Now it's all changed. Is there any way of getting it back to its old self?
U Oldfield, Selly Oak

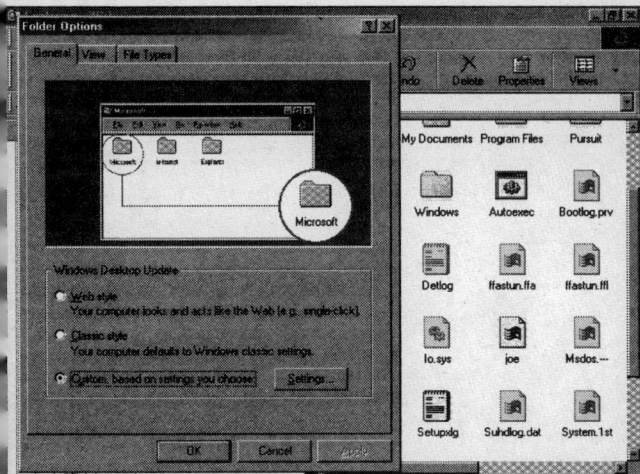

How to change the appearance of Explorer in a variety of different ways, including back to Windows 95 'classic' style

A If you open Explorer, then opt for View and Folder options, you can not only go back to what's called the Classic style, you can go forward to the convention used on the web and have a single click launch for applications.

A CHANGE OF ART

Q What graphics features come with Windows 98? Is it just good old Paint?

C Coates, Cheltenham

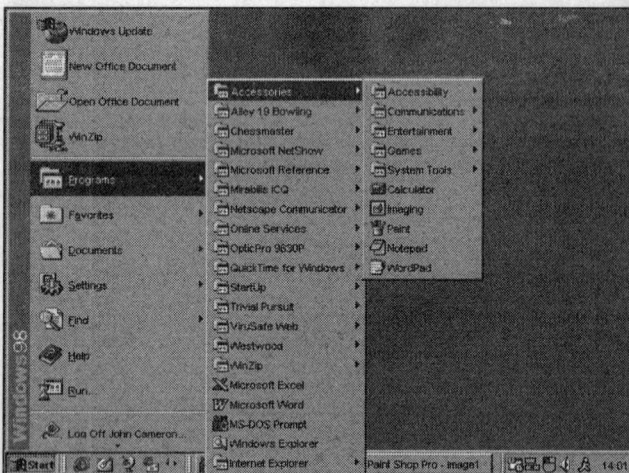

How to get to the Imaging program, via the Accessories menu

A Old perhaps, but not so good in some peoples eyes, as you can't save stuff in GIF or JPEG formats, the two formats for the web. There is an additional imaging program which is worth trying. You will find it on the Accessories continuation menu.

A GOOD BATCH

Q It would be nice to have a batch file system for Windows. Is there such a thing as a Windows batch file program?

Peter Arran, E Midlands

A There is now. It's called WSH, short for Windows Scripting Host.

SEARCHING FOR A SIGN

Q I do some part-time work drawing up astrological charts for people. I don't suppose there are any signs of the zodiac around that I can use in my documents?
Wendy Deer, Edinburgh

A There are indeed. If you load the Character Map (on the Accessories continuation menu) and opt for Windings as the font, you will find them all set out for you.

COLOUR WORRIES

Q Nothing important, just something that puzzles me. When I load an application, sometimes the colours in an existing application go all weird. What's happening?
Peter E Fetters, Wellington

A The answer is that, while your computer can indeed show millions of colours, it can't show them all at the same time, and if there is a conflict between one colour palette and another, strange things can indeed happen. But if you give focus to the oddly behaving window, you will find the colours return to their proper state.

AVOIDING THE BIN

Q How can I delete stuff without it being sent to the Recycle Bin?

D Derry, Maidstone

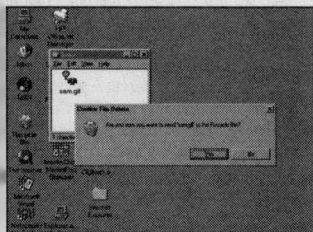

Even if you want to delete a file altogether, the system insists on double-checking with you

A When you opt to delete a file, what actually happens is that it is put into a kind of limbo (a word familiar to those with long memories of a certain PCW computer and a word processor called LocoScript), rather than being wiped off the face of the earth, so to speak. If you really want to delete a file or folder, right click on it, then press Shift+D. You will still be asked by the system if you really, really want to delete it.

WIN 95

CLIPBOARD HELP

Q The Clipboard is a bit of a nuisance. When I save something, whateve[r] I saved before is lost. Can I do anything about it?
Charlotte Findley, Huddersfield

A This sounds like you haven't loaded ClipBook Viewer. This program allows you to save CLP files on the Desktop or anywhere else. This technique can be used to grab bits of the screen or the whole screen, either when your graphics package can't seem to get at them for one rea[-] son or another, or when taking interesting images off the Internet for a DTP project.

Select Add/Remove Programs from the Windows 95 CD-ROM. Or start fro[m] Help, looking for Add/Remove Programs, and then installing a Windows component after Windows has been installed. Follow the on-screen instructions for adding ClipBook Viewer.

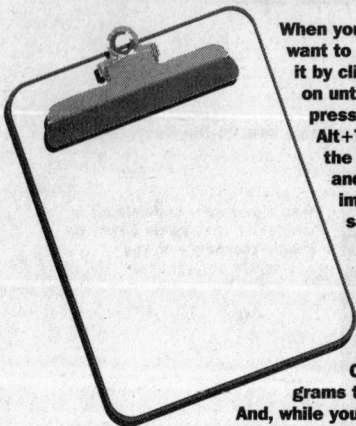

When you have the ClipBook Viewer and want to save images, load it, then minimise it by clicking on the menu bar. Next, carry on until you want to save a screen, then press Alt+Print Screen. After that, pres[s] Alt+Tab until ClipBook Viewer appears i[n] the task box. Alt+F then A comes next and now you can name and save the image. By default your chosen file is saved on the Desktop.

By the way, another reader wrote i[n] with a similar question about the Character Map. It seems that by default this isn't included auto-matically, nor, mystifyingly, is the Calculator. Use Add/Remove pro-grams to get your hands on them, too.
And, while you have the Add/Remove list in front of you, check to see if there aren't any other useful programs you could do with.

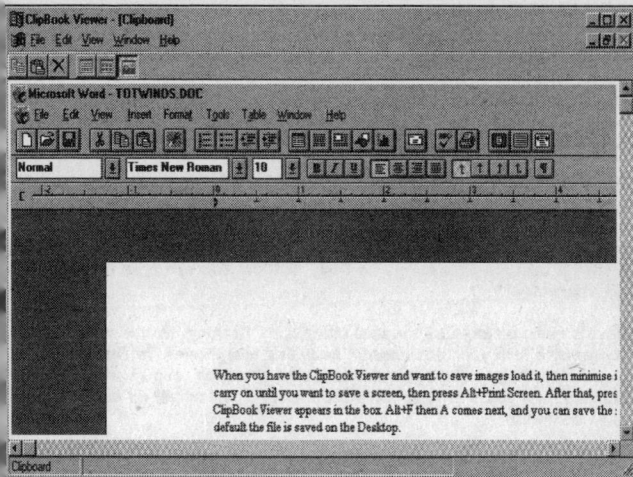

ClipBook Viewer - [Clipboard]
File Edit View Window Help

Microsoft Word - TOTWINDS.DOC
File Edit View Insert Format Tools Table Window Help

Normal | Times New Roman | 10

When you have the ClipBook Viewer and want to save images load it, then minimise i
carry on until you want to save a screen, then press Alt+Print Screen. After that, pres
ClipBook Viewer appears in the box Alt+F then A comes next, and you can save the :
default the file is saved on the Desktop.

Clipboard

The Clipbook Viewer with the text of this answer loaded and showing on the page

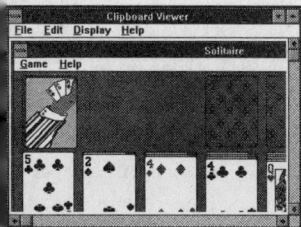

Using the Clipboard program you're able to grab any images displayed on your screen

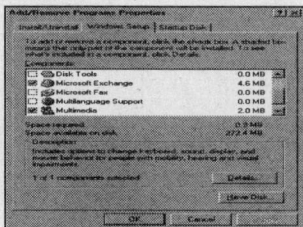

The Add/Remove Programs dialogue box in Windows 95

UNUSUAL CHARACTERS

Q I was looking at a document the other day, and was admiring the bullets which were used. They were square with a shadow on them. How is that done? And am I able to do this too?
Rex Jenkins, Carlisle

A What you need is the Character map, and pen and paper. When you hit a key on the keyboard, a particular

character appears on screen, and most of the time if you hit an "s", up comes an "s". However, there are some character sets which are not normal, like Cyrillic, Reference 1 and 2, and many others.

They generate a range of different character sets. The Wingdings set includes the bullet you are after, as well as a number of others - in fact, do explore that character set and Zapfdingbats as well.

With the Character map loaded, click and hold down the left mouse key over the character you want. You'll see a magnified version of it. A panel in the bottom right-hand corner of the Window will tell you which key or key combinations will get you the character. Double click on the character to load it into the Characters to Copy Window. You can type in more than one character.

There's quite a range of unusual characters floating around which you can incorporate into your documents, including telephones, letter, scissors, spectacles, floppy disks, clock faces and plenty of arrow variations. In Zapfdingbats you even get the Windows logo, which will no doubt be useful to someone.

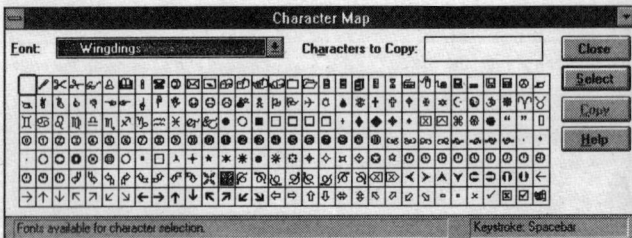

>Accessing Wingdings in the Character map screen - many unusual characters are available to use here

A FRESH START

Q I remember somewhere reading about how to put commonly used applications on the Startup menu. How's it done, please?
Stuart Brown, Bristol

A The first step is to find out where the application you want to run is on the hard disk. Then put that directory (folder) up on screen as a Window. Find the application, then hold the right mouse button down and drag the copy of the icon on to the Start menu. Release it and there it is. The next time you summon up the Start menu, you will see the application in a separate section of the menu above Programs. To refine the process when you have a number of items, rename them in the order in which they appear by prefacing each item with a number. Then you will only have to press Ctrl+Esc followed by the appropriate number to run your application instantaneously.

An alternative approach to adding items to the Start menu is to right click on the Taskbar, select "Properties" and then the Start menu. This will allow you to browse and add items to the Start menu.

When you want to change the name of the icon on the Start menu, click it twice with a pause in between - don't double click it quickly, otherwise it will just load and run. You will find the name selected and you will then be able to change it.

There's a little trick which doesn't appear to have been documented anywhere. Open a MS-DOS Window and type START followed by a space and the path to the directory you want. Up comes the folder in a Window. Or, if you are in the directory you want, type START followed by a space followed by a full stop. The full stop means "the current directory", and the double full stop in MS-DOS speak means "the next directory up."

WHY THE RESTART?

Q I was using an unfamiliar machine the other day and suddenly everything went wrong on the screen. I think I hit Alt+F and the Find facility appeared. The computer seemed locked on 95 Dialogue boxes. I had to restart the system to get everything back to normal. What went wrong? Did I hit a strange key combination? How can I put things to rights the next time round?
Steve Andrews, Bath

A It's very possible that the computer you were using has a Windows keyboard with special keys on it. One - or maybe two - of them will have the Windows logo on it, and another the pop-up menu logo. There are other variations, too, depending on the manufacturer.
What you did is inadvertently touch it, probably while you were aiming for the Alt key. What it does is activate certain Windows functions, so if you miss Alt+F and hit the Windows key +F you get the Find dialog box. Windows+P gets you the Programs continuation menu, Windows+H brings up Help, and so on.

The simplest way out is to go along with the system rather than fight against it. If you have just hit the Windows key, you get the Start menu. So if you then press Esc, everything resets itself back to normal. Sometimes you have to press another valid key, like P, before the Esc key clears the system.

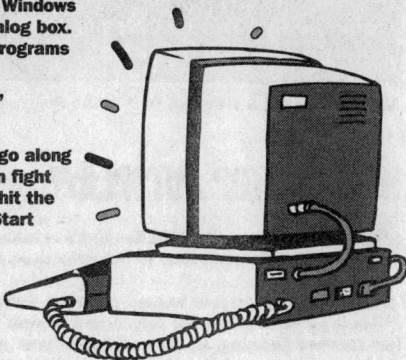

SCREEN TRAFFIC

Q When I'm online, the Network Explorer takes up the whole screen including the Taskbar. Does that mean I can't use the Start menu or anything else that was running?
Janet Prior, Newcastle-upon-Tyne

A Not at all. To access the Start button, just press Ctrl+Esc. To switch to an application which is currently running, Alt+Tab will take you round the other applications.

USER PROFILES

Q I want to go into more detail on the question of User Profiles. The help from Help (if you see what I mean) is OK, but I get the feeling that there is more to it. Can you - for want of a better word - help?
Terry Cole, Glasgow

A What you need is the Windows Resources kit Help, which provides a vast amount of assistance on all kinds of technical aspects of Windows.

> You will find the WIN95RK.HLP file on the Windows 95 D-ROM in the directory:
> D:\ADMIN\RESKIT\HELPFILE
> Copy the two Win95rk files to:
> C:\WINDOWS\HELP

and you can put a shortcut to it in the Programs folder.

HOW TO STOP AUTOPLAY?

Q How do I stop a CD-ROM like the Windows 95 upgrade CD-ROM from autoplaying when I load it? And why does it happen anyway?

A The way to stop it is to hold down the Shift key while the CD-ROM is being inserted into the drive - and do wait until the drive light really has finished flashing. As for part two of your question, there is a file in the root directory of the CD-ROM called AUTORUN.INF. That tells the computer to go through the autoplay process.

...udio CDs will also autoplay unless you stop them. To toggle Autoplay on
...nd off, double click on "My Computer, go for "View", then "Options", and
...nally for File types. Double click on Audio CD. You will see that the word
..."Play" is in bold. Click on Settings to toggle bold (and with it Autoplay)
...n and off.

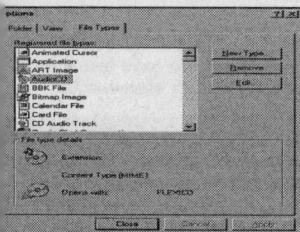

1 Double click on Audio CD to be able to turn Autoplay on and off

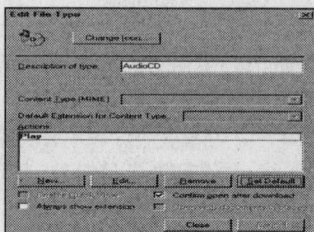

2 Changing the autoplay for audio CDs - click on the Settings button

...O ROOM!

Q I have a lot of stuff on my Start menu and it's beginning to dominate the screen. What can I do about it?
...ason Leonard, Grimsby

A Right click on the Taskbar, select Properties and tick the box marked Show small icons in Start menu. You'll see a demo of what happens ...the dialog box, and if you like the result, go for it.

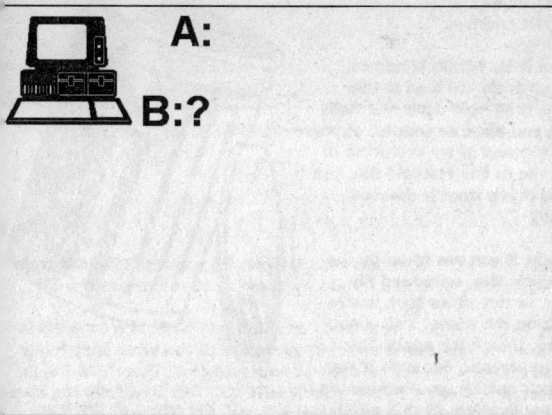

A:

B:?

The two different sizes of Start menu you'd get on your machine by varying the icon size

MINIMISING MENUS

Q It's a bit of a nuisance having to close the current Window to get at the Desktop. Is there a way round this?
Geoff Spiller, Birmingham

A All you do is to right click on an unoccupied part of the Taskbar [1] and select Minimise All Windows [2]. Once you have finished with your Desktop, right click again and opt for Undo Minimise All.

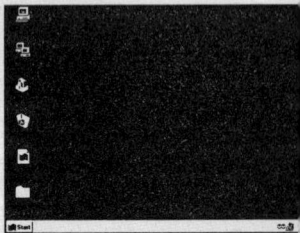

1 With lots of menus open the Desktop can barely be seen

2 Use the Minimize All Windows option to clear up your display

RENAME THE BIN

Q Is it possible to delete a file without sending it to the Recycle Bin, and can I change that rather silly name?
Tim Hunt, St Andrews

A Indeed it is. Within Windows, right click on the icon in the usual way, then hold down the Shift key when you click on Delete, or press Shift+D. Instead of an invitation to send the file to the Recycle Bin, you are asked if you want it deleted altogether.

Incidentally, if you are irked by the name Recycle Bin, or indeed My Computer, or any other icon name, then click on the name, wait a second or two, then click again. The pause is important, because if you double click quickly, you will launch the relevant application. At this point, you can edit the name of the icon.

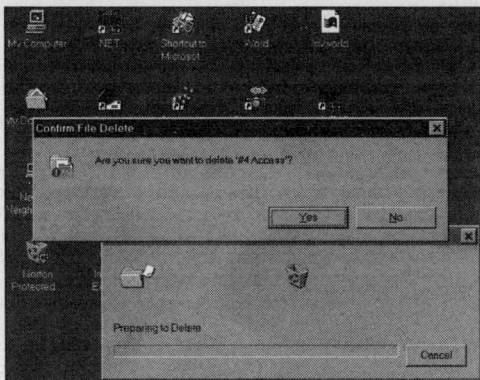

The normal option is to send the file to the Recycle Bin, where it stays until either you do something or the system ditches it in order to make space in the Bin

If you press Shift when deleting, the file is simply removed completely, but you do get a nice red warning sign

A STICKY SITUATION

Q I'm trying to help a severely disabled user who can type adequately, but has problems with holding down a key combination. I told him all about Sticky Shift keys - he was delighted and I went on my way rejoicing.

A day or so later, he rang up to say that the Sticky Shift had somehow reset itself and he had had to activate it himself. Can you explain?
Dominic Pendred, Hull

A That's not so much of a puzzle as you might think at first sight. Go to Accessibility features, and you will see the sticky shift options are on the Keyboard tab of the Accessibility Properties. To unravel the reset-ing problem, go to General and uncheck the box which offers the Automatic reset.

The keyboard panel of Accessibilities. Note the range of options available under Windows 95, which, to its credit, has concentrated heavily on helping those with disabilities

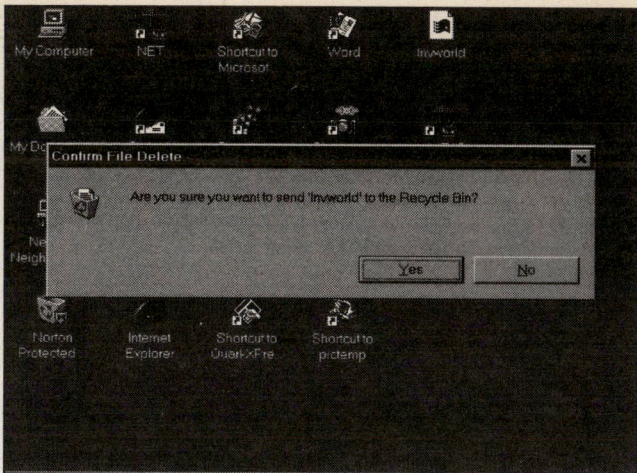

This is where you can stop the feature being turned off until after a specified number of minutes, or from being turned off at all

PRINTING PROBLEMS

Q I'm using Word and all of a sudden it's stopped printing images. Help!
Helen Storey, Glasgow

A This is a really spooky sensation, and it's quite unnerving to find the file which used to print intricate images now flatly refusing to do so. However, the answer to the problem is simpler than you think. Just cast your mind back to that longish document which you wanted to print in a hurry and that sent you into draft mode.

Now, one thing about draft mode is that it doesn't print images in order to speed things up. Simply go to Print Setup and Device options. Change back to high quality, and that's that.

Word 2's Printer Properties running under Windows 95

COLOURFUL LETTERS

Q You can print in different colours with a word processor, but I find it very fiddly having to hop back and forth to the right menu. Is there an easier way?
Matthew Taylor, London

A It depends on how much you want to fiddle around with colours. If there is a lot of work involved, why not use a graphics package, type out the text you want and use Flood fill for each of the colours? It will still involve swapping around a bit, however.

MAKING YOUR POINT

Q Sometimes I want to use caps to emphasise certain text, but all upper case seems to SHOUT TOO LOUD, if you see what I mean. What's the answer?
Chris Moore, Blackpool

A There are two ways round the problem. The first is to type out the caps and then reduce the point size until you get the effect you want, but that may not print out properly. The proper solution is to highlight the text you want to put in small caps, then go to the Alt+T (Format) menu and select Character. You will see an option for small caps.

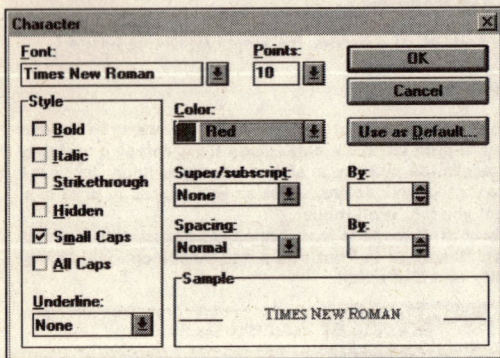

The Character options dialog box - notice just how many options there are

SMALL CAPS LOOK LIKE THIS, not so loud as
BIG CAPS, DON'T YOU THINK?

SAVE PAPER

Q I have a little bubble jet printer which won't accept A5 sheets in portrait format. It thinks there is no paper in the feed. This is quite a nuisance, as I use A5 sheets for inserts in the software I sell. I have to print on A4 and then cut the sheets down. It's a bit wasteful. Is there any way round this?
Ted Dickens, Stratford

A Apart from printing on A4 and getting out the scissors or the guillotine, there is a way round the problem. It just needs a touch of dexterity. Get your A5 sheet and a blank A4 sheet. Position the A5 sheet carefully on the top left-hand corner of the A4 sheet, and insert both into the printer mechanism.
The printer will think it's a proper sheet of paper and print happily away. The one problem that you might encounter is once the page is printed, the A5 sheet can slip back on one corner into the mechanism and get chewed to bits or at the best rather badly smudged. So you will have to sit over the printer and watch it to ensure that this doesn't happen to your work.

WRONG WINGDINGS

Q I thought I was being rather clever and used a dagger and double dagger sign (from the Wingdings font) to mark text and footnote comments, but when I sent it off to our club secretary to print, her machine came up with entirely the wrong characters. What went wrong and is there a way out?
Ross Drew, London

A This is Windows attempting to be helpful (or not, as the case may be). If you specify a typeface which is not installed on your machine, Windows will look for what it thinks is the nearest typeface.

Windows' idea of the nearest font can be quite peculiar, and most unhelpful if it's a font consisting of non-alphabetical characters, like Wingdings, Music and so on.

So, what do you do? A rather mundane answer is to use (1) and (2) for your footnote numbers. Plan B is to use superscript numbers, which are available from the Alt+T Format/Character dialog box.
Plan C, if you really want to retain a particular font, is to go to your favourite graphics package and create the text, then import it as a borderless image. That way no one can deprive you of your textual effect, large or small.

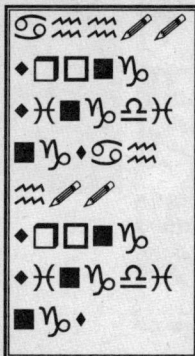

DECORATE YOUR DESKTOP

Q Can I make wallpaper easily on my machine?

Tom Rutherford, Grantham

A No problem, so long as you have a file in BMP format. Launch Paint, load the file, go for Alt+F, and select the file as wallpaper, either tiled or centred.

Now right click on the Taskbar, opt for Minimise all Windows, and you can see your efforts before your very eyes. What looks nice as a single image can be overwhelming when duplicated all over a screen. To get back to your favourite wallpaper, start up the Control Panel followed by Display.

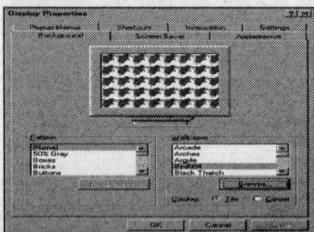

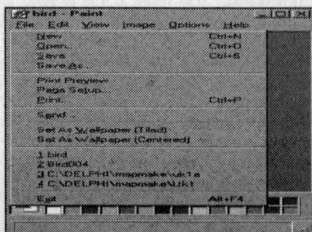

1 To change wallpaper, go to the Control Panel, Display, and select another option

2 The Set as Wallpaper options in the File menu of Paint

3 A garish piece of wallpaper using Paint and its Set as Wallpaper option on the File menu

OUT OF CONTROL

Q OK, so it's nice when Windows 95 changes your clock for you to Daylight Saving Time. But it's a bit over the top when Word 97 insists on overruling you by putting the "th" in 30th as a superscript, and also forces the format of numbered paragraphs. Don't you just love it when you're not in control?
Wendy Marson, Peterborough

A Too true. It was better in the bad old days of MS-DOS, when you were at least in control of what was going on and there was no one else to blame if the system blew up in your face. Now there is so much happening behind the scenes which you aren't aware of and which few of us have the knowledge to patch up when it all goes wrong.

The answer to your problem is buried away in the Tools menu. Click on the AutoCorrect item and you'll find options for switching on and off automatic correction for just about everything you can imagine, at least in a working Windows environment.

Do make a practice with this and other programs of checking out any items called Options or Preferences so that you can see to what extent you can tweak the way the program looks or works. Don't put up with something annoying because it looks complex to fix - usually it isn't.

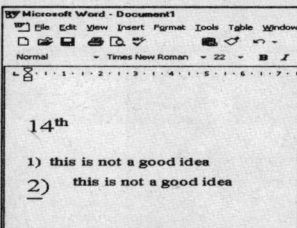

The muddle that Word 97 can get itself in with autocorrection - note the superscript it insists on putting in the second item on the list!

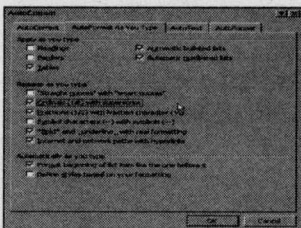

Buried away in Help is a pointer to AutoCorrect - it's accessed by the Tools menu item

SEEING DOUBLE

Q I have Word 2. Recently I wanted to remove all single hard carriage returns and convert double carriage returns to singles, but I got into a total mess, ending up with an unreadable slab of continuous text and a time-consuming manual edit. Is there a way round the problem?
Dawn Simmons, Canterbury

A This sounds a touch technical, but actually it can be a common problem. The answer is to go in two stages. Word allows you to Find and Replace hard carriage returns, using the sequence ^p.

This means a carriage return is an end of line marker, if you like. The expression goes back to the days of manual typewriters, when you had to reach out and give the arm sticking out a hard whack to get the carriage back to the beginning of the line, at the same time cranking the platen roller up enough for you to begin typing on a new line.

If you replace all the occurrences of ^p with nothing, then you are indeed in a mess. The way round the problem goes something like this. First, replace all double ^p^p sequences with a unique set of characters, like *****.

Then you can eradicate the single carriage returns. Finally, replace the ***** sequence with a single ^p. Hope you understand that!

HAVING A CLEAROUT

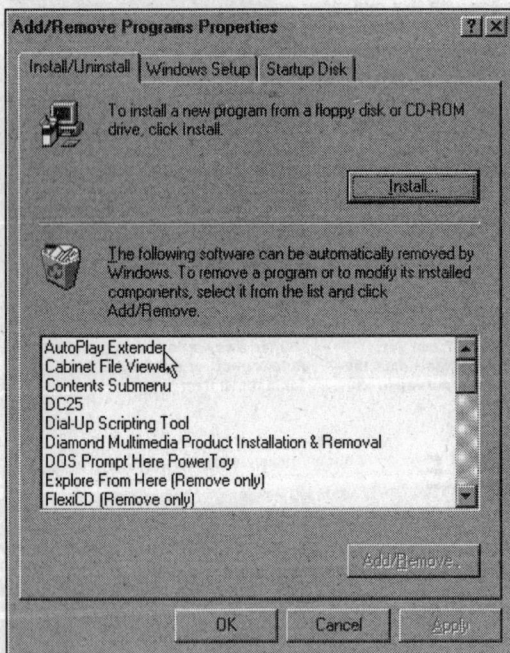

The Add/Remove Programs dialog box. Select a program and follow the instructions to delete it

Q My machine is cluttered up with a number of programs which I've loaded from time to time from CD-ROMs on the front of magazines, and I want to get rid of them. What's the best way?
Chris Hepplewaite, Bradford

A If you don't want to go to the expense of buying a special product, you can try one of three things. First, you can try deleting the unwanted applications yourself, using Windows Explorer. The trouble is, some of them will use shortcuts and there is no guarantee you will eradicate the files that are really cluttering up the system.

Plan B is to check to see if the applications are courteous enough to have an Uninstall function themselves. Some do, others - to their shame - do not.

The best approach is to use Windows 95 itself. And the easiest way is to load Help, type removing and home in on removing programs from your computer. Up comes a box inviting you to click to get to the Add/Remove Programs dialog box.

Note that you can only remove programs designed to run under Windows 95 with this technique.

However, the best way of tackling this problem is to avoid it by promptly removing any applications which you just load on a trial basis if you don't want to keep them.

169

THE NANNY STATE

Q I was having a grand clear out of files the other day, but when I checked the amount of space remaining on my hard drive, I found that hardly anything had changed. But the files have gone, haven't they? **Sue Phillips, Greater Manchester**

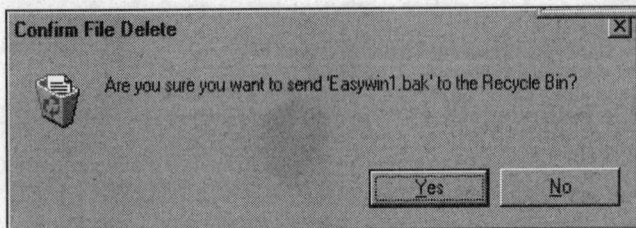

Confirm File Delete

Are you sure you want to send 'Easywin1.bak' to the Recycle Bin?

Yes   No

If you right click and opt to delete, this is the message you get - the file will be sent to the Recycle Bin

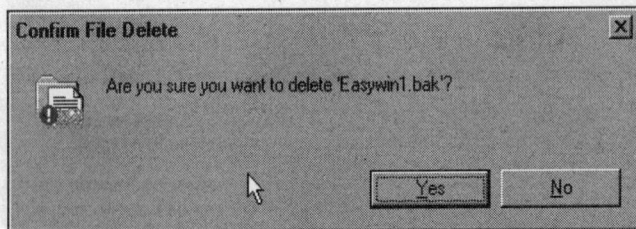

Confirm File Delete

Are you sure you want to delete 'Easywin1.bak'?

Yes   No

If you right click, hold down Shift and opt to delete, that will get rid of the file entirely

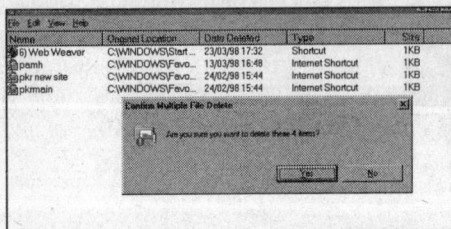

Name	Original Location	Date Deleted	Type	Size
6) Web Weaver	C:\WINDOWS\Start...	23/03/98 17:32	Shortcut	1KB
pamh	C:\WINDOWS\Favo...	13/03/98 16:48	Internet Shortcut	1KB
pkr new site	C:\WINDOWS\Favo...	24/02/98 15:44	Internet Shortcut	1KB
pkrmain	C:\WINDOWS\Favo...	24/02/98 15:44	Internet Shortcut	1KB

Confirm Multiple File Delete

Are you sure you want to delete these 4 items?

Yes   No

When you click on File, then Empty Recycle Bin, you get a Confirm delete message

A Well, it all depends. How's that for a crisp and positive answer? A little more precisely answered. Way back in the bad old days of MS-DOS and nothing else, if you erased a file that was that - in the earlier versions at least. Unless you were a bit of a rocket scientist and knew how to tinker with the FAT (File Allocation Table), an erased file was on a par with the famous Monty Python deceased parrot.

170

Along comes Windows 95 and the Nanny State, or to put it more nicely, a Helping Hand, known as the Recycle Bin. If using Windows 95 you opt to erase a file, you are simply sending it to the Recycle Bin, a holding area which retains the deleted files.

If you want to delete the file altogether, right click on the file icon in Windows Explorer, hold down Shift and opt to delete. Then if you decide to erase it, it will be lost once and for all.

Also, double click on the Recycle Bin icon and explore its contents. To empty the Bin, click on File, then opt for Empty Recycle Bin.

GRUNTS, GROANS, TOILETS...

Q I left a friend of mine (at least, I thought he was a friend) play some game or other on my machine, and when he left there was a rather mysterious smirk on his face. I put that down to his having achieved genius status at noughts and crosses, but I soon discovered that he had somehow messed around with the sounds on the machine.
Instead of the normal bells and raspberries, I heard all these strange animalistic grunts and groans, some of them hinting at an animal in a deal of pain or in urgent need of the toilet. What's he done and how can I reverse the damage?
Anna Burton, Perth

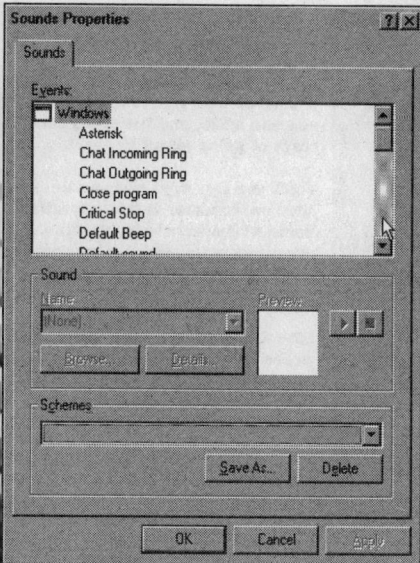

You access the Sounds Properties dialog box via the Control Panel's Sounds icon

A Trade him in for another friend. Then go to the Control Panel, double click on Sounds and up will come Sounds Properties. It's most probable that you will find under Schemes a reference to jungle sounds. You can change that back to the Windows default, replace it with your own scheme, or turn the wretched things off altogether.

FLOPPY PROBLEMS

Q I still use the MS-DOS Window for file copying and other housekeeping activities. When copying a backup file to a floppy disk, what do I do if I get a Disk-full message and the system seems to stop working? I have to reset the system and sometimes lose the work I have been doing.
Gabriel Harding, North Wales

A The golden rule with MS-DOS is to ensure that you have saved any current work before you start copying to a floppy disk. Then, if something goes wrong, you haven't lost anything serious. The first line of defence is to keep hitting Ctrl+C, and with any luck you will get back to the prompt and you can continue in business.
Even simpler, do check that the disk you are backing up to has enough space on it!

WHAT'S IN A NAME?

Q I hate the phrase "My Computer". It's boring, twee and must have been thought up on a bad Friday afternoon. Can I please change it?
Gene Gordon, Aberdeenshire

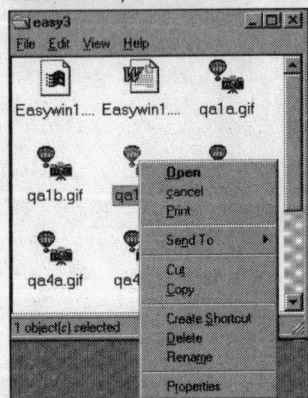

After a right click, you can opt for Rename and then change the name of the folder or file

A Here at Windows Made Easy we agree with you. It's very simple to rename a file, and there are two ways of going about it.

First, you can right click on the icon, then on Rename. At this point the name of the item is highlighted, a cursor appears, and you can rename it. Press Enter when you have finished.

Plan B is to click on the name, then pause for a second, then click again - and that gets you into Edit mode. Now you can call "My Computer" what you want!

RECYCLED FILES

Q Two questions, really. First, where are the recycled files, and what happens when the Bin is full?
F B Carter, County Down

A They are in a hidden system folder called \Recycled, and it's in the root folder (or directory, to give it its 3.1 name). The Bin, by default, can take up 10 per cent of each drive (or partition), and when full, the oldest files are erased first, but you are given no warning of this. You can vary the size of the Bin by right clicking on it, selecting Properties, and making the necessary adjustments. At the same time, you can disable the Bin altogether.

HIDING THE TASKBAR

Q I noticed on another machine in the office that the Taskbar wasn't visible all the time, thus not cluttering up the screen. How is this done and how do you make it visible?
Melanie Green, Cumbria

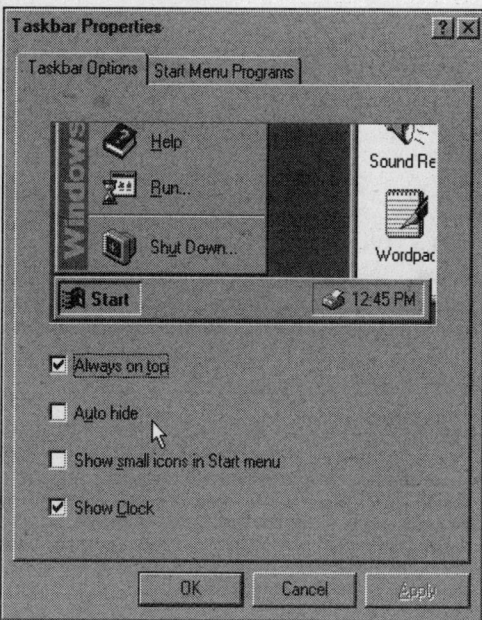

The Taskbar Properties dialog box, which also allows you to change the size of icons on the Start menu - and hence vary the amount of space it takes up

173

A Right click on a spare bit of the Taskbar. Click on Taskbar Properties to bring up the dialog box which enables you to Auto hide the Taskbar. Then move the cursor to the bottom of the screen (if that's where the hidden Taskbar is) to reveal it again.

Here's some related information: CTRL+ALT+Delete lets you see all the programs running. If you hold down ALT and keep pressing Tab, you will move one by one through the programs currently running. Release Tab when you want to give focus to a particular program.

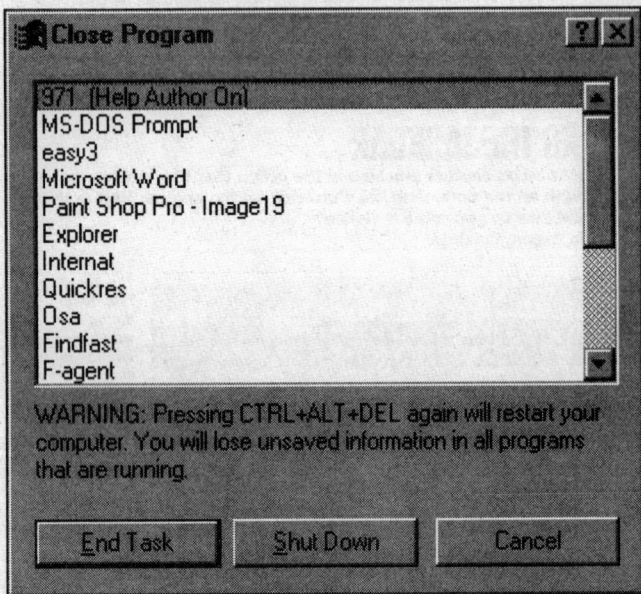

Close Program	?	X

971 [Help Author On]
MS-DOS Prompt
easy3
Microsoft Word
Paint Shop Pro - Image19
Explorer
Internat
Quickres
Osa
Findfast
F-agent

WARNING: Pressing CTRL+ALT+DEL again will restart your computer. You will lose unsaved information in all programs that are running.

End Task	Shut Down	Cancel

When you press CTRL+ALT+Delete, you get a view of what's running behind the scenes

CAN'T GET STARTED

Q I have two different versions of the CD-ROM player on the Taskbar and I want to get rid of one. How do I get access to the stuff on that little box in the right-hand corner of the Taskbar where the clock is? Also, when I loaded the latest version of Paint Shop Pro, I find that it now loads automatically together with the README file in Word. Sorry to ask two different questions, but how do I stop that happening?
J Wilkins, Castleford

The StartUp folder with short cuts to two CD-ROM programs and Paint Shop Pro and its Read Me file

A In fact, these aren't two very different questions at all. The answer for both of them lies in the StartUp folder. This is where you will find it:

C:\WINDOWS\START MENU\PROGRAMS\STARTUP

To remove an item from the folder, just right click on it and click on Delete. This applies whether you want to get rid of an extra item or an Autorun program. If you want to Autorun an application at StartUp, add a corresponding shortcut to the folder.

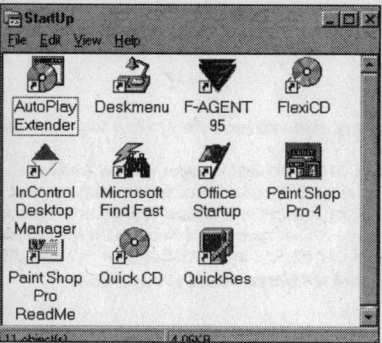

EXPLORING THE WAY

Q When using Explorer, I often want to look for a particular file starting from the directory I've found my way to. How can this be done - or can it be done at all?
Sam Walton, South Shields

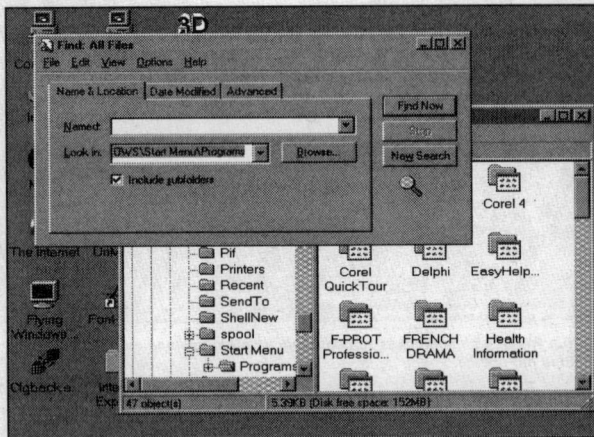

With Explorer open, all you have to do to get to Find File is to press F3

A When you have arrived at your target directory, press F3 and the Find File dialog box will pop up starting in that directory.

GETTING UNSTUCK

Q How do I undo the last command I executed in Explorer?

W Quentin, S London

A This tip applies to Move, Copy, Rename (or Delete) Files and Folders. All you do is press Ctrl+Z.

A QUICK JOURNEY

Q Is there a way of getting quickly from the Control Panel to My Computer?
Peter Banks, Cumbria

A There's a very swift route into My Computer from the Control Panel, which I came across quite by chance. Hit the backspace (left delete) key when the Control Panel has focus, and up it comes.

SCRABBLING AROUND

Q I have a shareware Scrabble game called Scrabout which I have put into a folder called Scrabble (I tend to be imaginative like that). When I opened the folder and copied the EXE file to the Desktop, it wouldn't run. It crashed because of a dictionary error, but it works if you double click it from within the folder. What's going on?
P Butterwick, North Shields

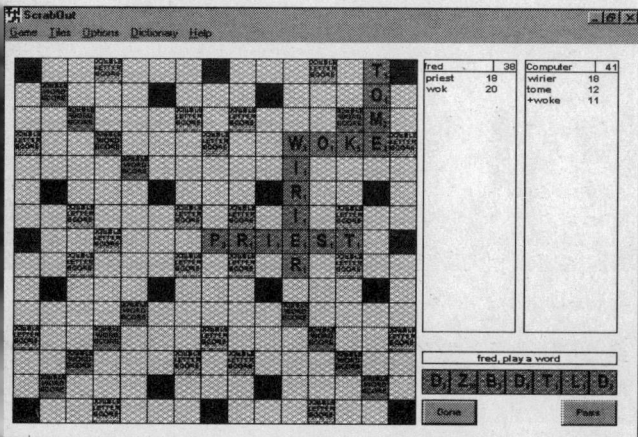

A scrabble game in full cry with one player doing slightly better than the other

A Nice little program for anyone who likes word games. Anyway, it can easily be resolved. Open the Scrabble folder and check to see if you moved the EXE file to the Desktop or copied it.

If you moved it, move it back - hold down the right mouse button and drag it to the folder. If you copied it, right click on the Desktop icon and delete it, ignoring the dire warnings about what happens when you delete EXE files.

Now drag the EXE file from the folder to the Desktop and this time click on Create a Shortcut here. The program should work now.

Why? Because when you copied or moved the file to the Desktop and ran it, it couldn't find the other files it needs in the same directory, so it burst into tears and refused to play. The shortcut simply points to the Scrabble folder, which means the associated files are all in the right place.

SMILE FOR THE CAMERA

Q Help! I have just bought a digital camera and can't use it to upload pictures to my own computer, because there is a hardware conflict and try as I might, I cannot resolve it even with the Wizard. I have a network card that I don't use and that's causing the trouble. Is there a way round the problem?

J Jones, Wolverhampton

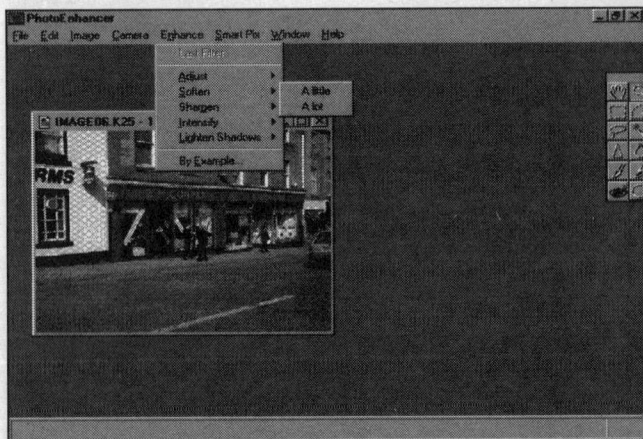

Kodak's software for digital camera use offers a range of valuable options

A The COM2 port is your the problem, and it sounds as if you bought a top of the range machine where the network card came bundled with it. No problem arose until you tried plugging a cable into the spare - as you thought - COM2 port.

This is a pain; back in the old days of the IBM PC, no one believed anyone would want to hang more than a couple of devices on to the computer. Now we have CD-Roms, ZIP drives, scanners, and heaven knows what else. And now on top of that, digital cameras.

If you are sure you don't need the network card, remove it, or if you don't feel competent to do so, take it to your local computer shop and get them to do it. Otherwise, some hairy reprogramming needs to be done; again, that is best carried out by experts.

By the way, if you do take the machine to a professional, take the opportunity to upgrade your memory if you have 16Mb or less. You will be amazed at the improved performance at a very cheap price.

LIFE'S A DRAG

Q I have used the tip of dragging icons on to the Start button, which enables me to run common applications quickly and easily. But I bet you can't do the same for the Control Panel. Or can you?
Peter Smith, North London

A You have just lost your bet. This is what you do. Open the Windows folder, and find Control.exe. Move the cursor over it, hold down the right button and drag the icon over the Start button. Let go. Now you can launch the Control Panel from your Start menu.

GETTING INTO A FIZZ WITH NUMBERS

Q There's one aspect of Windows which makes me fizz with fury. When I boot up, the Num Lock is on and I keep forgetting to switch it off before trying to use the keys on the right-hand side of the keyboard. Can it be done automatically?
Sally Barnes, Gloucestershire

A What? You mean there's only one aspect of Windows which gets you cross? There are quite a few, for example, such as the genius who put the Close Window box right next to the Maximise box, so a simple slip loses a Window. Anyway, to your problem.

The Windows 95 version of MS-DOS allows you to add to your CONFIG.SYS file, which is in the root directory, the line: numlock=off

Go into an MS-DOS Window, change to the root directory (CD \), then type: EDIT CONFIG.SYS

- and add that line at the end. To save the new version, type Alt+X then Y.

A NOSY PARKER

Q I guess I'm just nosy, but what is going on behind the scenes when the opening Windows 95 screen is running? And while I'm being curious, what happens if you forget your password?
William Paterson, Fife

A Press Esc while the Windows 95 opening screen is doing it's thing, and you will be able to peep behind the scenes. Whether you understand what is going on or not is a different matter altogether.

> *Now for the password. This will not exactly bolster your faith in the system's security, but here goes. When you get to the password dialog box, press Esc. Go for the MS-DOS prompt and in the Windows folder type: DIR *.PWL*

Delete the file with your name on it, using the DEL command. Start the system again and you will be invited to type in and confirm a new password.

RE-FORMAT THE QUICK WAY

Q Quite often I want to erase and reuse floppy disks which contain various subdirectories. It is quite a fiddly business. Is there a really quick way of doing it?
S W Patten, Scarborough

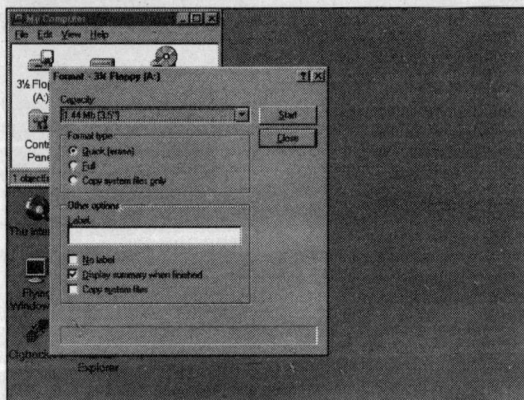

Using My Computer to get to Quick Format which rapidly wipes your disks

A Open an MS-DOS Window, type: Format A:/Q - and follow the instructions. A quick format takes a couple of seconds only. For those who insist on using Windows 95 for everything, this way is nearly as quick.

Open My Computer, right click on the floppy drive, select format and Quick format (erase). The MS-DOS way of doing things allows you to give a volume label to the disk as part of the process.

FIGHTING BACK AGAINST THE SYSTEM

Q I don't like being beaten by the system. I can't find where the Documents files are located on the Start Menu. I'd like to tinker with them rather than just having the blunt instrument option of deleting the lot. Can you help?
J Farmer, West Midlands

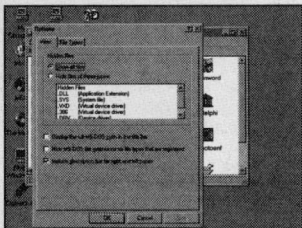

Finding hidden folders using Explorer

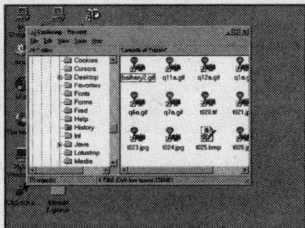

This is the Recent folder containing the files in the Document menu

A You'd better get used to being beaten by the system - it happens to everyone with monotonous regularity! On this occasion, though, help is at hand. There is a folder in the Windows folder called Recent, but you can't see it because it's what's known as a hidden file.

Files have attributes: they can be read-only, hidden archive or system. Attributes also apply to folders, which are if you like a special kind of file which can contain other files. Question is, how do we get our grubby paws on the Recent folder?

Open up Windows using Explorer. Click on View, Options, and then on the radio button to Show all files. Recent will then pop up among the folders; all you have to do is open it and it's putty in your hands. Incidentally, showing all files will also cause the History folder, used by Internet explorer, to emerge into the light of day.

KEYS TO SUCCESS

Q I am handicapped and find it difficult to right click on the mouse, but I am quite good at the keyboard. Is there a way of doing it with

keys?
Pam Wells, Portsmouth

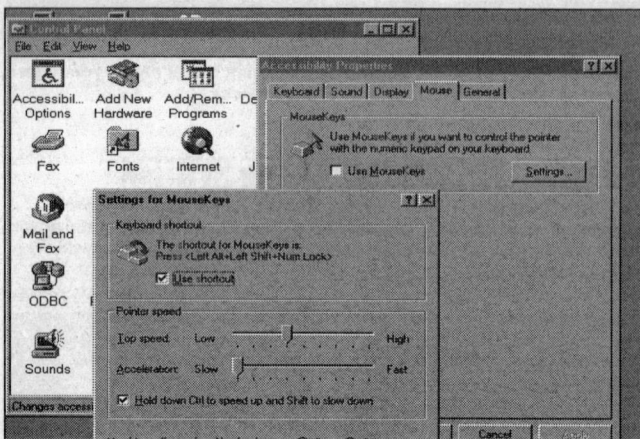

Finding the mouse options under Accessibility options

A The answer is quite simple: Shift+F10 will get you there. Look at mouse options under Accessibility on the Control Panel for a more complete solution which allows you to use the numeric keypad as an alternative to the mouse.

DECODING FILE EXTENSIONS

Q I like wandering round the system, and have noticed quite a range of different file extension names. Those like EXE are, I assume, executable programs. DOC is for documents in a word processor, and TXT is for text files. There are a couple which puzzle me, though. They are BAT and CPL. What do they stand for?
P H Feltham, Surrey

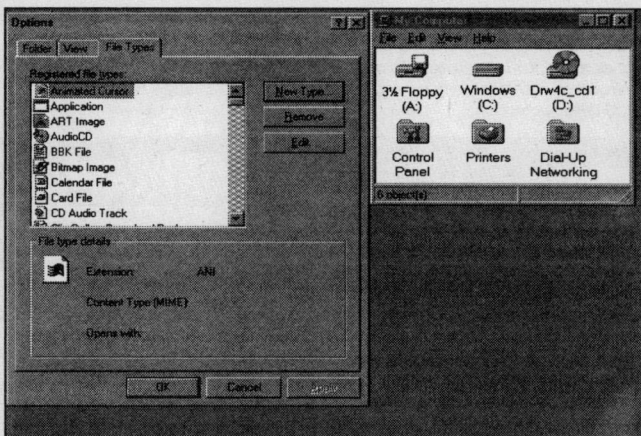

File types under the Options menu of My Computer shows you the registered types

A There are large numbers of extension names which are known to the system. Windows calls these 'registered files', and to inspect or alter them (the latter is not recommended), open My Computer and from the View menu, go for Options, then click on the File Types tab.

Highlight any item in the list, and you will see the extension name. You would expect to find CPL files in WINDOWS\SYSTEM. They are the files which contain the applications in the Control Panel.

As for BAT, that's an MS-DOS file type. It stands for batch file, and is a text file containing a list of MS-DOS commands which are executed when you type the name of the batch file. The file you probably have come across is AUTOEXEC.BAT, which runs automatically when the system starts up if it is present.

RETRO COMPUTING, DOS STYLE

Q I know it's supposed to be naff and passé to use the MS-DOS Window, but I think it's quicker to use XCOPY, for example, than to prat about with Explorer. However, it's a bore when it opens in the Windows sub-directory (sorry, folder). How can I change it?
L U Dite, Luton

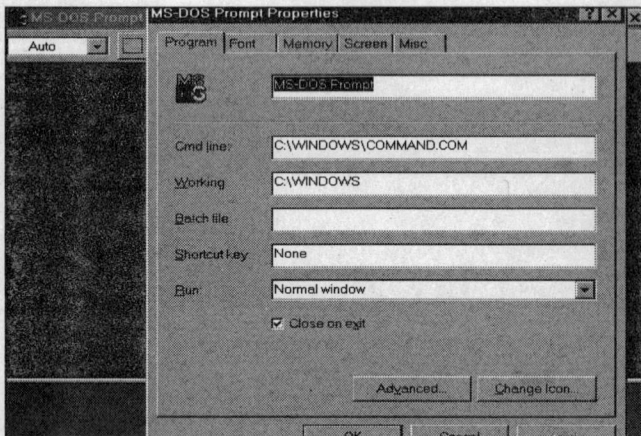

The Properties tab of the MS-DOS Window allows you to change the starting directory - note that the window runs Doskey in insert mode when it opens

A No, it's not naff. It's just that people brought up exclusively on Windows 95 don't know that it's a real Man's World out there with command line programming. Open an MS-DOS Window, right click on the colourful icon in the top left hand corner, and go for Properties.

Change the Working directory to the one you want MS-DOS to open in. Also spend a moment or two looking at the options which the other tabs offer. For those with visual problems, you can vary the type face and size, and there are other ways in which you can usefully tweak the way it works.

KEYS TO SUCCESS II

Q I have discovered that once an icon is highlighted, you can move around icons, say on the Desktop, with the cursor keys. Is there anything else you can do from the keyboard?
J Stewart, Grampian

A]If an icon is highlighted, you can launch the application by pressing Enter. Also, a little known fact is that if you hold down the Alt key, then double click, up comes the Properties panel of the highlighted icon. If you hold down the Shift key as you move around the icons, you can select more than one.

MOUSE TROUBLE

Q I have problems with the mouse. Can I access Start from the keyboard?
J Finchley, Somerset

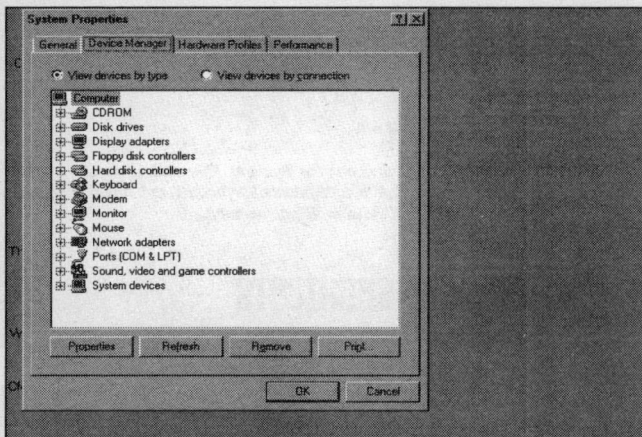

The Device Manger can be accessed from the Control Panel Systems icon, or by pressing Win+Break

A Not just Start, also the continuation menus. To put up the first menu, press Ctrl+Esc. Then press, say, P for Programs and up comes the Programs menu. Press A for Accessories and up comes the appropriate continuation menu. To go back a step, press Esc. To get WordPad, press W plus Enter. If there is more than one item beginning with the same letter, press the letter until you get to the item you want, then Enter.

It's a bit tricky, as there is no indication on the menu as to which item you are currently highlighting, but you will soon get the hang of it. If there is no submenu and just one item beginning with a particular letter, it's launched right away. For example, Ctrl+Esc, S, C gets you to the Control Panel.

On the desktop, press the initial letter to get to the first icon beginning with that letter. If there is more than one, a second press gets you to the next one, and so on.

FIND YOUR WAY AROUND

Q I often use Find all Files, but is there a quick way of launching it?

A Hamilton, Buckingham

A Yes, but you would never guess it in a million years. Press Ctrl+Esc, then Esc again. Now press F3 and up comes Find all Files.

Alternatively, if you have a Windows keyboard, press Ctrl+Win+F (Win = Windows key).

WHERE'S THE DEVICE MANAGER?

Q I can never seem to find the Device Manager. Where have they hidden it?

Ron Palmer, Weston-Super-Mare

A Go to the Control Panel and opt for System. Then click on the Device Manager tab. Or, if you have a Windows keyboard, cut out the middle man by pressing Win+Break (Win = Windows key).

MORE KEYBOARD SHORTCUTS

Q I love using the Internet, but I'm handicapped and don't have strong control over the mouse. I see on some sites the instruction to press Ctrl+D to add the page to Favourites. Are there any other keyboard short-cuts?

Wendy Williams, Ely

A To get to a new web page, press Ctrl+N. That brings up the Open dialog box, from which you can, of course, browse if you wish.

Forward and Back buttons can be emulated by Alt+Right Arrow and Alt+Left Arrow. You mentioned Ctrl+D in relation to the Favourites list, and to get into Organise Favourites press Ctrl+B.

To open the History list, press Ctrl+H. And to refresh the current page, press Ctrl+R.

FILES: GET THE FULL STORY

Q I'd like to see full information about files in a folder, and it is a bit fiddly having to right click on them one at a time to find out what I want. Is there a way round this?

AThe simplest route is to open an MS-DOS Window. Use My Computer to get where you want, then right click on the folder you want. Click on MS-DOS prompt here, then type: DIR/V/P

That produces a verbose directory listing which tells you a great deal of information about each file. Note also the difference between the file size and the allocation units the file takes up. For small files, quite a chunk of space is wasted, as you will see.

To vary the DIR listing, type DIR/? and note the wide range of other options, for example, listing in alphabetical or date order.

RUNAWAY ICONS

Q The caption to one of the icons on my desktop overlaps the icon underneath it. What can I do?
Jim Williams, Canterbury

You can see one extremely long file name here which could drown several icons below it

Even the Confirm Delete dialogue box is struggling to cope with even part of the file name in its message!

A Plan A is to place it as the last icon on the desktop. Plan B is to move it to an empty space on the desktop. Plan C is to click on the caption, pause, then click again: now you can edit the caption and make it as short as you wish.

PUT IT ON THE DESK

Q I like the idea of keeping documents on my desktop. What's the easiest way of putting them there?
Roberta Haycliffe, W Midlands

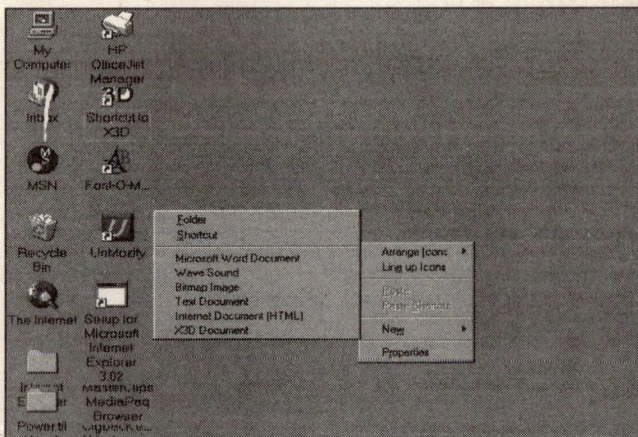

The first stage in setting up a new Word document. Right click on the desktop, then opt for New

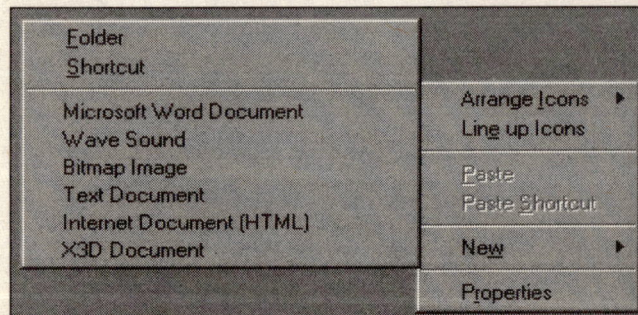

A I suspect you have been dragging them from an existing folder to the desktop. Why not try right clicking on the desktop, then opting for New and, say, Create a new Word document, which places an icon called 'New Microsoft Word Document.DOC' on the desktop. Double click on it, and you're in Word right away.

DODGY CHARACTERS

Q I've an old text file which I wrote under MS-DOS. The special characters - accents, and so on - don't convert properly when I load it as text into Works. Help!
F Farmer, Ely

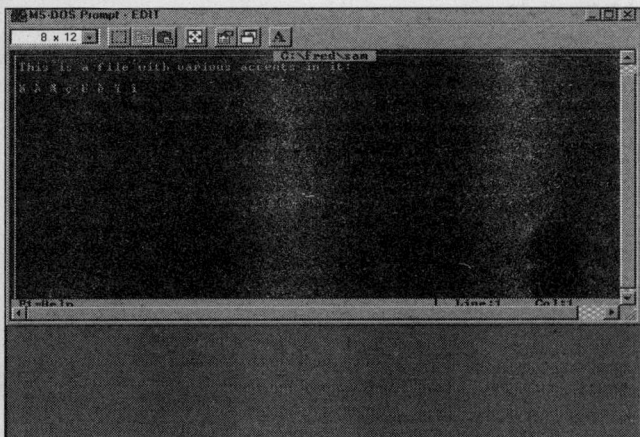

Here's some text in ASCII format created by using the MS-DOS Editor, quite a powerful beast for its age

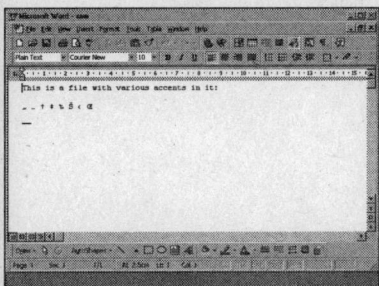

And this is what happens when you copy it into Word 7. All the values appear to go crackers

A If you have an early version of Word, you can open it as DOS Text, which brings back the old values. In Word 97, click on the ANSI characters topic in Help. The problem is that MS-DOS uses character values according to ASCII, and Windows uses ANSI, which are - as you can see - different when you get beyond the normal letters, numbers and punctuation.

TRASH IT - FOR GOOD!

Q When I want to get rid of a file, I want to get rid of it, and if it's an EXE file, I don't want Nanny Windows asking me if I mean what I mean. Can I cut out that message?
B R Temple, Windsor

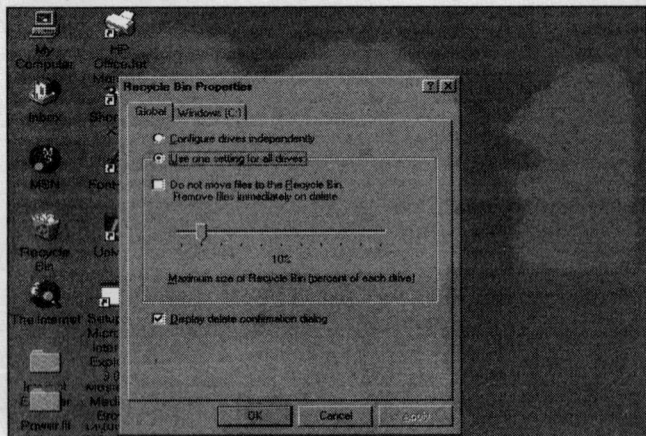

Right click on the Recycle Bin and then from the Global tab you can opt to get rid of the Confirm delete and also send stuff straight into limbo

A The Confirm Delete message for EXE files (and why just for EXE files, by the way?) can be switched off by right clicking on the Recycle Bin, going for Properties and then unticking the Confirm Delete box on the Global tab.

LIFE'S STILL A DRAG...

Q When I drag a file from one part of my hard drive to another, I expect to be moving it, not copying it, and that's what happens. But when I drag a file from, say, the hard drive to the floppy, it just copies it. What's going on?
W R Freedom, Isle of Wight

A Windows is being inconsistent, that's what's going on. As you say, dragging implies moving from one place to another (or in your case, C: to A:). With an EXE file, a shortcut is created, and, just to make things even more untidy, no move takes place. The best solution is to drag using the right mouse button. Then when you release the button, up comes a pop-up menu giving you a range of choices.

AN ANIMATED ISSUE

Q I have installed some utility that show windows growing when I maximise them and shows them shrinking when I minimise them. I want to uninstall it but I don't remember its name or where it is.
Oliver Smith, Birmingham

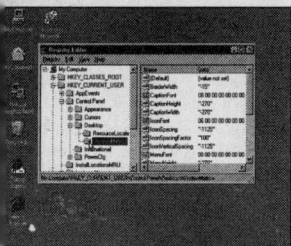

A Go to: Start|Settings |Control panel| TweakUI|General and uncheck the Window Animation option to stop it.
Or If you don't have TweakUI, use RegEdit.
HKEY_CURRENT_USER\Control Panel\desktop\WindowMetrics There will be an option MinAnimate. If it is not there, add a new string value called MinAnimate. Modify this and change it to 0 (zero). Remember to backup the registry before making ANY changes. Hope this helps.

CURSOR COLOUR BLUES

Q Can anyone tell me how to change the colour of the cursor in W95 from white to black? With many programs running a white background (such as Eudora), I'm forever looking where the cursor is. You'd think Bill Gates would have made that an easily executed option. Thanks for whatever help you can give me.
John Samson, Kent

A First, you need to get an icon editor to create a black (or other colour) cursor. I would suggest downloading IconForge from http://www.cursorarts.com/ to make the cursor. Next, you need to open the Windows Control Panel and click on the Mouse icon. Under the Pointers tab, you can choose the cursor file(s) you made.

CREATING A BOOT DISK

Q Can you tell me what files are needed to create a win 95 boot disk? This is a simple procedure. click on start|settings|control panel select Add Remove programs and then select the 3rd tab start-up disk. H does the rest for you.
Harry Fairhead, Yorkshire

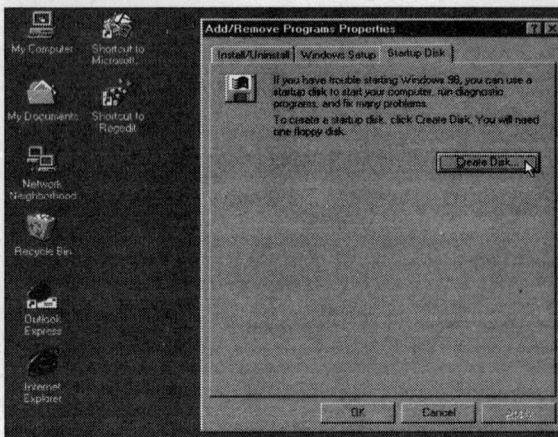

A If you want a basic start-up disk without the added resource tools (scandisk, chdsk, sys, etc.) then all you need is command.com, io.sys and msdos.sys. Note the last two are hidden files. After you do a FORMA A: /S to the disk, here are some handy commands to have on it: FDISK FORMAT EDIT (to create/edit your AUTOEXEC.BAT and CONFIG.SYS files if you have to) HIMEM.SYSCHKDSK a CD-ROM driver for

Copy these files to your hard drive after you make it bootable so that
you won't need to access the floppy so often.

OLD MAC, NEW PC

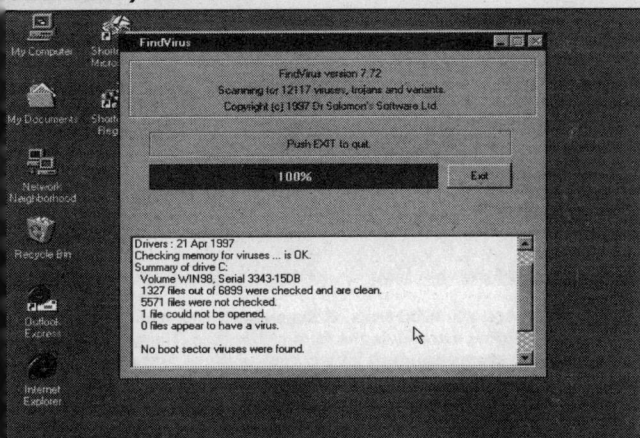

Q I am new to Windows after six years on a Mac. The only non-system
utility that I had on my Mac was Norton Utilities. Is Norton the best
available for the PC? Also, I have always heard that viruses are a more
serious problem for the PC. As I use the Internet, what is the standard
virus program for the PC? Any other utility programs that I should look
at? Thanks loads...
Stuart Sutherland, Hitching

A About the virus scanner: I think the real problem is actually spam
mail, but viruses are indeed very bad and naughty. Try Thunderbyte-
antivirus, Norton antivirus or F-prot. As far as virus protection goes, go
for McAfee; though when a virus got onto my system once, the only program that found it was IBM Antivirus. They're all pretty good, but just
make sure you get one that has frequent updates over the web.

MEMORY LOSS

Q I have an 80MB EDO RAM PC. On booting up Windows 98, when I
check my physical memory, I get only 37MB of free ram and the rest
is allocated to Win98. Is this normal? Does Win98 actually need that
much to run??? How do I free up more memory?
Karen Bell, Parkstone

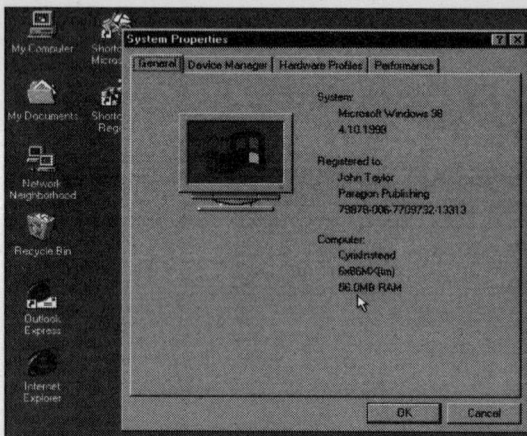

A This is normal. Win95/98 hogs all the memory it can and, when it runs out, uses virtual memory in the form of Swapfile. There are share/freeware programs which let you control these features. In Win98, go to Start/Programs/Accessories/System Tools/System Information. Next Choose Tools/System Configuration Utility. Then, choose the Startup Tab and uncheck the lines that are not needed for starting up Win 98. This helped me a lot when my RAM and system resources were low.

PERSISTENT PASSWORDS

Q On starting Windows, I get a box asking for a password with a tip saying that if I don't enter a password this prompt won't be shown again at start up. But it does! This is something new and I've no idea what has caused it. Also, I've changed the font size on the taskbar but am unable to change to another font
Pete, Email

A Did you just click cancel? You need to key a non-blank user ID and leave the password blank. Click OK to confirm if it asks you to. This should stop it asking.

CALLING A CAB

Q I am trying to find out the purpose of the .cab extension file. I have a folder on my system that is called FLAT. I do not ever remember creating it, but that is beside the point. In this folder are 26 files: Win 95_1.cab through to Win 95_27.cab. and they are all 1,667 k in size. I

would love to know what they are and if I can delete them. Thanks
Ann, Email

A They are your cabinet files, the compressed installation files for
Windows 95. When your machine was setup these files were copied
from the CD to the hard disk. If you're not desperate for space on your
hard disk, it makes the installation of Windows components much easier
and faster, because the SETUP SourcePath probably points to this folder
(FLAT) on your hard disk. If you want to delete these files you'll have to
make a registry change.

DISAPPEARING TASKBAR

Q I booted my computer this morning and my taskbar was gone. I had
it on autohide at the bottom of the screen and it won't show up now.
After much searching, I realised it is now on the left side of my screen.
But I cannot see the Start button nor can I switch programs without
using Alt-Tab. Now the problem. I can get to the start menu by pressing
Ctrl-Esc and now the pop up box is in the upper left corner. I went into
the taskbar properties and unchecked autohide and checked Always on
top. I can now see a thin, grey bar pop up on the left side. If I go over to
that side and right click, I can bring up the taskbar properties, and so
on. But - no taskbar. I cannot raise the size of the task bar because the
mouse icon will not switch to the resize icon. I originally thought that it
had somehow switched from
one level to zero, but, alas, it will not raise up (or out in this case).
Any ideas or suggestions will be greatly appreciated.
Jillian Wakefield, Worcester

A Have you tried left clicking and dragging it back to the bottom border? Alternatively, you might also need to resize it. Move the cursor to the edge of the screen where it is. When the cursor turns to double arrows, click and hold the left mouse button and move the cursor away from the edge of the screen (drag).Once the task bar is the width you want, release the mouse button.

PC PROPERTIES

Q I want to know if there is something on my PC that will tell me about its properties, such as the processor, how many megahertz, and so on. I am running Windows 95, but I don't know where to find this kind of information.
Ryanne schrieb, Email

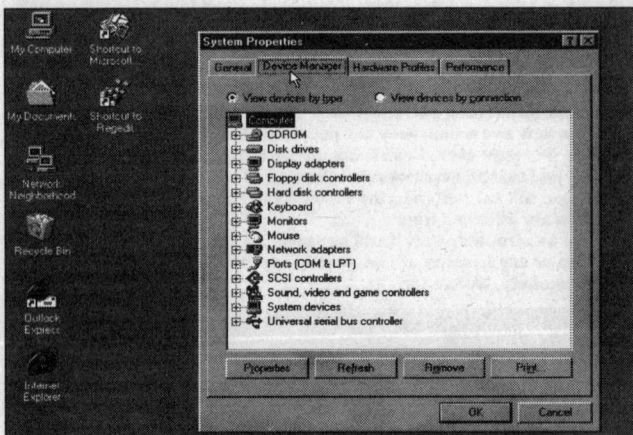

A You get all this Information when you click "My Computer" Icon with the right Mouse button and select "Properties" from the drop down menu. There are four tabs with several buttons to explore. At the DOS-Prompt, you can type "MSD" to get all the information too. If you get the error message "bad command or file name" you will have to copy the file "msd.exe" from your Win95-CD-ROM into your Windows\command folder. The msd.exe file is in CD-ROM folder \other\oldmsdos.

LOGO NO-GO

Q Can you tell me how to change that ugly Win95 logo picture which is displayed at Startup and Shutdown. We have a small network running in the office and I would like to have our company logo on the screen

when starting and closing.
Jerry Cartwright, Woodgreen

A To change the Win95 startup logo: Open your picture in a graphics program. (Paint or whatever) Resize or crop it to 640x480 in 256 colours and save it as a bitmap. Then squeeze it to 320x400 (I know it looks funny, but it'll work). Rename it "logo.sys" and copy it to your root directory.

OH DEAR...

Q I was so stupid to format my hard disk with Windows 95. Is there someone who knows about unformat?
Silly Billy, Email

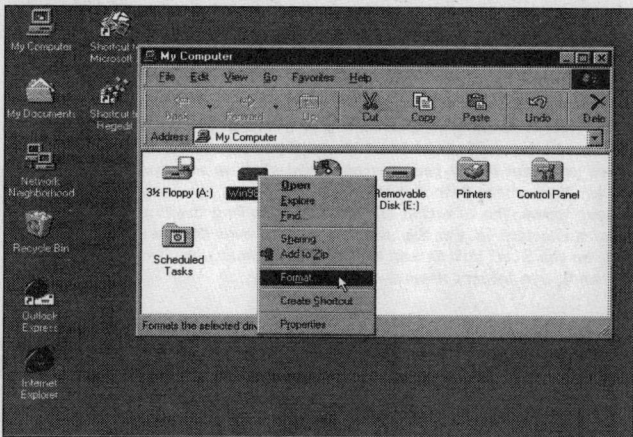

A You have to be so careful when formatting any disk as this is just about the most permanent thing you can do to your computer. We don't suggest a beginner ever formats a hard drive. All you can do now is reformat it, but there is nothing you can do to restore what was previously on it. You will have to reinstall every thing from scratch.

ADDING SHORTCUTS

Q I find the short cuts on the start menu very easy to use and very helpful I would like to add my own items to the Start Menu but I am unsure as to how I go about this. Could please give me some guidance?
Jerald Smithy, Email

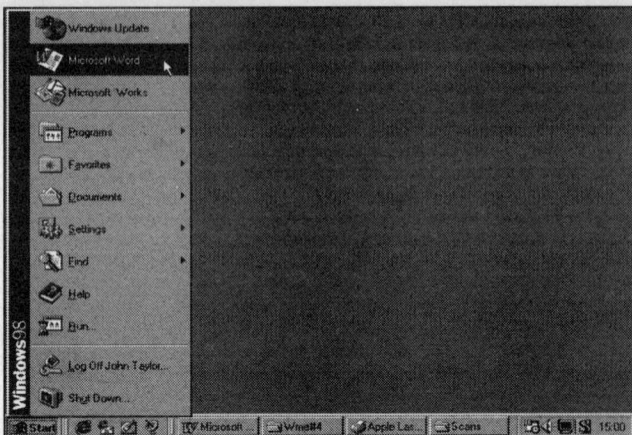

A The Start Menu's just filled with shortcut files. The easiest way to add an item is to drag an icon on top of the Start button. This creates a shortcut in the root of the Start Menu. If you're a bit more selective on where you want to put the shortcut, right click on any open Taskbar space and hit Properties. Select "Start Menu Programs" and you can add or remove items. The Shortcut Wizard helps you find the item you want to make a shortcut to. For the ultimate control over the Start Menu, right click on the Start button and hit Open or Explore, and then you can drag shortcuts and folders around at will.

TSR?

Q I know this might be a stupid question but I really want to know what a TSR is.
Ross Andrews, Manchester

A It was a technique used primarily in pre-Windows days for a program to be available while you were running other programs-a primitive form of multi-tasking, if you like. TSRs were normally loaded in autoexec.bat. In a multi-tasking operating system like Windows, there's no longer any need for TSRs, and it's pretty much an obsolete technique.

BETTER SAFE

Q I went to have my first delve into the Registry today, but thought I should heed the oft-given advice to back up user.dat and system.dat files. The only problem is that the system.dat file is 2.2Mb and since I

don't have a zip drive, I am stumped. I tried emailing the file to myself, but it was too big for that also. Is 2.2Mb the usual size for this file? If so, are there any other ways I can back it up? If not, is there a remedy?
George Pecan, Email

AYou can use Export Registry File (Start | Run | Regedit | Registry) to a directory on your hard drive (being sure that Export Range covers All). Then compress the file using WinZip or similar utility and copy the compressed file to a floppy. Another tool is Cfgback.exe, which resides in C:\Windows\System. After you double click it, it will be self-explanatory.

BIN TROUBLE

QAre the recycle bins for each drive supposed to be separate from each other? For example, if a file is deleted from a file folder on C, it is placed in the recycle bin on C; but should it also be put in the "recycle bin" of other drives? If I delete a file on a drive (C: D: E: etc.), all the recycle bins on each Drive contain the same deleted files, regardless of where they were deleted from. It is as though there is only one recycle bin for all drives. Since you can allocate different size recycle bins for each drive, through the Properties menu, I assumed each bin would be separate.
Simon Lanes, Leeds

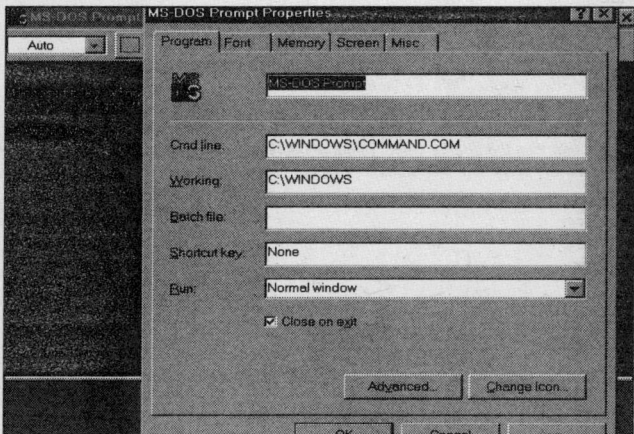

AYes, they are separate. If you delete from C: it will remain in C: If you delete from D: it will remain in D: Even though it all shows up in the "combine" recycle bin, when restored the files will return to their original homes.

COLOUR BLIND

Q Maybe I'm worrying unnecessarily, but from time to time the colours on one of my applications goes weird. If I click on it, the colours return to normal. This also happens from time to time inside my graphics package. Is there something wrong with my display?

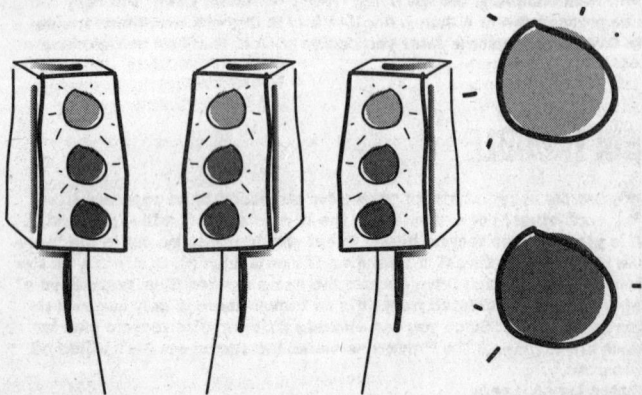

A First of all, to put you out of your misery: no, there is nothing wrong with the display. It's all to do with the concept of palettes. Whereas an image can choose from 16.5 million colours, it can't choose them all, and if its palette clashes with that of a Window which doesn't have focus, the result can be pretty psychedelic. There is no cure as such, since there really isn't a problem in the first place.

RETURN OF THE RIGHT MENU

Q How do you get the right mouse floating menu in Word with copy and paste options, Font and the rest on it if the wretched program has marked the word or phrase with a coloured squiggly line beefing about the spelling or grammar?
S S Harmer, Wolverhampton

A Word 97 allows you to right click on any word or selection and the floating menu which appears contains the Cut, Copy and Paste options, as well as Font, Paragraph, Bullets and Draw table. However, if the word is underlined with a squiggle in red (a spelling problem) or green (grammar problem), you get the menu appropriate to spelling or

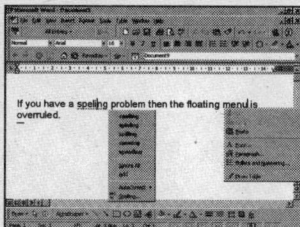

A doctored image showing the right mouse menu when there's a spelling or grammatical error, plus the usual menu

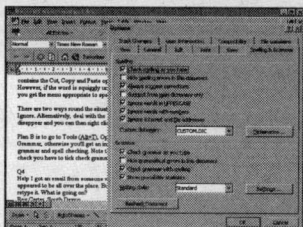

This is the dialog box you want on the Tools menu, Options, to switch grammar and spell checking on and off

grammar instead.

There are two ways round the situation. The first is to right click on the underlined word, then click on Ignore. Alternatively, deal with the spelling or grammar problem. In either case, the underline will disappear and you can then right click on the word to arrive at the standard floating menu.

Plan B is to go to Tools (Alt+T), Options, Spelling and Grammar. Don't go to Tools, Spelling and Grammar, otherwise you'll get an instant spelling and grammar check. Here you can switch off grammar and spell checking. Note that if you want to have readability statistics at the end of a spell check you have to tick check grammar with spelling.

MINIMISE YOUR PROBLEMS

Q Sometimes, when I want to close a Window or minimise all Windows, I can't. I have to close a dialog box like a Save As box or something

before I'm allowed to do so. Why not?
H R Diamond, Winchester
*Here's a situation where you cannot minimise the Window using Win+M - you have
to close the dialog box first*

AThis is quite an insidious problem if it is hidden behind another Window.
You may think the system has seized up. Look on your taskbar, and min-

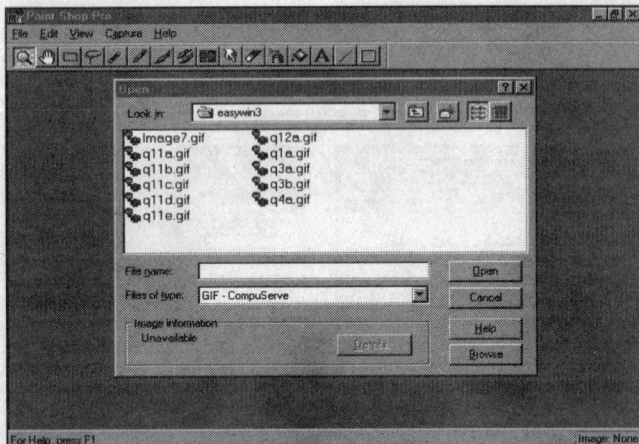

imise other Windows or poll round Windows with Alt+Tab and close the
dialog box which is causing the bother. It's known as a modal dialog box
because it won't let you close it until you have made a positive response
to it by clicking on one or another of its buttons. Bafflingly, though, you
can still minimise that Window individually by clicking on the Minimise
button.

DIRECTORY LISTINGS

QI used to find the old MS-DOS DIR command very useful in getting a
list of files, like documents for example. There seems to be no easy
way to get such a list in Windows 95, especially, for example, a list in
date or size order. Is there a means of doing this?
W Arthur, Scarborough

APerhaps the best route is to open My Computer and go to the folder
you want. Open it, then go for File (Alt+F) and DOS Prompt here, which
opens up an MS-DOS Window in the current folder.
Now you can do directory listings to your heart's content. Here are some

examples to remind you:

An MS-DOS Window with a directory listing, verbose, in alphabetical order, and a page at a time

A sample page from the full MS-DOS help which came with Version 6 of MS-DOS

DIR > PRN (a straightforward listing to the printer)
DIR/OD (in date order)
DIR *.DOC/ON (DOC files in alphabetical order

For fuller information, type DIR /? at the MS-DOS prompt, or HELP DIR if you loaded Windows 95 on top of 3.1 - your fuller version of MS-DOS help should still be around, so long as you haven't removed QBASIC.

RETRIEVING THE TASKBAR

Q When I got back to my machine the other day, I found some comedian had moved the Taskbar to the top of the screen. How can I get it back?
F Carry, Humberside

A Find an empty space on the Taskbar, move the mouse pointer over it, hold it down and drag it to the edge of the screen you want it on. You can increase or decrease the width of the Taskbar, just in case your comedian has also made it half fill the screen when it's visible (that's as

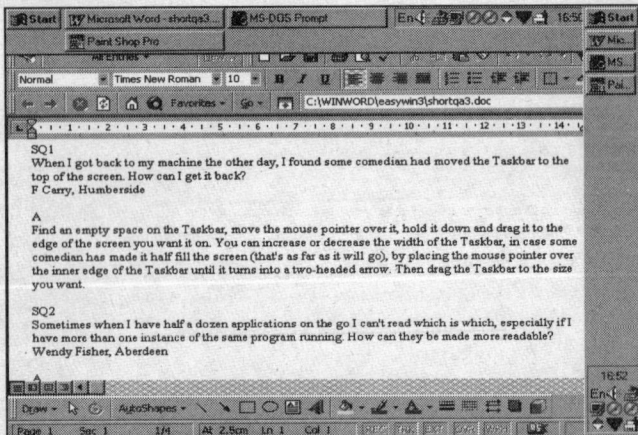

A Word session running with these questions and answers sitting in it - with the Taskbar at the top of the screen and (by a bit of trickery) simultaneously at the right of the screen

far as it will go), by placing the mouse pointer over the inner edge of the Taskbar until it turns into a two-headed arrow. Then drag the Taskbar to the size you want.

ANOTHER TASKBAR PROBLEM

Q Sometimes when I have half a dozen applications on the go I can't read which is which, especially if I have more than one instance of the same program running. How can they be made more readable?
Wendy Fisher, Aberdeen

A Another Taskbar problem. You can increase the size by dragging the edge towards the centre of the screen. If you do so - and you are working with a smallish screen resolution (640 x 480) - it's best to put

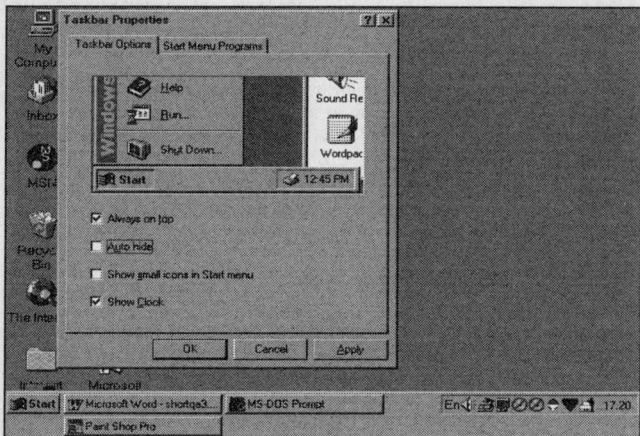

The Taskbar Properties dialog box with the Autohide option sitting on top of a two-row Taskbar

Autohide on, so that the Taskbar only appears when you move the mouse pointer to the edge of the screen where the Taskbar would normally be. Right click on the Taskbar, select Properties and Auto hide.

TASKBARS (AGAIN...)

Q My Startup tray in the right-hand corner of my Taskbar contains seven or eight items. Very occasionally they don't all appear when I power up. Why not?
Terry Grainger, Dorset

A This is a tricky one which took quite a bit of digging to solve. What appears to have happened is that you clicked on the Start button while the system was completing the loading process. If you do this at a particular moment, the Taskbar stops filling the tray up. So hold your fire until everything has settled down - it's as simple as that. Incidentally, the contents of the Taskbar are in the folder Windows\Startup.grp - an extension name which will be familiar to Windows 3.1 users.

MISSING DISKS

Q I have a hand-me-down computer with Windows 95 and I tried as a first exercise to create a safety disk. I followed the instructions until I got to the point of creating a disk. A message asked me to insert a disk labelled Windows 96 CD-ROM. I don't have such a disk. What do I do?
C W Mackness, Milton Keynes

A First, if anyone buys or is given a second hand machine, ensure that you have all the disks and so on which go with it. Second, don't confuse a disk (3.5 inch floppy) with a CD-ROM. You need the CD-ROM which was used to install Windows 95 on your machine. Then you can continue with the process of creating an emergency Startup disk, which is what I assume you were doing.

SAVE AS WORRIES I

Q I was using a graphics program the other day and tried Save As. I was asked if I wanted to increase the number of colours to 16 million. What happened?
B Ellingham, Dorset

A You had a file in a format which probably had 256 colours, for example, a GIF file. To save it as a JPEG file, which I guess is what you are doing, the number of colours has to be increased. It should not make a

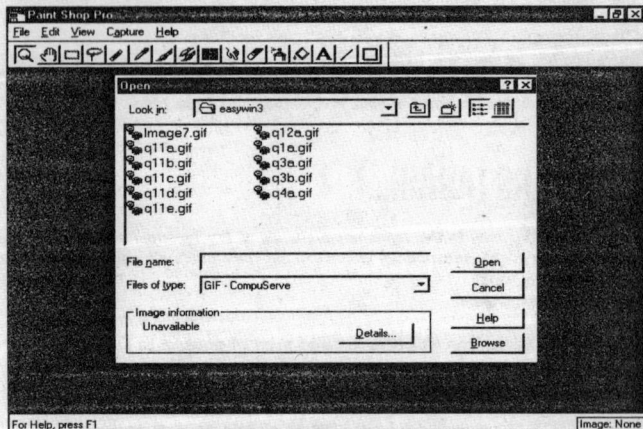

A CDR file is about to be saved in JPEG format, and up comes a reminder that it requires conversion to 16 million colours

dramatic impact on the appearance of the file. In fact, if you have a JPEG file which looks grainy, go the other way and convert it to a GIF. The colours will usually smooth out. Both JPEG and GIF files are usable in web site programming.

SAVE AS WORRIES II

Q I tried Save As with a file the other day and couldn't find it. What did I do wrong and how can I get it back if that happens again?
W Williams, Coventry

A What may have happened is that the package you were working with was set to open files from one folder and to Save As in another folder. That can often happen if you don't check which folder is current when you have the Save As dialog box open. The obvious thing to do is to check before you save. To find out where the file is, use Find on the Start menu. Alternatively, open an MS-DOS Window, go to the root directory (with the command CD\) and type DIR filename/S - where the filename is in DOS format. You can also use wildcards.

BRANCHING OUT WITH TREE STRUCTURES

Q Is there a Windows equivalent to the TREE command in MS-DOS which lets you view part or all the tree structure of a disk?
C Long, Ipswich

A Indeed there is, and a much more flexible one it is too. The great disadvantage of TREE is that you can't ask for it a page at a time, so the best thing to do is to type TREE > TMPFILE (or some other such name) and view the TMPFILE

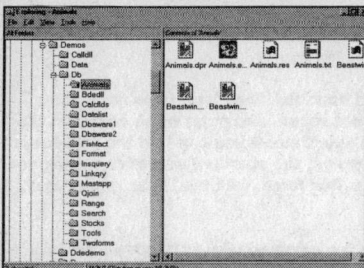

in EDIT. Under Windows, simply open Explorer. In the left-hand window, you have a tree structure ready made. Click on the plus sign to show the contents of any folder, double click on the folder name to display the contents in the right-hand window and, remember, you can resize the windows by dragging the bar which separates them.

Explorer with a number of folders and subfolders opened up and the dividing bar between the Windows moved to the centre of the screen

AOL

Q At random, the add for AOL messaging appears. As there is no box that says "Don't show me this again", it keeps coming back. I have deleted all the AOL and other rubbish cluttering my hard drive to no avail. How can I banish this from my Start Up screen forever?
Cheers,
Steve Huntley, Email

A There is a set-up button (or preferences or something like that) at the bottom left of the AIM screen. Clicking it brings up a tabbed display. In the middle of the Misc. tab is a check box to stop AIM from running at start-up. It is buried in the middle and is easy to miss. That is preferable to using Regedit.

NO BOOT

Q My computer (which runs Win95) is failing to boot on its own,it just freezes up. So I booted to a floppy disk and got the A: prompt, but when I tried to access the C: drivel got a message saying it is an invalid drive. I then booted the computer using the Norton Anti-Virus emergency disks. Norton found a virus and I got the followingmessage:

Master boot record of drive 0 isinfected with the Bloodhound.MBR virus. When Norton tried to fix the virus it failed, giving me a message that it couldn't access the C: drive.I called my PC's tech support line and they told me to use their kit which will reformt the hard drive and reinstall Win95.

However, I have some very important data on the HD which I need to get at. Does anybody know how I can access the C: drive so I can transfer that data to a floppy disk? Any replies would be greatly appreciated, thanks in advance. Jeff Spartley, Northants.

A Try to boot with a uninfected boot disk then type fdisk /mbr. That should refresh the master boot record and put a fresh one from the boot disk on it. It will not affect your data. If you can find the "fdisk.exe" program on one of your boot floppies, the standard way of re-writing your Master Boot Record is to do this: Run fdisk, with the "/mbr" parameter, as: fdisk /mbr <enter>

As long as the fdisk.exe is from the same version of Windows 95, this may solve the problem. To protect against infecting your boot floppy (or any other floppy you insert into the system) with the virus, set the tab on the floppy to make it "read-only" before you use it. Boot with a Win95 floppy. Run " fdisk /mbr " and " sys a: c: "

MEMORY TROUBLES

Q Hi: I have a clean install of Win98 and the machine crashes constantly at startup: "Windows Protection error. You need to restart your computer."Yesterday the error message referenced VxD PCI(04)VxD CDVSD(01) ... this fileCDVSD.VxD is located in c:\Windows\system\iosub-sys

I removed my new CD-ROM 24X drive and re-installed the old quad speed drive and driver. This has been going on non-stop for the past month. I even removed my new scroll point mouse and am using the old one, with no success. I keep getting the same message, and it usually refers to a VxD problem...and I think that's a driver problem.

I am using the Microsoft drivers except for the modem, printer and tape drives. I am not using a config.sys and the only entries in the autoexec.bat were put there by the Microsoft McAffee anti-virus install. I have formatted and re-installed the whole system at least 12 times!

Also, I have made several $35 calls to Microsoft support, and various peripherals mfgrs with no change whatsoever. I am so nervous that I'm afraid to install anything at all for fear of another crash at startup! The system runs just fine once I reboot. If I use the machine and reboot or shutdown and restart, no problem - it only happens when the system has been turned off for several hours and is cold.

If you have any insights into this, I sure hope you'll respond.
 Thanks for your help,
MikeG in Philly, KrashKing

A This problem turned out to be bad memory. The reader invested in some new memory and all is now well (Ed.)

BIG HARD DRIVES

Q What is the largest drive Win 95a can accommodate? I want to add another drive to 120megahertz system with 1.5 gig.
T B Mansfield, London

A It Depends on your BIOS. Partition size is limited to a shade over 2GB, but you can have 20+ partitions. Fairly recent BIOS should recognise drives larger than 2.1GB (one of the BIOS thresholds). Get the 4 (I assume you meant GB) drive and put it in 2 partitions. If/when you upgrade the OS, you can reset the partitions to FAT32 if you wish. Even if your BIOS doesn't meet spec, it's a small matter of a BIOS flash upgrade. I recently flashed my AMI 10/10/94 BIOS up to spec.
If you add it as an IDE drive, your BIOS may give you some troubles if you go above an 8GB drive. Win95a will require you to partition such a drive into sections of not more than 2Gb; each are seen as separate

drives
from the system - but you can have as many as the letters in the
alphabet will run to. Or, move on to Win98 and have unlimited partition
size.

HIMEM WORRIES

Q What is HIMEM? After running Disk Optimizer on my notebook it
rebooted and told me HIMEM is missing. I found HIMEM on my boot-
disk but don't know how to copy off of it to where ever it goes on C:, I'm
totally desktop dependent. Is this a problem with my notebook (hardware)
or is it software? Would my notebook work better with Win98? My notebook is a Jetta with 64M RAM, 200 MMX. Thanks, Mark Hamilton, Torquay

A It is an essential file (HIMEM.SYS) for getting Windows loaded - it is
loaded normally by the boot program, from the C:\windows directory.
Check that it is there, by giving DIR C:\Windows\HIMEM.SYS from the boot
disk: if not, copy it there from the boot disk with COPY A:\HIMEM.SYS
C:\windows\HIMEM.SYSWhat is likely to have happened is that D.O. has
either changed your hidden MSDOS.SYS file so that the [Paths] at the
start no longer has the line:

```
WInDir=C:\windows or, very likely, has made a file
C:\winboot.ini, which ought to have
been deleted and hasn't -
DEL C:\WINBOOT.INI
```

ICONS

Q Hello, When my computer boots up and the desktop screen first
appears, the icons are awhite background with the Windows Logo in
them. Then, they gradually change to the proper appearance for each particular icon. Does anyone have an idea as to what is going on. This has
never happened before. Is it dangerous or an indication that something is
wrong?
Harold A. Climer
Lab Instructor
Dept.Of Physics & Astronomy

A The explorer has decided that the icons in the icon cache can't be
trusted, so it is going around and finding the primary source for each
icon, extracting them and re-building the cache. This tends to happen
after a bad close, with scandisk subsequently run at the boot.
The problem should go away provided you close cleanly each time: if it
persists look for something which might be changing the size of icons so
they don't match the cache. A virus might have been written to do this,

for example.

It also happens with Win 98 because the default max size for the icon cache is too small - this certainly causes trouble in Win 98, resulting in weird icons in the Quick Launch. The suggested fix is:

```
Make the lines below, after - - start and before - - end
into a file - say, patch.reg
Don't let it wrap the line [HKEY. . explorer] around.
Then, double click to enter into the registry.
- - start REGEDIT4
[HKEY_LOCAL_MACHINE\Software\Microsoft\Windows\CurrentVersion\explorer]
"Max Cached Icons"="2048"
```

SHUTTING DOWN FOR GOOD

Q The story is that one night after choosing to Shut Down the computer hung on the "Windows is shutting down" screen, and has hung there ever since. It had been shutting down fine for months, and I did not add any new software that day, did not run low on disk space, and I am pretty sure that the moon was not full. I saw a few suggestions on the MS support pages, but none applied. Any ideas?
Dave, Email

A Go to Start/Run and enter Msconfig.On the General Tab, click on the advanced button.Check the box to disable fast shutdown.
This will sometimes correct this problem. We did not notice any speed difference between the two settings on our computers.

SWAP FILE: SIZE MATTERS

Q Can somebody tell me why my win386.swp file (located in C: directory)is so big? Is it normal to be a little over 100meg?
Seems huge to me...
Tia Brent, Email

A It is a dynamic file, growing and shrinking to suit system demands. The less physical memory you have, the bigger this file gets. I'm not sure why it is so big but it is unusual for it to be so large. Win386.swp is the swap file used for virtual memory. You can decrease it's size by setting the virtual memory yourself. Go into the system icon in the control panel, then the performance tab, and click on the virtual memory button. Now, there are many different ways to set this, but I'll tell you the way that has worked the best for me. Click on the Set my own virtual memory radio button (little white dot) and set your minimum to the amount of RAM in your computer and set the maximum to 2 1/2 times that.

STARTUP SOUND

Q When windows boots up and the Microsoft start wave plays, it sound broken up. When you play it with a wave player it's fine. Any ideas would be appreciated.
Gary, Email

A This is common. During boot, the system is busy doing 10+ other items in addition to playing the sound file. Sometimes the hard drive/system is busy loading something else and is not available to give more attention to the sound file.

It's probably due to a large number of programs being loaded as Windows starts up. Since the .wav file is on the hard disk and is being read off it at the same time as the other programs are loading, then this causes the break up. This is normal if you have a large number of programs that need to load as soon as Windows gets started.

OFF SCREEN WINDOWS

Q Hi I should know how to do this, but...I have a window that is off the screen at the top so I cannot access the Title bar to click and drag the window down again. How can I move the window so I can see it all again, does anyone know???
PLEASE HELP....Thanks in advance
Renee, Email

A Holding the <Alt> key, press <tab> until your off-the-screen application is selected.

Then press <Alt><spacebar> which opens up the menu that would normally open if you clicked in the top-left corner of the window. Press "m" for move. Using the <down arrow> key, move the window back onto your desktop.

BAD SECTORS

Q What causes the hard drive to develop "bad sectors"? My computer seems to run fine (with regular scandisk and defrag), but defrag indicates a bad sector on the drive. What causes this? Thanks.
Maxine, Email

A Simply old age or perhaps a manufacturing flaw. Some hard drives come from the factory with sectors already marked as bad.
Those sectors are ones that can't reliably and flawlessly hold data.
I believe the standard for the mfg. industry is that 1% of the total sectors
on the drive may be 'bad' and still be considered a perfectly serviceable drive.
The key is that the sectors that can't prove themselves 100% reliable during testing (with ScanDisk, for example) ARE marked bad.
Marking them bad simply prevents any data from ever being written there again, thus helping to ensure the safety of your data.
If you removed the 'bad sector table' (by low-level formatting the drive, for example) from the drive, sooner or later you will lose data that you didn't want to lose.

CHANGING OWNERS

Q The computer I am using is second-hand. I was looking in my cookie folder and the cookies are registering under the previous owners name. All of the browser and connection settings have been changed to my name. Is his name registered somewhere in the Win 95 settings? If so, does anyone know how to change this?

A Back up C:\Windows\system.da0 & user.da0 Then, click on: START—>RUN In the box, type = regedit <Press enter> Navigate to:

```
HKEY_LOCAL_MACHINE\SOFTWARE\Microsoft\Windows\
CurrentVersion
```

Right click on Registered Owner & Company, & choose "Modify". Then, enter your own info. Save the file & exit Doing this will allow you to change Registered Owner & Company for the version of Win 95.

LONG NAMES

Q I would like to copy or move files with long file names with a batch-file (.bat) but I can only type the dos-filenames in the copy command and sometimes the result of the command is a file with short name. Is there a solution?

A You can type the long filenames if you run your batch in a DOS window under Windows 95/98/NT. Just type them between quotation marks like this:

```
COPY "my long filename.ext" "other name.ext"
In a pure DOS session (no window), you will be able to
do neither. You will always have to use the short names.
```

copy "drive:\folder\long file name" "newdrive:\folder\long file name"

DEFRAG BLUES

Q I am running Win 98 and when I want to do a defrag the program starts up, but when it gets to 10% complete a message comes up saying "Disk contents have changed - restarting" or something to that effect. It seems to keep looping like this too. Any suggestions would be appreciated!!
H J Farnley, Bath

A This is happening because something is running in the background. Likely suspects are an anti-virus checker or the fast find feature of Office97. Make sure that you don't have anything running in the background. If you do, close it before running defrag; i.e. anything in the task tray. You don't necessarily have to close virus scanners. I leave mine running and it doesn't interfere. You might also want to set the screensaver to none, since every time the screen saver starts the contents on the hard drive will change.

GENERATION X

Q What does the Direct X drivers do? Are the different versions really that different? I'm not big on games, but I see them offered online and in magazines as something that helps games. If I don't play games, do I need them? Will they help with anything else? Should I be running them on my computer? Are there any drawbacks (configuration problems) that need to be considered? Any insight into this would be helpful
J.M, Email

A Direct X drivers are used by Windows to interface with your hardware i.e. video card, sound card and various other cards when you play a Windows 95 game.

Generally, if you don't play video games you usually don't need Direct X drivers. There are some applications that require them in order to run and

will tell you so when you install them. So far as drawbacks are concerned,
there really aren't any. They are only used when an application or game needs them. At all other times, Windows uses the drivers that have been installed for your hardware.

ZIPS

Q What is the best way to make zip files? Will Winzip do it or should I look for a different utility?

A Yes Winzip will do the job. There are many zip utilities around, and most do a fine job of creating zip files. WinZip (now version 7) has been around a long time and is shareware. There are several freeware compression programs available from: http://www.completelyfreesoftware.com/
Personally, I use ZipMagic by Mijenix, for, amongst other things, its ability to treat files as folders:

EMAIL

Q Every time I leave my PC on for a while and just let it sit I get a MSGSRV32 error and it freezes what do I do......

A Most likely your PC is set to check for mail periodically. Try turning that off.

NO SOUND!

Q I deleted my sound recorder - I will not even get into the circumstances surrounding this blunder.I tried to find it on the MS website, but to no avail.

Can someone send it to me with all the related files?? It would be a big help!!
Shawn, Email

A It should be on your Windows 95 CD. Go to the Add/Remove Programs in the Control panel and select the Windows Setup tab. Check off the Multimedia option and Windows should re-install the sound recorder.

GLOSSARY

ACTIVE DESKTOP:

A new feature that allows you to use Web pages or channels as your desktop wallpaper. See also Channel, Wallpaper.

ACTIVEX:

A Microsoft technology that provides interactive content on Web pages.

ADDRESS:

The location of a file. You can use addresses to locate files on the Internet and your PC. Internet addresses are also known as URLs. See also the Address Bar.

ADDRESS BAR:

A method of opening files that are on the Internet or your computer. When you type an address in the Address Bar, you open the file at that address.

CHANNEL:

A Web site that delivers content from the Internet to your computer. Channels automatically copy content from the Internet to your computer when you subscribe to a Web site. See also Channel Bar. Channel Bar: A desktop option that lists the channels available on your computer.

CLASSIC STYLE:

A desktop display option that resembles the Windows 95 desktop.

CLIENT:

A computer that connects to another, central computer called a server. A client computer uses files, printers, and other resources shared by the server.

CONTENT PROVIDER:

A business that uses the Internet to supply you with information such as news, weather, business reports and entertainment.

DOMAIN:

A group of networked computers that share information and resources.

DVD:

Digital Video Disk – a high-capacity compact disc. This disc can store enough data – sounds and pictures – for a full-length movie. You must have a DVD disc drive or player to use DVD discs.

EXPLORER BAR:

A pane that opens on the left side of windows, such as when you click the Search button or Favorites button.

FAVORITE:

A link to a particular Web page, saving you having to type in the same address time after time.

FILE SYSTEM:

The overall structure in which files are named, stored, and organised by the operating system. For example, MS-DOS and earlier versions of Windows use the FAT16 file system. Windows 98 can use the FAT16 or FAT32 file system.

SUBSCRIBE:

To set up Internet Explorer to check a Web page for new content. The program can then notify you about the new content or automatically download it to your computer.

UNIVERSAL SERIAL BUS:

A hardware standard for external device connections (such as a mouse, modems, game controllers and keyboards). USB supports plug-and-play installation so that you can easily add new devices to your computer.

WALLPAPER:

The background on your desktop. You can select a background from bitmaps and HTML documents included in Windows 98, or you can choose from your own files.

WINDOW:

The rectangular portion of your screen that displays an open program or the contents of a folder or disk. You can have multiple windows open at the same time.

WINDOWS EXPLORER:

A feature you can use to view the contents of your computer and network drives in a structure.

24-BIT COLOUR:

24-Bit colour images are composed of three 8-bit colour channels. Each colour channel, similar to an 8-bit greyscale image, contains up to 256 colours. When combined, the red, green and blue channels provide up to 16.7 million colours. 24-Bit colour is also known as True Color and Photo-realistic Color.

32-BIT COLOUR:

32-Bit colour images have four colour channels of 8 bits each, one channel each for red, green and blue, plus eight bits of greyscale data to provide higher detail.

8-BIT GREYSCALE:

Images that contain 256 possible shades of grey.

A/D CONVERTER:

A device used to convert analogue data to digital data. Analogue data is continuously variable, while digital data contains discrete steps.

ADDITIVE PRIMARIES:

This is red, green and blue light that, when put together, produce white light. These are known as the primary colours of light, from which all other colours can be made.

ANALOGUE:

There are two main ways of doing things electronically: analogue or digital. In the analogue method, signals are continuously variable and the slightest change may be significant. Analogue circuits are subject to drift, distortion and noise, but they are capable of handling complex signals with relatively simple circuitry. Analogue data transmissions require amplifiers, due to attenuation of the signal with distance, magnify signal.

ANSI:

An abbreviation for the American National Standards Institute. It is a non-governmental organisation founded in 1918 that proposes, modifies, approves and publishes data processing standards for voluntary use in the United States. ANSI is also the US representative to the International Standards Organisation (ISO) in Paris, and the International Electrotechnical commission (IEC). Any programming language that claims to conform to ANSI standards must pass all the tests for the standard syntax rules as set forth by the ANSI body.

APPLICATION SOFTWARE:

The general term for software programs that perform specific tasks such as accounting, word processing and database management.

ARCHIVE FILES (*.ARC *.ZIP): I

n the true definition, an archive file is one that has been copied onto an auxiliary storage medium such as disk or magnetic tape for the purpose of long-term retention. In the microcomputer world, an archive file is one that has been compressed, squashed, squeezed, crunched and/or packed with a file archiving program in order to use less disk space and to reduce the transfer time when sending files between computers. File libraries also store program and data files in compressed format. The most common PC archiving program is PKZIP, which labels its compressed files with the extension .zip. In the UNIX world, similar archiving is achieved with pack (.z), compress (.Z), or gzip (.gz).

ASCII (AMERICAN STANDARD CODE FOR INFORMATION INTERCHANGE):

Standard by which many computers assign code numbers to letters, numbers and symbols. Used for text exchange between computer platforms. ASCII, pronounced "ask-key", is the common code for microcomputer equipment. The standard ASCII character set consists of 128 decimal numbers ranging from zero through 127 assigned to letters, numbers, punctuation marks and the most common special characters. The extended ASCII character set also consists of 128 decimal numbers and ranges from 128 through 255, representing additional special, mathematical, graphic and foreign characters.

ASYNCHRONOUS:

When signals are sent to a computer at irregular intervals, they are described as asynchronous. When data are transmitted asynchronously, they are sent at irregular intervals by preceding each character with a start bit and following it with a stop bit. Asynchronous transmission allows a character to be sent at random after the preceding character has been sent, without regard to any timing device.

AT COMMAND SET:

The set of commands that is used to control the operation of a modem is called the standard Hayes AT Command Set. Most of the commands are prefaced with an AT which stands for ATtention. For example, to dial the phone, the communications program would send the command "ATD" (ATtention, Dial) to the modem.

ATTRIBUTE:

An attribute is a characteristic that describes data, or a data structure, or an element of a data model. An attribute is a word that describes the manner in which a variable is handled by the computer. For example, typical file attributes would be the file's size and the length of a record in a file. The DOS file attributes are stored in byte 11 of a directory entry and determine whether or not a file is declared read-only, hidden, a system file, or if the archive bit is on or off.

AUTOEXEC.BAT:

A special batch file used by DOS and OS/2: they search for it when booting up the computer. If DOS finds the AUTOEXEC.BAT file, it automatically carries out the commands contained in the file.

BANDING:

A visible stair-stepping of shades in a gradient.

BACKUP:

Copies of data and program files, intended to safeguard against the loss of those files,

219

are called backups. It is always advisable to make backups of your data and programs. Microcomputers, like all things manufactured, are prey to human error and mechanical failure. No matter what type of backup hardware you choose, you still need a backup system, a strict routine for making backups. Most backup systems utilise either tape or disk.

BASIC:

Is a computer programming language, an acronym for Beginner's All-purpose Symbolic Instruction Code. Although it is a simple language to learn and use, it contains many advanced features for handling mathematical formulas and character strings. In its early form, as devised by Andrew Kemeny at Dartmouth, BASIC was an interpreted language, which means that each statement is translated and executed as it is encountered rather than having all the program statements compiled before execution. Bill Gates made his first $50 writing a basic interpreter for the PC. There are now compilers for BASIC so that final versions of programs can be translated to executable code for faster run-time performance.

BATCH FILE:

Executable text files that save you from having to retype often-used commands. To use a batch file, you just type in the batch file's name, and the PC carries out the commands contained in the batch file as if you had typed them from the keyboard. In UNIX, such files are called scripts, or shell scripts. These are much less widely used under Windows than under DOS or UNIX.

BAUD:

Baud is a unit of measurement that denotes the number of discrete signal elements, such as bits, that can be transmitted per second. Bits per second (bps) means the number of binary digits transmitted in one second. There is a difference between bps and baud rate, and the two are often confused. For example, a device such as a modem said to transmit at 2400 baud is not correct, it actually transmits 2400 bits per second. It is important to note that both baud rate and bps refer to the rate at which the bits within a single frame are transmitted. The gaps between the frames can be of variable length. Accordingly, neither baud rate nor bps refers to the rate at which information is actually being transferred.

BBS: A bulletin board system is a computer that operates with a program and a modem to allow other computers with modems to communicate with it, often on a round-the-clock basis. There are thousands of MS-DOS, Windows and UNIX-related bulletin board systems in the United States offering a wealth of information including libraries of freeware and shareware programs that can be downloaded.

BENCHMARK:

A benchmark is a process or program that can be executed to measure and compare the performance of one system against another.

BETA TESTING:

The pre-testing of hardware or software products with selected typical customers to discover inadequate features or possible product enhancements before it is released to the general public.

BEZIER CURVES:

In object-oriented programs, a curve whose shape is defined by anchor points set along its arc.

BILEVEL:

A type of image containing only black and white pixels.

BINARY:

A number system based on 2. In binary, only two numbers, 0 and 1, represent all possible mathematical values. Computers use the binary number system because it best represents what a computer understands: on and off.

BIOS: The basic input/output system, resident on a chip which plugs into the motherboard of a microcomputer, is a system program. The BIOS is responsible for handling the details of the input and output operations, including the task of relating a program's logical records to a peripheral device's physical records. The BIOS contains routines tailored to the specific requirements of each peripheral device. These routines are called drivers, or device handlers.

BIT:

The smallest unit of data recognisable by a computer. Eight bits equals one byte (or one character). A bit can be either off or on, representing a value of 0 or 1. Bits can be used in combination to represent higher numbers.

BITMAP:

An image formed by rectangular grid of picture elements (pixels). The computer assigns a value to each pixel, from one bit of information (indicating black or white) to 24 bits per pixel (for full-colour computer displays), to as many as 64 bits per pixel for some types of full-colour images. A bitmap is an image defined by a collection of dots, as opposed to a vector image, which is defined by mathematical formulas.

BOOT UP:

The term describing the series of steps that takes place when you turn on the computer. In the boot process, the operating system (DOS for example), is loaded into the computer's internal memory (RAM). It derives from the ancient advice, "Pull yourself up by your own bootstraps!"

BROWSER:

a program allowing viewing of information transmitted by a site on the world-wide web; the information may combine text, still graphics, sound and video. The leading browsers at this time are produced by Netscape (Mozilla) and Microsoft (Internet Explorer).

BTW:

By the way. An abbreviation widely used in email and newsgroups.

BUFFER:

A buffer is often a block of memory that the operating system uses to store data temporarily. Several buffers can be defined at system configuration time based on your applications. A buffer can also be part of a peripheral device containing its own memory to receive the output of a task quicker than the device can perform the task's instructions, thus freeing the processor for other operations.

BUG:

an error in a program or hardware setup that causes it to work other than as intended. See Debug.

BUNDLED SOFTWARE:

Software sold with the computer hardware as part of the system's total price, also known as pre-loaded or packaged software.

BUS:

A bus is a set of wires or lines used for data transfer among the various components of a computer system. The bus is made up of traces on the printed circuit boards. All the major components such as the microprocessor, the disk-drive controller, random access memory (RAM) and the input/output ports are electrically connected by the bus so that information can be passed. The first IBM microcomputers and compatibles such as the PC and the PC-XT (8086 and the 8088) utilised an 8-bit data bus. The IBM-AT (80286) systems provided both the 8-bit and the 16-bit bus. Systems with the 80386 and 80486 microprocessors can transfer data along a 32-bit bus.

BYTE:

Consisting of eight bits, a byte is the amount of storage space required to hold one alphanumeric character such as the letter A, the number 5, a comma, question mark, and so on.

CACHE MEMORY:

A cache is a memory medium that provides faster access than the medium where the data is customarily stored. A cache memory architecture combines SRAM's speed with DRAM's cost effectiveness. It provides a small amount (usually 64kb or less) of fast SRAM (the cache) that is logically located between the processor and main memory (which is usually simple DRAM).

CALIBRATION:

Setting equipment to a standard measure to produce reliable results.

CD-ROM:

Compact disk, read-only memory. A form of data storage that uses laser optics rather than magnetic means for reading data. CD-ROM drives read compact discs similar to the audio CDs available in music stores, and indeed, most of them can play audio CDs.

CLIP ART:

Graphic images or files that can be imported to word processing and desktop publishing documents are called electronic clip art. Clip art for computers, just as in the printing and art industry, is available in various graphics file formats and is typically available as specialised

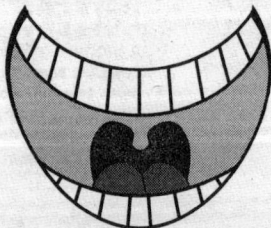

...ibraries for different purposes such as medical, business, holiday seasons, sports, and so on.

COLOUR CHANNEL:

Colour images on the computer are created by combining different colour channels. In RGB, the most commonly used colour model, the channels are red, green and blue.

COLOUR CORRECTION:

The process of adjusting an image to compensate for scanner deficiencies or for the characteristics of the output device. Colour picker: A utility for specifying colours on the monitor.

COLOUR PROOF:

A representation of what the final printed composition will look like. The resolution and quality of different types of colour proofs can vary greatly.

COLOUR SEPARATION:

The division of an image into its component colours for printing. Each colour separation is a piece of negative or positive film.

COLOUR TRANSPARENCY:

A photographic image on transparent film used as artwork. 35mm, 4x5" and 8x10" formats are commonly used.

COMPRESSION:

Encoding the bits of information in an image file so that it takes up less space when stored. Compression results in little or no distortion.

CONTRAST:

The relationship between the light and dark areas of an image. The more extreme the difference, the greater the contrast.

CLOCK SPEED:

Computers contain internal clocks. Like a wristwatch, the microprocessor uses regulated vibrations to measure speed. The faster the clock speed, the faster the computer will execute (carry out) commands.

CLONE:

The term clone most often refers to a computer system that resembles one of IBM's personal computers. Shortly after IBM introduced the PC, the XT and the AT, clones appeared on the market claiming to be IBM-compatible. Some clones were more compatible than others.

COM PORT:

A COM port is a communications channel or pathway over which data is transferred between remote computing devices. Microcomputers operating under DOS or Windows can have as many as four COM ports: COM1, COM2, COM3 and COM4. These COM ports are actually serial ports most often used with a modem to establish a communications channel over the telephone lines. The COM ports are also used to send data to a serial printer or to connect a serial mouse.

CONFIG.SYS:

A text file which is used by DOS and OS/2 during system startup. This file contains commands that tell DOS how to communicate with hardware, how to customise communication, or how to adjust the computer's memory usage.

CONVENTIONAL MEMORY:

RAM (random access memory) used by DOS to run software programs. Conventional memory is limited to 640 kilobytes.

CPU:

Central processing unit. Every computer has a central processing unit. The CPU is the portion of a computer where instructions are fetched, decoded and executed. The overall activity of the computer is controlled by the CPU. It consists essentially of an arithmetic unit, a control unit and an internal memory. A minimum requirement is three registers, a decode and control section, an adder and two memory buffers. The control of other functions is exercised through the interpretation and execution of instructions. Today's CPUs for microcomputers are cortained in chips small enough to fi easily in the palm of one's hand.

CROP MARKS:

Lines printed showing the dimensions of the final printed page. These marks are used for final trimming.

CRASH:

the sudden, unexpected cessatio of operation of a program or of the computer.

CRT:

Literally, cathode ray tube; an older term for the video display unit, or monitor.

CURRENT DRIVE:

The disk drive currently accessed by your computer. It is displayed in the prompt, such as C> or A>. C stands for the first hard drive and A stands for the floppy drive (in most cases). (If the computer has two floppy drives, A represents the first drive and B represents the second.) UNIX names multiple drives, or can treat additional drives as subdirectories of the first one.

CURSOR:

A short blinking line or box that appearson the monitor either underneath or just in front of the space where the next character is to be typed or deleted. The curso indicates that the computer is waiting for the user to input a command or information.

DATABASE:

A collection of information organised for easy retrieval. Databases are organised into a hierarchy of files, records and fields. A file is a group of related information, such as personal information about a group of employees. Information about a particular employee (name, national insurance number, address, etc.) is stored in a record. A record is a collection of related data items called fields. For example, a company's employee file stores information about each employee in a single record consisting of fields for the employee's name, national insurance number, and address.

DATA COMPRESSION:

"Squeezing" of data for the purpose of transmission throughput or storage efficiency. Portions of the data are removed using an algorithm that will restore the data when needed.

DDE:

Dynamic Data Exchange. DDE is a form of interprocess communication implemented in mutitasking operating systems such as Microsoft Windows and OS/2. Information, commands and status information can be exchanged between two or more pro-

grams if they support DDE and are executing simultaneously. For example, a spreadsheet with a DDE link to a communications program could keep its stock prices current with the trading information received over the communications channel. An exchange of data in DDE is called a conversation and an application can participate simultaneously in multiple DDE conversations with any number of other applications. A conversation is organised around three conceptual descriptors: service, topic and item.

DECOMPRESSION:

The expansion of compressed image files.

DEFAULT:
Command or parameter that takes effect if no other option is specified.

DEBUG:
locate and remove errors in a program or computer.

DEFAULT:
a value or state assumed to be true by the computer unless contrary instructions are given.

DESKTOP PUBLISHING (DTP):
One of the fastest-growing applications in personal computing. Desktop Publishing software offers a relatively inexpensive way for a PC to generate typeset-quality text and graphics.

DEVICE DRIVER:
A program loaded by the CONFIG.SYS file or AUTOEXEC.BAT file that controls devices such as a mouse or CD-ROM drive.

DIALOG BOX:
An on-screen box found in graphical user interfaces which provides users with information and explains limited options.

DIGITAL:
Method of data storage and/or transmission wherein each element of information is given a unique combination of numerical values (bits). Each bit indicates either the presence or absence of a condition (such as on-off, yes-no, true-false, open-closed). Digital data or voltages consists of discrete steps or levels, as opposed to continuously variable analogue data.

DIGITAL-TO-ANALOGUE CONVERSION (D/A):
Conversion of digital information into a state of fluctuating voltage levels. (DAC) Interface to convert digital data (represented in discrete, discontinuous form) into analogue data (represented in continuous form).

DISPLAY:
Temporary visual representation of computer output on a CRT or other electronic device.

DITHERING:

The process of specifying colour to adjacent pixels in order simulate a third colour in a bitmapped image. This technique is used when a full range of colours is not available.

DIRECTORY:

A directory is an area on a disk for storing files. Directories consist of files and/or subdirectories. A directory listing will show the names of files and subdirectories subordinate to that directory along with file sizes, creation dates and times. Each formatted disk contains a main directory also called the root directory. In DOS, the most common hard disk root directory is referred to as "C:\" or just "C:".

DIRECTORY TREE:

A way of organising data into a hierarchical structure, beginning with a root directory and branching into subdirectories and files.

DISK CACHE:

A disk cache is a software technique of speeding data access times. Copies of recently accessed disk sectors are stored in memory to a reserved area called cache RAM. When the executing program or the operating system requests to read a sector from the disk, the disk caching software checks to see if the sector is stored in cache RAM. If it is, the sector is retrieved from RAM and returned; no disk access is required. If the desired sector is not in cache RAM, the software reads the requested sector from the disk, stores it in cache RAM, and returns it to the program. When the info is found in the cache, it's a hit. When the info must be retrieved from the disk, it's a miss. Some disk-caching programs also check for sector writes.

DISK DRIVE:

the mechanical apparatus, consisting of a shaft and motor for rotating the disk, and a magnetising head for reading/writing the disk.

DISKETTE:

A flat piece of flexible plastic covered with a magnetic coating which is used to store data (also called a floppy diskette). The former standard for diskette size was 5.25 inch; they were truly flexible, hence the descriptor "floppy". Newer 3.5 inch diskettes are encased in a hard plastic coating (which makes them more durable).

DLLS:

Dynamically linked libraries. DLLs are libraries of object files or executable code modules available to programmers writing code for the Microsoft Windows operating environment. Functions and procedures written in languages like Pascal and C can be compiled and the object file stored in a DLL. These modules can be loaded at run time, and then unloaded when the code is no longer needed. The use of DLLs allows for a high degree of customisation. If a particular development language doesn't support a required function, it could be written in another language and made available through the DLL.

DMA:

After a sector of data has been read from a disk drive into the disk controller's onboard buffer it must be moved into the computer. This is done with a process known as DMA or (direct memory access). The transfer of data takes place directly along an input/output channel at high speed between memory and the device. The CPU only initiates the transfer on a DMA request and therefore is not involved.

DNS:

Domain name system. The database for translating IP addresses in verbal format into numeric format.

DOS:

Disk operating system. Software that translates the user's commands and allows application programs to interact with the computer's hardware. DOS supplies a file management system for disk input and output.

DOS PROMPT:

The signal that DOS is awaiting your command. The prompt is usually displayed as the current drive letter and the greater-than symbol (>). Thus C> is a DOS prompt with C representing the hard drive as the current drive (i.e. C:\>, A:>, or C:\DOS>). Other operating systems use prompts, of course, each with its own format.

DOT:

Smallest visible point that can be displayed on a display surface.

DOT MATRIX PRINTER (DMP):

A type of printer that employs a movable printhead with pins, or wires, that shoot out and strike a ribbon. Each strike of a single pin creates a dot on the paper. Letters are formed as a pattern, or matrix, of dots. The most common are nine- or 24-pin printers.

DOWN TIME:

when the computer isn't working. DRAM: Dynamic random access memory. It is a kind of memory chip in which data is stored capacitively and which must be energised or recharged hundreds of times a second or the data will be lost. While DRAM is being refreshed, it cannot be read by the processor. If the processor attempts to read the DRAM while it is being refreshed, one or more wait states occur. DRAMs offer high-bit densities, low cost, input/output compatibility with TTL levels, and speed compatibility with most microprocessors. The operational speed of DRAM chips is measured in nanoseconds, such as 100, 80, and 70ns.

DRIVER:

A software program that allows the operating system (like DOS or UNIX) to work with a specific hardware device like a printer, a mouse or trackball (see also device driver).

DPI (dots per inch): A method of denoting the resolution of a scanned image, a digitised image in a file, or an image as rendered by an output device. Also, used interchangeably with pixels per inch (PPI).

EISA:

The industry standard architecture (ISA) for IBM-compatible microcomputers defines the use of the data bus and the eight- and 16-bit expansion slots on the PC-XT and PC-AT models. EISA is the extended ISA. With an EISA bus, eight- or 16-bit add-in boards based on the (ISA) can be fitted to the new machines.

EPS:

Encapsulated PostScript: The best quality graphics are vector graphics in which the image is made up of lines, curves, and filled regions rather than a series of data points as in bit-mapped graphics. EPS refers to a condensed graphics file containing actual PostScript language in a special format. EPS files can become quite large, and some contain a bit-mapped image of the graphic so that if the output is sent to a non-PostScript printer, the bit-mapped image is used. To get the best results, however, EPS files should be output on a PostScript device.

EXPANDED MEMORY (EMS):

Memory outside the one megabyte (Mb) limit of DOS that is accessed in revolving blocks.

EXPANSION CARDS:

Electronic circuit cards that fit into slots on the main circuit board inside the case of the computer. Expansion cards are used to add such items as modems, sound capability, ports, etc. to a PC.

Expansion Slot: A socket inside the computer case that is designed to hold expansion cards.

Extended Memory (XMS): Linear memory extending beyond the one megabyte (MB) limit of DOS. Extended memory is only available on 80286 and above machines; it is off-limits to 8088s and 8086s. The distinction between conventional, expanded, and extended memory does not exist on a UNIX machine.

EXPORT:

To output data in a form that another program can read.

FAQ:

Frequently asked questions. A list of frequently asked questions and their answers. Most usenet news groups maintain a FAQ so that participants won't have to answer the same questions over and over for each issue.

FAT:

The file allocation table is a system area on a disk that keeps track of disk clusters allocated to all the files on a DOS partitioned disk. The FAT also keeps track of available disk space. In the case of a hard disk, the size of the FAT limits the amount of storage capacity that can be handled under DOS. Under DOS 3.3 and earlier versions, hard disks were limited to 32 megabytes of storage. Hard drives with more than 32 megabytes of available storage can be partitioned into smaller segments. These higher capacity hard disks come with special drivers that modify the FAT, thereby allowing DOS to use the additional storage space.

FAX Board: A FAX board is an add-in printed circuit board for a personal computer that allows the system to send and receive text and graphics data over the telephone lines. A FAX board is actually a facsimile machine in a personal computer.

FILE:

A named collection of information treated as a unit by the computer; it may contain text, data, or executable programs.

FILENAME EXTENSIONS:

In DOS, filenames are from one to eight characters long and can be followed by an optional short tag called an extension. An extension starts with a full stop, has one, two or three characters, and follows immediately after the filename. The following are examples of extensions used to identify the type of data or the format of data to be found in the file: .EXE – executable program, used to run a program; .COM – executable program, also usually used to run a program; .BAT – a batch file consisting of a series of commands; .SYS – a system file, often a device driver; .TXT – usually a text (ASCII) file created with a text editor.

FILM:

Photosensitive material, generally on a transparent base, which will receive character images, and may be chemically processed to expose those images. In image-setting, any photosensitive material, transparent or not, may be called film.

Format:

To prepare a disk or diskette so it can store information. Formatting organises the tracks and sectors that store information. When one formats a disk, any information already stored on it is erased. In some of the newer operating systems one has the capability to "UN-Format" a formatted diskette, depending on how it was formatted and if nothing has been re-written to the diskette.

FTP:

File transfer protocol. The standard for file transmission between computers using a TCP connection. Programs that accomplish the transfer are called FTP programs.

FULL-DUPLEX, HALF-DUPLEX:

The term full-duplex designates the transmission of data in two directions at the same time as from a terminal to a computer or from the computer to the terminal. Full-duplex (FDX) is simultaneous two-way communication. The term half-duplex (HDX) designates the transmission of data in either direction but only one direction at a time.

FUNCTION KEYS:

Keys that act as shortcuts for performing certain functions, such as saving or printing data. These keys are labelled F1 through F10 (or F12) and they run across the top or down the side of the keyboard. Some keyboards allow you to program these keys for any application, but they are usually controlled by the software running.

FUZZY LOGIC:

Fuzzy logic provides an approach to approximate reasoning in which the rules of inference are approximate rather than exact. Fuzzy logic is useful in manipulating information that is incomplete, imprecise, or unreliable. Also called fuzzy set theory, fuzzy logic extends the simple Boolean operators, can express implication, and is used extensively in Artificial Intelligence (AI) programs.

GIF:

Graphics interchange format . Early in 1987, CompuServe's graphics engineers introduced this protocol as a standard for exchanging raster-based images among various computers. GIF can handle up to 256 simultaneous colours, and uses a sophisticated data compression method to reduce the file size to less than half, saving in download time. It is one of two standard formats for display of images on the World-Wide Web.

GIGABYTE:

A unit of measure of stored data corresponding to one billion bytes of information, 1,024 megabytes or 1,048,576 kilobytes of digital data.

GIGO:

Garbage in, garbage out. A computer user acronym, meaning that no matter how good the program or the computer, if one inputs bad data one outputs bad results.

GUI:

Graphical user interface. Pronounced "gooey." A GUI is a user-friendly alternative to character-based interfaces such as DOS or UNIX. GUIs allow the user to point at a list of command options or click on an icon, instead of typing a character-based command. Two of the more popular GUIs for PCs are Microsoft Windows and OS/2. UNIX has both X-Window and Open GL interfaces.

HALFTONE:

An simulation of continuous tones by the use of black or overlapping process colour dots of varying size or position.

HARD COPY:

Information on paper as opposed to a screen or diskette.

HARD DISK:

A data storage device for personal computers that consists of a rigid platter that is fixed inside a sealed case. A hard disk can store more information and retrieve data faster than a diskette.

HARD DISK PARTITION:

Partitioning divides a single physical hard disk into multiple logical partitions. The partitions on a drive, even if there's only one, are managed by a special sector called the partition table, which is located at the very beginning of every hard disk. It defines the starting and ending locations for each partition. Each partition on a hard disk is blind to the existence of any others. By universal agreement, the operation of software inside a partition is completely contained within the bounds of that partition.

HAYES COMPATIBLE:

The originator of the de facto standard for modems in the world of microcomputers was Hayes Microcomputer Products, Inc. In 1981, the company produced the first modem to operate with a command set. The set of commands that is used to control the operation of a modem is called the standard Hayes AT Command Set. Most of the commands are prefaced with an AT which stands for ATtention. Today, the term Hayes-compatible is used as an adjective to describe modems from other manufacturers that operate with the same command set as the popular Hayes modems.

HEXADECIMAL:

The hexadecimal number system has 16 as its base.

HTML:

Hypertext markup language. The formatting language in which display pages for the World-Wide Web are created. The formatting instructs the browser about how to display the information. In many ways, an HTML document resembles a word processed document from the days before WYSIWYG. For example, words to be italicised are preceded by <I> and followed by </I>.

HTTP:

Hypertext transfer protocol. The protocol (agreed-upon standard) describing how HTML documents are to be transmitted from one computer to another over the Internet.

ICON:

A visual symbol used to represent programs or documents in a GUI. For example, in a DOS interface you see LETTER.DOC in a directory listing. In a GUI, you'd see a little picture (such as a piece of paper and pen) representing the same document.

INKJET PRINTER:

This type of printer uses a printhead which has a series of little nozzles. In each nozzle, the ink heats up, and bubbles. When the bubbles burst, ink sprays out onto the print surface.

INPUT:

what goes into a computer; also used as a verb meaning to enter input.

INPUT DEVICES:

A piece of computer hardware (the keyboard and the mouse being the most popular examples) that is used to enter and manipulate information on a computer. Other input devices include, but are not limited to, light pens, touch screens, graphics tablets and trackballs.

INTEGRATED CIRCUITS:

An arrangement of miniature transistors (silicon chips) used for electronic data transmission. Also known as ICs.

INTEGRATED SOFTWARE:

Integrated software programs pack several applications into one package. These packages usually contain scaled down versions of spreadsheets, word processors and database programs. Some packages even include communication modules for connecting to a transferring data between two PCs via a modem and phone line. Once such example of an Integrated Software package is Microsoft(R) Works. Works for Windows does not contain a communications module.

INTERLACED, NON-INTERLACED:

Interlacing is a technique used by some video displays in which the electron beam repaints the screen by alternately displaying all the odd lines and then all the even lines. Thus, interlacing updates any single line on the screen only 30 times per second, yet it provides a refresh rate equivalent to 60 cycles per second. The electron beam of a non-interlaced monitor refreshes all the lines on the display sequentially from top to bottom. Each pixel on every line of the screen is repainted. Non-interlaced methods require twice as much signal information in the same time frame as interlaced methods.

INTERNET:

The network of networks.

Interpreted Language: A high-level programming language that is translated into machine code line by line as it is executed. BASIC and LISP are interpreted languages. The chief advantage of an interpreted language is rapid alteration of the program, the penalty for which is slow execution.

INTERPRETER:

A program that translates a program in an interpreted language into executable machine code.

IP:

Internet protocol. A layer on TCP, for routing data packets across the networks that form the Internet.

IP ADDRESS:

The identifier for a site on the Internet. It may be expressed either as a multiply dotted number (e.g. 130.111.58.95) or in equivalent words: adamantane.umeche.maine.edu.

INPUT:

Raw data, text, graphics, imagery or commands inserted into a computer.

INTERPOLATION:

The process of increasing the resolution of an image by the addition of new pixels throughout the image, the colours of which are based on neighbouring pixels.

IRQ:

Interrupt request lines are physical connections between external hardware devices and the interrupt controllers. When a device, such as a floppy controller or a printer needs the attention of the CPU, handshaking signals are sent back and forth until a task is completed. On PCs there are 16 IRQ lines numbered IRQ0 through IRQ15. In a particular system, the goal is to configure expansion boards so that each board has its own IRQ line. If you have two serial ports on your system, you know that IRQ3 and IRQ4 are taken.

ISA BUS:

Industry standard architecture bus. It is an unofficial designation for the bus design of the PCs and compatibles. This original bus design allows for various adapter cards (printed circuit boards) to be plugged into expansion slots on the system board (motherboard). Originally introduced with an eight-bit data path on the IBM PCs and PC-XTs, the ISA bus was expanded in 1984 with the PC-AT computer and its 16-bit path, and is now commonly 32 bits.

JOYSTICK:

A joystick is a two-dimensional potentiometer, an electromechanical input device with a vertical lever, pivoted so that it may be manipulated within 360 degrees. When connected to a computer via a cable, it can provide positional information for the movement of the cursor on a video display screen. The application program that is designed to receive input from a joystick, responds by moving a cursor or an image on the screen in the same direction as the movement of the joystick lever. Joysticks are primarily used to play video games.

JPEG (JOINT PHOTOGRAPHIC EXPERT GROUP):

An image compression/decompression standard that divides the image area into cells to condense information based on content analysis.

JUMPER:

Often on printed circuit boards the designer will allow the board to be set-up in a variety of ways depending on the particular needs of the user. This is accomplished by placing a pair of jumper pins in the circuit. If a small plastic-covered metal clip is placed over the open pair of pins, the circuit becomes closed.

KB (KILOBYTE):

A unit of measure of digital information corresponding to 1024 bytes. Abbreviated and referred to as K. 1,024 bytes of digital data.

LAN (LOCAL AREA NETWORK):

When two or more computers are linked together for the purpose of sharing information and/or peripheral devices, a network is created. When the network is confined to a geographically restricted area, such as within the same building or perhaps on a college campus, it is referred to as a local area network. There are three types of data transmission media used on most of today's LANs.

LASER PRINTER:

Computer output device that uses a laser to generate the character image. It uses some of the same methods to produce the final image as a copier. with a laser beam as the light source. Laser printers produce high-resolution copy and are especially popular with business users. Laser printers are also very quiet and usually faster than DMPs (dot matrix printers).

LPT1, LPT2, LPT3:

These are logical device names for parallel printers or ports. With DOS operating system, LPT1, LPT2, and LPT3 are reserved names for up to three parallel printer ports. LPT1 is usually the same as the primary DOS hard-copy output device PRN. UNIX uses "lpr" as the acronym for the printer or printer port.

MASS STORAGE:

Non-memory storage for data. Floppies are mass storage.

MB, MEGABYTE:

A unit of measure for computer memory or storage equivalent to approximately one million (1,048,576) bytes.

MEMORY:

The area where your computer stores data. Data can be permanently stored in ROM (read only memory) or stored temporarily in the computer's RAM (random access memory). A computer's RAM storage space is emptied when the power is turned off;

whereas ROMs will retain information with no power.

MENU:

A list of available services or functions provided by an application program. One selects an option by using a mouse or arrow key to highlight it, and clicking the mouse or pressing Enter. Most menus are pull-down menus located at the top of the screen, and the options for a particular heading appear when that category is selected.

MHZ, MEGAHERTZ:

A unit of frequency measurement. One hertz (Hz) is equal to one cycle per second. Heinrich R. Hertz, a German physicist, first detected electromagnetic waves in 1883. One megahertz is one million electrical vibration cycles per second. The original IBM personal computers in the early 1980s were controlled by central processing units (CPUs) that were synchronised with clock crystals vibrating at 4.77 MHz. Present PCs operate at frequencies as high as 200 MHz.

MICROPROCESSOR:

A single large-scale integrated circuit containing all of the central processing functions of a computer (see also CPU).

MIDI:

Musical instrument digital interface. An interface card or adapter board for connecting a musical instrument to a microcomputer is called a MIDI adapter. Multiple musical instrument keyboards can be daisy-chained together (linked in series) and played simultaneously with the help of the computer and related software. The various operations of the musical keyboard can be captured, saved, edited and played back to one or more musical instruments. Each instrument, of course, must be MIDI compatible. Music can be digitally recorded and then played back as new tracks are recorded, creating the sound of an entire orchestra.

MIME:

Multipurpose Internet mail extensions. An encoding scheme for allowing non-ASCII data, such as word processor formatting, to be included in an e-mail message.

MIPS:

Million instructions per second. MIPS is a unit for measuring the average number of machine language instructions a computer can perform or execute in one second. However, it can be shown that the same computer can execute two different loops of code to estimate MIPS, and their execution times will differ significantly. A MIPS value should therefore be used only as a very general measure of performance when comparing different types of computers. In order to obtain accurate performance data to compare similar computers, each subsystem must be isolated, and practically speaking, this is an almost impossible task. More realistic benchmark testing occurs at the application level. MIPS is sometimes jokingly referred to as meaningless indicator of processor speed.

MODEM:

Modulator–demodulator. A piece of computer hardware that allows a computer to communicate with other computers (if they also have a modem attached) via a telephone line. Originally, modems converted electrical signals to audio tones and sent them through a telephone mouthpiece; current modems introduce the electrical signals directly into the phone line.

MONITOR:

The part of the computer containing the video display unit; so called because it allows you to monitor processes visually.

MONITOR CALIBRATION:

The process of optimising the colour settings of a monitor to match selected colours of a printed output.

MOTHERBOARD:

The printed circuit board that is the foundation of a PC or workstation system. This board contains the computer's CPU (central processing unit), RAM (random access memory) chips and expansion slots that enable one to add more functions/features to the machine.

MOUSE:

A device about the size of the palm of your hand that one rolls around on a flat, smooth surface to move the computer's cursor (pointer) quickly over the screen. As the mouse moves, a plastic ball on the bottom creates signals that move the cursor on the screen. Clicking the buttons on the mouse sends signals equivalent to those that are generated by various keyboard combinations. For example, clicking the left button rapidly twice in succession usually is equivalent to pressing the Enter key. So named because its slender connecting cable reminded someone of a mouse's hairless tail.

MPC:

Multimedia PC. A specification developed by Tandy and Microsoft for the minimum platform capable of running multimedia software. PCs carrying the MPC logo are able to run any software that also displays the MPC logo, which consists of rainbow-coloured letters on a black background.

MULTIMEDIA:

The presentation of information on a computer using a

combination of sound, still graphics, animation and video.

MULTI-SYNC MONITOR:

A video display monitor that is capable of automatically adjusting to the synchronisation frequency of the video board that is sending signals to it.

NETWORK:

When two or more computers are linked together for the purpose of sharing information and/or peripheral devices, a network is created. A network is also a database design technique for managing a collection of related programs for loading, accessing, and controlling the information that makes up the database.

NODE:

When any number of computers are connected together in a network, each of the workstations or terminals is referred to as a node, and is assigned a unique address within that network. A node is also an electrical connection point on a printed circuit board or component. With online services, a node is the local collection of relay modems.

OCR (OPTICAL CHARACTER RECOGNITION):

The analysis of scanned data to recognise characters so that these can be converted into editable text.

OLE:

Object linking and embedding. Pronounced oh-lay, OLE is a software technology, an inter-process communication within the Windows operating environment. It allows the operator to embed one object within another, even though the different types of objects may have been created using different programs. OLE differs from traditional export/import methods. If the embedded object is updated by the originating program, the changes are also reflected in the embedding program. For example, a graph from a spreadsheet can be embedded in a word processing document. If the numbers in the spreadsheet are changed, the updates are reflected in the graph in the word processing document.

ONLINE SERVICE:

A dial-up service that provides news, information and discussion "forums" for users with modem-equipped computers. Some of the more popular Online Services are America Online, Compuserve, Prodigy and GEnie.

OPTICAL RESOLUTION:

In the scanning context, this refers to the number of truly separate readings taken from an original within a given distance, as opposed to the subsequent increase in resolution (but not detail) created by software interpolation.

OPERATING SYSTEM:

The master control program that translates the user's commands and allows application programs to interact with the computer's hardware. The most common operating systems are Windows/DOS, OS/2 and UNIX.

OUTPUT:

Process of sending computer results to a CRT or printer.

ORPHANS:

A printing term, meaning the first line of a paragraph that appears at the foot of a column of text. These are usually avoided to ensure ease of reading. See also Widows.

PARALLEL PORT:

A parallel port is an electrical channel to which a peripheral device, such as a dot matrix printer, can be connected. In parallel transmission, the bits of data representing characters are transmitted over several lines simultaneously. Typically, parallel transmission of data is faster than serial (RS-232) transmission.

PATH:

The route that tells DOS where to search for a program or batch file if it is not found in the current directory. The PATH statement is usually found in the AUTOEXEC.BAT file for DOS.

PCMCIA:

The personal computer memory card international association and the Japanese Electronic Industry Development Association developed a standard for integrated circuit cards called PCMCIA and it establishes a standard for input/output cards and creates a new I/O bus for portable computers. The cards are about the size of a credit card, 85.6 by 54 mm, and are plugged into portable and pen-based microcomputers. Cards from different manufacturers, if they conform to the standard, can be interchanged between computers. The cards are lightweight, small and rugged, and are used for a variety of functions. There are modem, network interface and other cards.

PIXEL:

Another term for picture element; the smallest raster display element, represented as a point with a specified colour or intensity level. A two-dimensional array of dots that define the form and colour of an image. Measurement is indicated as PPI. (pixels per inch) The term pixel is usually interchangeable with dot, but pixel most often refers to screen dots rather than image dots. The eye merges differently coloured pixels into continuous tones.

PLOTTER:

A plotter is a pen-based output peripheral device attached to a computer for making drawings. There are basically two kinds of plotters, flatbed and drum. The most common way of transmitting graphics to a plotter is using HPGL, Hewlett-Packard graphics language.

POINTER:

An item of information containing

the location of, thus "pointing" to, another item of information.

PORT:

Either (a) a number that identifies a particular Internet application with which communication is desired, as in "telnet to port 1000"; or (b) an actual physical input/output channel on the computer.

POSTSCRIPT:

The standard device-independent language developed by Adobe Systems that describes the appearance of pages in documents. PostScript describes a page in its final form, ready for imaging on an output device. Encapsulated PostScript describes a graphic, image or complete page in a final form in a way that can be exchanged between application programs so that one PostScript described item can be included in another layout.

PPP:

Point to point protocol. A protocol for using TCP/IP over a standard telephone line. It is a newer and purportedly more efficient protocol than SLIP.

PROMPT:

A request by the computer for input. The DOS prompt usually takes the form of either C>, C:\DOS>, or A>, blinking on the monitor screen. A typical UNIX prompt is the name of the user or computer, a command number, and a % sign.

PROTOCOL:

A protocol is a set of rules governing the communication and the transfer of data between two or more devices. The rules define the handling of certain communication problems, such as framing, error control, sequence control, transparency, line control and start-up control. There are three basic types of protocol: character oriented, byte-count oriented and bit oriented.

QWERTY KEYBOARD:

The standard typewriter or computer keyboard, with the characters "Q, W, E, R, T, and Y" on the top row of letters. The QWERTY keyboard was developed in the 1800's to slow-down swift typists and to prevent jamming of the old mechanical typewriters.

RAM (RANDOM ACCESS MEMORY):

The memory a computer needs to store the information it is processing at any given moment. This is short-term memory and is lost when the power is shut off. RAM may be expanded by adding memory chips or memory boards. Also referred to as dynamic or volatile memory, in that data is stored in RAM only temporarily. A computer's RAM storage space is emptied when the power is turned off.

RGB (RED, GREEN AND BLUE):

The colour model in which colour images are composed of red, green and blue colour channels. Most computer displays and image editing programs use the ROB colour model.

ROM:

Read-only memory: Also referred to as permanent or non-volatile memory, in that the data stored in ROM is permanent or not affected by a power loss. The computer's BIOS is stored in ROM.

RESOLUTION:

The measure of image details. The smallest discernible detail in visual rendering. Resolution may be stated in terms of spot diameter, line width, pixel matrix dimension, raster lines or dots/inch. It defines the capability of an optical system, such as a video screen, or of a scanning device such as an OCR, or of a printer, to make clear and distinguishable the separate parts or components of an object. In video graphics, the resolution is the number of pixels into which the display area can be divided, counted as the number of horizontal and vertical pixels. For example, a resolution of 640 by 200 pixels indicates a display area with 640 pixels across the screen and 200 pixels vertically. The greater the resolution, the more display memory is needed to produce the screen image. Printer and scanner resolution usually is expressed in dpi, dots per inch.

ROOT DIRECTORY:

The root directory is the base level of the directory structure. Branching from the root are various subdirectories, each of which can contain one or more files and subdirectories of its own.

Individual files can also reside at the root directory level. In DOS, the root directory of every disk drive is identified with the back-slash character (\) and is the main directory on that drive. For example, C:\ represents the root directory of drive C.

ROUTER:

A system that transfers data between two networks that use the same protocols, even if they are different in physical characteristics, such as an EtherNet and a telephone line.

SCANNER:

A scanner is a peripheral device for capturing graphic images from a page and converting the data into a binary code. Once captured, the image can be edited with a painting program, pasted into a desktop publishing document, or sent over the telephone lines with a facsimile device. Scanners work similarly to copiers, except that the pattern of charged particles is converted to bits rather than being used to attract pigment.

SCALE:

To change the proportion of an image by increasing or decreasing its size.

SCSI (SMALL COMPUTER SYSTEM INTERFACE):

An internal communications standard for computers, through

which hard drives, scanners, and other peripherals transfer data.

SERIAL PORT:

A serial port is an asynchronous communication channel or address to which a peripheral device such as a modem, a character printer, or a mouse, can be connected. Serial ports are also referred to as COM ports, (COM1, COM2, etc.) In serial communications, bits of data are transmitted sequentially over a single line as opposed to parallel communications, in which multiple wires in the cable allow data to be sent multiple bits at a time. Serial interfaces are also called RS232 ports, from the IEEE standard for their wiring.

SERVER:

Software that allows a computer to offer a service to another computer, such as the ftp server that allows ftp downloading by client software. Also applied to the computer on which the server software runs.

SHADOW RAM:

In random access memory (RAM), stored information can be accessed directly and quickly without having to follow a sequence of storage locations, regardless of which memory location was last accessed. The system BIOS, normally stored in ROM, is responsible for handling the details of the input and output operations, including the task of relating a program's logical records to a peripheral device's physical records. Shadow RAM is a technology that loads the system BIOS and/or video BIOS into RAM during the boot procedure, thereby allowing the BIOS to operate much faster.

SHAREWARE:

Shareware is a distribution method for software programs developed by independent programmers or authors. It is a marketing technique rather than a type of software. It allows the author to market the program with minimal start-up expenses while encouraging feedback from the users. Programs acquired through the shareware method may be freely copied and passed on to others, but each user is expected to register with the author and pay a usage fee. The fee may include some or all of the following: printed documentation, the latest version of the program on disk, telephone support, free updates, and commissions, but most importantly a legal license to continue using the software.

SOFTWARE:

A general term for all types of programs used to manage a computer's operations. Software is essentially a set of instructions the computer uses to perform a task. The commonly seen phrase "software program" is redundant, and should not be used.

SPREADSHEET:

A program that simulates an accountant's worksheet, made up of rows and columns. It is mainly used to calculate budgets and perform financial analyses. By using a spreadsheet, one can set up and monitor budgets, checking accounts, brokerage accounts, and so on.

SUBDIRECTORY:

A directory located within another directory (called the Parent directory). The root directory (C:\>, A:\>, or B:\>) is the only directory which is not also a subdirectory.

SVGA:

Super video graphics array provides for a screen resolution of 1024x768 pixels. Its predecessor, VGA, gave a resolution of 640x480 pixel, still the most common PC screen resolution.

SYNTAX:

The rules governing the structure and sequence of statements in a programming or a natural language.

TIFF (TAGGED IMAGE FILE FORMAT):

A file format developed by Aldus Corporation for exchanging bitmapped, monochrome and full-colour images between applications.

TRANSPARENCY SCANNER:

An optical input system for digitising images from small format positive or negative transparency film.

TRACKBALL:

Is usually described as an upside-down mouse. A trackball remains stationary on your desk; as you move the sphere (ball) in the center with your fingers or palm, sensors detect movement and cause the on-screen cursor to move. Some of the newer notebook computers have this type of directional device that attaches to one edge of the computer.

UPPER MEMORY:

The area of memory on a DOS-based machine located between the 640K DOS conventional memory constraint and the 1024K (1 megabyte) limit of DOS.

VARIABLE:

A parameter that can have several values; the symbol used in a program to represent the parameter.

VGA:

Video graphics array: The VGA is

an analogue video controller. It handles colour in much the same way as a TV receiver. The VGA produces a signal that can vary in small increments over a large spectrum of colours. The VGA requires an analogue colour monitor. The VGA provides a text mode with a 9 by 16 dot box for characters, it emulates the EGA modes and the two graphics modes of MCGA, and it provides its own graphics mode with 16 colours and 640-by-480 pixel resolution.

appears to be held entirely in memory. The virtual memory system allows a program to be broken up into segments, called pages. Instead of bringing the entire program into memory, it brings in as many pages that will fit and leaves the remaining pages on disk. When instructions are called for that are not in memory, the appropriate disk page is read in, overlaying a page in memory. The input and output of program pages is called paging or swapping.

VIRTUAL MEMORY:

When a program requires more space than is available in main memory, a direct access (mass) storage device can be used to hold program segments until needed in memory. The swapping of information between actual memory and virtual memory is transparent, so that the program utilising virtual storage

VOLATILE MEMORY:

Computer memory, made up of dynamic RAM or static RAM chips, is called volatile memory because its contents are lost when the power is shut down. Non-volatile memory, also called firmware, is capable of retaining its contents without power. Examples of non-volatile memory chips: ROM's, PROM's, EPROM's, and EEPROM's.

VRAM:

Video random access memory chips are modified DRAM's on video boards to allow them to transfer a large number of bits from the memory array to a separate internal serial-shift register. After making the transfer, the contents of the shift register are independently shifted out to the video display.

WARM BOOT:

A computer's operating system is initiated with a boot procedure, a start-up from scratch. It is not always necessary to turn-off the power and then re-apply it to start the boot procedure. If your PC hasn't completly locked up, and the keyboard is active, the system can be warm booted by depressing the following three keys simultaneously: Ctrl-Alt-Del. This procedure is known as the "three finger salute." UNIX machines cannot be similarly restarted.

WILDCARDS:

In DOS, the two characters, * and ?, can be used when specifying one or more filenames in an operation. These characters are called wildcards. For example, the DOS command DIR *.COM will cause a directory listing of all the files that have the extension .COM to be displayed on the screen. The asterisk (*) character can represent any valid set of up to eight characters. The question mark (?) can represent any single character in a filename. For example, the DOS directory command, DIR SEPT??.DAT would show directory information any files with names starting with SEPT, followed by two characters, with a .DAT extension).

WIDOWS:

The last short line of a paragraph that appears at the top of a column of text. As with Orphans, these are avoided to ensure ease of reading.

WORM MEMORY:

Write once, read many. A CD-ROM is worm memory.

WYSIWYG:

What you see is what you get. WYSIWYG, pronounced "wizzy-wig", or "wissy-wig", describes computer programs, such as Windows word processors, that generate screen images that are identical in position and type appearance to the final document, as opposed to those that show the formatting or special type requested only when the document is printed, such as the UNIX typesetting program, TeX. The advantages are twofold: the planning of a visually pleasing final document is easier and errors in the printed document can be found more quickly when the document is on the screen.

NOTES

NOTES

NOTES

NOTES

NOTES

NOTES

NOTES

NOTES